**THE MODERN LIBRARY**
*of the World's Best Books*

*Four*

# CONTEMPORARY
# FRENCH PLAYS

*Antigone*

by JEAN ANOUILH

*No Exit*

by JEAN-PAUL SARTRE

*Caligula*

by ALBERT CAMUS

*The Madwoman
of Chaillot*

by JEAN GIRAUDOUX

# *Four* CONTEMPORARY FRENCH PLAYS

Introduction by **RUBY COHN**
*Associate Professor of English, San Francisco State College*

*The Modern Library*

NEW YORK

CAUTION: *Professionals and amateurs are hereby warned that all the plays in this volume, being fully protected under the Copyright Laws of the United States of America, the British Commonwealth, including the Dominion of Canada, and all other countries of the Berne and Universal Copyright Conventions, are subject to royalty. All rights, including professional, amateur, motion picture, recitation, lecturing, public reading, radio and television broadcasting, and the rights of translation into foreign languages, are strictly reserved. All inquiries should be addressed to the publishers named in the following acknowledgment.*

Acknowledgment is due the following for permission to reprint the selections in this volume:

Alfred A. Knopf, Inc., and Hamish Hamilton Ltd., London, for *No Exit* by Jean-Paul Sartre, translated by Stuart Gilbert. Copyright, 1946, by Stuart Gilbert. Reprinted from *No Exit and Three Other Plays.* First published in France by Librarie Gallimard as *Huis Clos.* Copyright, 1945, by Librarie Gallimard.

Alfred A. Knopf, Inc., and Hamish Hamilton Ltd., London, for *Caligula* by Albert Camus, translated by Stuart Gilbert. © Copyright, 1958, by Alfred A. Knopf, Inc. From *Caligula and Three Other Plays*, by Albert Camus. First published in France by Librarie Gallimard. Copyright, 1944, by Librarie Gallimard.

Random House, Inc., for *Antigone*, by Jean Anouilh, adapted by Lewis Galantière. Copyright, 1946, by Random House, Inc.

Random House, Inc., for *The Madwoman of Chaillot* by Jean Giraudoux, adapted by Maurice Valency. Copyright, 1947, by Maurice Valency, under the title "La Folle de Chaillot" by Jean Giraudoux. English version, Copyright, 1949, by Maurice Valency.

LIBRARY OF CONGRESS CATALOG CARD NUMBER: 67–12137

Manufactured in the United States of America

THE MODERN LIBRARY
is published by *Random House, Inc.*

# Introduction

Produced in Paris within a two-year period that saw the end of World War II, the four plays of this collection herald the vigor of French drama that continues to this day. When they were first performed these four plays seemed daring because they showed the shift from the dominant realistic mode of the Paris stage, with its psychological and sociological problems. All of them exemplify the trend from specific problems to the generally problematic. Rather than mirrors, these plays provide theatrical metaphors of the world at large.

Upon a surface reading of the dramas, one would not suspect that they were written or revised in a world at war. Two of them, *Antigone* and *No Exit,* were produced during the Occupation, and had to pass German censorship; the other two, *Caligula* and *The Madwoman of Chaillot,* were performed in the heady air of peace. But all four plays indirectly reflect the war in that three lean toward the tragic and only one toward the comic; none of the four plays is free of evil, suffering, and death, as none of the four is free of grotesque or grim humor.

Jean Anouilh's *Antigone,* produced in February, 1944, is the work of a skilled and experienced playwright. Like his mentors, Jean Cocteau and Jean Giraudoux, Anouilh sometimes turned to Greek myth for his subject matter. Early in his *Antigone,* the Chorus announces: "In a tragedy, nothing is in doubt and everyone's destiny is known." But everyone's destiny is known in Anouilh's drama because he adapts in 1944 what Sophocles dramatized in 442 B.C. Faithful to the events of the Greek tragedy, Anouilh re-views them in a contemporary context; into the neutral setting, Anouilh deliberately introduces anachronisms, and his drama is always played in black-and-white modern evening clothes.

In his *Eurydice* (written just before *Antigone*), one of Anouilh's characters explains the principle upon which the playwright constructs many of his own dramatic conflicts: "There are two races of beings. The masses, teeming and happy—common clay, if you like—mating, breeding, working, counting their pennies; people who just live; ordinary people; people you can't imagine dead. And then, there are the others—the noble ones, the heroes. The ones you can quite well imagine lying shot, pale and tragic: one minute triumphant with a guard of honor, and the next being marched away between two gendarmes" (Kitty Black translation). In our last view of Anouilh's Antigone, she is marched away by three gendarmes; she is a noble one, a heroine.

In sharp contrast to Sophocles' heroine, Anouilh's Antigone does not act according to strict dictates of Greek burial rites. Defying a wise and weary Creon, Anouilh's Antigone announces that she acts "For nobody. For myself." In her last letter, she admits, "I no longer know why I am dying." Nor does the audience learn, for the Chorus pronounces the final judgment: "Antigone is calm tonight, and we shall never know the name of the fever that consumed her." Though "we shall never know" within the context of the single play, we may perhaps guess within the context of Anouilh's *oeuvre*. Like other Anouilh protagonists, classical and contemporary, Antigone dies to preserve a purity that would be tarnished by exposure to the reality represented by Creon. The play's kernel lies in the confrontation of Antigone the absolutist and Creon the relativist.

When first performed, the play was admired both by French patriots who saw Antigone as a symbol of the Resistance, and by collaborators who viewed Creon as a figure of sensible moderation. Jean-Paul Sartre, who was working with the Resistance, considered Anouilh a kindred spirit, a "Forger of Myth." Sartre interpreted Anouilh's *Antigone* as "a free woman without any features at all until she chooses them for herself in the moment when she asserts her freedom to die despite the triumphant tyrant" (Rosamond Gilder translation). The description fits Sartre's Orestes better than Anouilh's Antigone. For Anouilh was an adapter rather than a forger of myth. In spite of colloquial dialogue, comic anachronism, and modern clothes, Anouilh's play insists upon the unchangeable tragic essence of his heroine.

It was against such an Essentialist conception of man that Sartre reacted in his own first play. *The Flies* (produced in Paris in 1943) reinterprets, reforges the Greek Orestes story to show the fallacy of tragic doom, for Sartre's Orestes has free choice of action; existence precedes essence. In Sartre's second play, *No Exit,* the philosophically trained playwright dramatizes the obverse situation—the time when choice is no longer possible, when one is dead. Negatively, then, Sartre insists upon man's ability to choose freely, and his play was performed in Paris three months before Parisians chose their own freedom from German occupation.

As in Dante's *Inferno,* the sinners of *No Exit* are sentenced according to their sin. With three characters lifted from newspaper scandals, Sartre constructs what Eric Bentley has aptly called a "philosophic melodrama." Having tortured others during their lifetime, Sartre's trio will torture one another throughout eternity. Early in the play, Garcin asks the Valet about the instruments of torture, Inez takes Garcin for the torturer, and Estelle mistakes Garcin for the man she has tortured on earth. Each of them will be tortured and torturer during the single act of mounting intensity. Their heated exchanges will replace traditional fire and brimstone; finally, Garcin will realize: "There's no need for red-hot pokers. Hell is—other people."

Garcin, Inez, and Estelle make separate entrances into the Second Empire drawing room; the furnishings reflect the period—inefficient and ugly. The initial familiarity of such a room makes Hell seem "homey," like other ugly, familiar rooms. Once Garcin begins to speak, however, we discover the hidden threats in the room— a massive bronze, a paper cutter, no light switch to control the anachronistic electricity; no window or mirror; no blinking and no sleep. By the time Inez enters, we know that the ordinary appearance of the room is false, as we know that Garcin's apparent calmness is false. By the time Estelle arrives, the menace of the room renders her etiquette grotesque. When Estelle high-handedly tells the Valet, "You can go. I'll ring when I want you," we have already witnessed Garcin's frenzied, futile ringing for the Valet, and we suspect that no ringing will summon the Valet again—or anyone outside the trio, now become a literal eternal triangle.

The eternal triangle is not equiangular, for Garcin is at its apex. Garcin is first on stage, but we do not learn the full details of his life until the play is nearly over. Garcin brings about the climactic opening of the door, and Garcin has the final lines of the play. Although all three characters have been torturers in their private lives, Garcin alone has committed a public sin, desertion, and he cannot admit that his desertion was due to cowardice rather than pacifism. Garcin's inability to define himself defines his punishment in Sartre's Hell; Inez came to Hell with self-knowledge, Estelle is incapable of it, and Garcin dares not face it. And that is their fate, for their lives are over; they can no longer act in existential freedom; death has reduced them to eternal essence.

Albert Camus is also preoccupied with death in *Caligula,* whose original title was "The Meaning of Death." Camus' Caligula announces, "Men die and they are not happy," and then he prepares to kill men and render them unhappy, so that they will comprehend the meaningless absurdity of being-in-the-world. Explicitly, he says, "There's no understanding fate; therefore I choose to play the part of fate." And yet, despite its somber theme, Camus' play is full of verve. Written by a twenty-five-year-old author about a twenty-five-year-old emperor, the play was not produced until after the end of World War II, when the role of Caligula was a stage triumph for twenty-three-year-old Gérard Philipe.

Camus' source, the Roman historian Suetonius, divides Caligula's biography into two parts, The Emperor and The Monster. Camus, however, dramatizes a monster of wit, élan, and passion for the impossible. In each of the four acts, it is through play and display that Caligula undermines the legal, emotional, religious, and artistic traditions of his (and our) heritage. Emperor Caligula is at once a Lord of Rule and of Misrule; his apparent madness creates absurdist chaos. Each of Camus' four acts is built on the same three-part pattern: 1) an opening crowd scene dissolves into the entrance of Caligula, 2) Caligula presides at a public ceremony, 3) the ceremony fades off into a personal encounter for Caligula. Within each act, as in the total drama, the movement is from the denseness of the crowd to the solitude of the hero, whose dedication fails of its purpose. He can kill men, but he cannot make them conscious of absurdity.

In his preface to the American edition of the play, Camus wrote: "Caligula accepts death because he has understood that no one can save himself all alone—and that one cannot be free at the expense of others." In the play itself, however, Caligula does not quite accept death; his dying words are a defiant expression of absurdity—"I'm still alive." At this distance from Camus' own accidental death in 1960, Caligula seems to speak for his creator, whose works are still alive to tell us energetically that men die and are not happy.

Even the whimsical fantasy of Giraudoux' last complete play, *The Madwoman of Chaillot* (produced just before Christmas, 1945), cannot hide that men die and are not happy. Thus, the genial and ingenious mad countess bends her efforts to save a young man from death, to make young lovers happy, and to rid the world of evil. But the evil is mildly comic, for though *The Madwoman* was the last of our four plays to reach the stage, it is a play in an older mode wherein drama is conceived primarily as entertainment.

Elegant and erudite, Jean Giraudoux was scholar, diplomat, novelist, and playwright. After dramatizing his novel *Siegfried* in 1928, he collaborated with actor-director Louis Jouvet, and together they imposed style upon a barren period of French theater. Giraudoux availed himself of myth and history, of his native province (Limousin) and his adopted city (Paris). Though all his plays contain an undercurrent of serious significance, it rarely interferes with the surface froth. So, in *The Madwoman of Chaillot,* the good and pure inherit the earth, while tawdry industrio-commercialism is consigned to the nether regions. The play's charm lies in familiar items—madwomen who are ethically sane, city slickers who are innocent and kind, cats and cafés of Paris—garbed in a prose as dated and distinctive as the Madwoman's wardrobe. Ironic intelligence supersedes the passion of the other three plays—an intellectual satire-play after a tragic trilogy.

When closely contemplated, the four plays pair off provocatively: two by established playwrights and two by neophytes; two produced in the shadow of the Occupation and two in the radiance of peace; two stripped linear actions and two dense profusions; two Essentialist and two Existentialist views of man; two male-centered dramas and two frail heroines; two stylistically rich plays and two riddled with colloquialism; two classical backgrounds and two contemporary fantasies. But however such juxtapositions may illuminate, each drama must finally make its own way on the stage, on the page, in the world.

**Ruby Cohn**

*San Francisco State College*

# Contents

# *Antigone*

## by
## JEAN ANOUILH

A Play in One Act

*Translated by*
*LEWIS GALANTIÈRE*

# CHARACTERS

CHORUS
ANTIGONE
NURSE
ISMENE
HAEMON
CREON
FIRST GUARD, *Jonas*
SECOND GUARD, *a Corporal*
THIRD GUARD
MESSENGER
PAGE
EURYDICE

Antigone *was first presented at the Théâtre de l'Atelier, Paris, in February, 1944.*

# Scene

ANTIGONE, *her hands clasped round her knees, sits on the top step. The* THREE GUARDS *sit on the steps, in a small group, playing cards. The* CHORUS *stands on the top step.* EURYDICE *sits on the top step, just left of center, knitting. The* NURSE *sits on the second step, left of* EURYDICE. ISMENE *stands in front of arch, left, facing* HAEMON, *who stands left of her.* CREON *sits in the chair at right end of the table, his arm over the shoulder of his* PAGE, *who sits on the stool beside his chair. The* MESSENGER *is leaning against the downstage portal of the right arch. The curtain rises slowly; then the* CHORUS *turns and moves downstage.*

CHORUS Well, here we are.

These people are about to act out for you the story of Antigone.

That thin little creature sitting by herself, staring straight ahead, seeing nothing, is Antigone. She is thinking. She is thinking that the instant I finish telling you who's who and what's what in this play, she will burst forth as the tense, sallow, wilful girl whose family would never take her seriously and who is about to rise up alone against Creon, her uncle, the King.

Another thing that she is thinking is this: she is going to die. Antigone is young. She would much rather live than die. But there is no help for it. When your name is Antigone, there is only one part you can play; and she will have to play hers through to the end.

From the moment the curtain went up, she began to feel that inhuman forces were whirling her out of this world, snatching her away from her sister, Ismene, whom you see smiling and chatting with that young man; from all of us who sit or stand here, looking at her, not in the least upset ourselves—for we are not doomed to die tonight.

(CHORUS *turns and indicates* HAEMON)

The young man talking to Ismene—to the gay and beautiful Ismene—is Haemon. He is the King's son, Creon's son. Antigone and he are engaged to be married. You wouldn't have thought she was his type. He likes dancing, sports, competition; he likes women, too. Now look at Ismene again. She is certainly more beautiful than Antigone. She is the girl you'd think he'd go for. Well . . . There was a ball one night. Ismene wore a new evening frock. She was radiant. Haemon danced every dance with her. And yet, that same night, before the dance was over, suddenly he went in search of Antigone, found her sitting alone— like that, with her arms clasped round her knees—and asked her to marry him. We still don't know how it happened. It didn't seem to surprise Antigone in the least. She looked up at him out of those solemn eyes of hers, smiled sort of sadly and said "yes." That was all. The band struck up another dance. Ismene, surrounded by a group of young men, laughed out loud. And . . . well, here is Haemon expecting to marry Antigone. He won't, of course. He didn't know, when he asked her, that the earth wasn't meant to hold a husband of Antigone, and that this princely distinction was to earn him no more than the right to die sooner than he might otherwise have done.

(CHORUS *turns toward* CREON)

That gray-haired, powerfully built man sitting lost in thought, with his little page at his side, is Creon, the King. His face is lined. He is tired. He practices the

difficult art of a leader of men. When he was younger,
when Oedipus was King and Creon was no more than
the King's brother-in-law, he was different. He loved
music, bought rare manuscripts, was a kind of art
patron. He would while away whole afternoons in the
antique shops of this city of Thebes. But Oedipus
died. Oedipus' sons died. Creon had to roll up his
sleeves and take over the kingdom. Now and then,
when he goes to bed weary with the day's work, he
wonders whether this business of being a leader of
men is worth the trouble. But when he wakes up, the
problems are there to be solved; and like a conscientious workman, he does his job.

Creon has a wife, a Queen. Her name is Eurydice.
There she sits, the old lady with the knitting, next to
the Nurse who brought up the two girls. She will go
on knitting all through the play, till the time comes
for her to go to her room and die. She is a good
woman, a worthy, loving soul. But she is no help to
her husband. Creon has to face the music alone. Alone
with his Page, who is too young to be of any help.
The others? Well, let's see.

(*He points toward the* MESSENGER)

That pale young man leaning against the wall is the
Messenger. Later on, he will come running in to announce that Haemon is dead. He has a premonition
of catastrophe. That's what he is brooding over.
That's why he won't mingle with the others.

As for those three red-faced card players—they are
the guards. One smells of garlic, another of beer; but
they're not a bad lot. They have wives they are afraid
of, kids who are afraid of them; they're bothered by
the little day-to-day worries that beset us all. At the
same time—they are policemen: eternally innocent,
no matter what crimes are committed; eternally indifferent, for nothing that happens can matter to
them. They are quite prepared to arrest anybody at

all, including Creon himself, should the order be
given by a new leader.

That's the lot. Now for the play.

Oedipus, who was the father of the two girls, Antigone
and Ismene, had also two sons, Eteocles and Polynices. After Oedipus died, it was agreed that the two
sons should share his throne, each to reign over
Thebes in alternate years.

(*Gradually, the lights on the stage have been
dimmed*)

But when Eteocles, the elder son, had reigned a full
year, and time had come for him to step down, he
refused to yield up the throne to his younger brother.
There was civil war. Polynices brought up allies—six
foreign princes; and in the course of the war he and
his foreigners were defeated, each in front of one of
the seven gates of the city. The two brothers fought,
and they killed one another in single combat just
outside the city walls. Now Creon is King.

(CHORUS *is leaning, at this point, against the left
proscenium arch. By now the stage is dark, with
only the cyclorama bathed in dark blue. A single
spot lights up the face of* CHORUS)

Creon has issued a solemn edict that Eteocles, with
whom he had sided, is to be buried with pomp and
honors, and that Polynices is to be left to rot. The
vultures and the dogs are to bloat themselves on his
carcass. Nobody is to go into mourning for him. No
gravestone is to be set up in his memory. And above
all, any person who attempts to give him religious
burial will himself be put to death.

(*While* CHORUS *has been speaking the characters
have gone out one by one.* CHORUS *disappears
through the left arch.*

*It is dawn, gray and ashen, in a house asleep.*
ANTIGONE *steals in from out-of-doors, through the
arch, right. She is carrying her sandals in her*

*hand. She pauses, looking off through the arch,
taut, listening, then turns and moves across downstage. As she reaches the table, she sees the* NURSE
*approaching through the arch, left. She runs
quickly toward the exit. As she reaches the steps,
the* NURSE *enters through arch and stands still
when she sees* ANTIGONE)

NURSE  Where have you been?

ANTIGONE  Nowhere. It was beautiful. The whole world
was gray when I went out. And now—you wouldn't
recognize it. It's like a postcard: all pink, and green,
and yellow. You'll have to get up earlier, Nurse, if
you want to see a world without color.

NURSE  It was still pitch black when I got up. I went
to your room, for I thought you might have flung off
your blanket in the night. You weren't there.

ANTIGONE  (*Comes down the steps*)  The garden was
lovely. It was still asleep. Have you ever thought how
lovely a garden is when it is not yet thinking of men?

NURSE  You hadn't slept in your bed. I couldn't find
you. I went to the back door. You'd left it open.

ANTIGONE  The fields were wet. They were waiting for
something to happen. The whole world was breathless, waiting. I can't tell you what a roaring noise I
seemed to make alone on the road. It bothered me
that whatever was waiting, wasn't waiting for me.
I took off my sandals and slipped into a field. (*She
moves down to the stool and sits*)

NURSE  (*Kneels at* ANTIGONE's *feet to chafe them and
put on the sandals*)  You'll do well to wash your feet
before you go back to bed, Miss.

ANTIGONE  I'm not going back to bed.

NURSE  Don't be a fool! You get some sleep! And me,
getting up to see if she hasn't flung off her blanket;
and I find her bed cold and nobody in it!

ANTIGONE  Do you think that if a person got up every

morning like this, it would be just as thrilling every
morning to be the first girl out of doors?

(NURSE *puts* ANTIGONE's *left foot down, lifts her
other foot and chafes it*)

NURSE  Morning, my grandmother! It was night. It still
is. And now, my girl, you'll stop trying to squirm out
of this and tell me what you were up to. Where've
you been?

ANTIGONE  That's true. It was still night. There wasn't
a soul out of doors but me who thought that it was
morning. Don't you think it's marvelous—to be the
first person who is aware that it is morning?

NURSE  Oh, my little flibbertigibbet! Just can't imagine
what I'm talking about, can she? Go on with you!
I know that game. Where have you been, wicked girl?

ANTIGONE  (*Soberly*)  No. Not wicked.

NURSE  You went out to meet someone, didn't you?
Deny it if you can.

ANTIGONE  Yes. I went out to meet someone.

NURSE  A lover?

ANTIGONE  Yes, Nurse. Yes, the poor dear. I have a
lover.

NURSE  (*Stands up; bursting out*)  Ah, that's very nice
now, isn't it? Such goings-on! You, the daughter of
a king, running out to meet lovers. And we work our
fingers to the bone for you, we slave to bring you
up like young ladies! (*She sits on chair, right of table*)
You're all alike, all of you. Even you—who never used
to stop to primp in front of a looking-glass, or smear
your mouth with rouge, or dindle and dandle to make
the boys ogle you, and you ogle back. How many
times I'd say to myself, "Now that one, now: I wish
she was a little more of a coquette—always wearing
the same dress, her hair tumbling round her face. One
thing's sure," I'd say to myself, "none of the boys will
look at her while Ismene's about, all curled and cute
and tidy and trim. I'll have this one on my hands for

the rest of my life." And now, you see? Just like your sister, after all. Only worse: a hypocrite. Who is the lad? Some little scamp, eh? Somebody you can't bring home and show to your family, and say, "Well, this is him, and I mean to marry him and no other." That's how it is, is it? Answer me!

ANTIGONE (*Smiling faintly*) That's how it is. Yes, Nurse.

NURSE Yes, says she! God save us! I took her when she wasn't that high. I promised her poor mother I'd make a lady of her. And look at her! But don't you go thinking this is the end of this, my young 'un. I'm only your nurse and you can play deaf and dumb with me; I don't count. But your Uncle Creon will hear of this! That, I promise you.

ANTIGONE (*A little weary*) Yes. Creon will hear of this.

NURSE And we'll hear what he has to say when he finds out that you go wandering alone o' nights. Not to mention Haemon. For the girl's engaged! Going to be married! Going to be married, and she hops out of bed at four in the morning to meet somebody else in a field. Do you know what I ought to do to you? Take you over my knee the way I used to do when you were little.

ANTIGONE Please, Nurse, I want to be alone.

NURSE And if you so much as speak of it, she says she wants to be alone!

ANTIGONE Nanny, you shouldn't scold, dear. This isn't a day when you should be losing your temper.

NURSE Not scold, indeed! Along with the rest of it, I'm to like it. Didn't I promise your mother? What would she say if she was here? "Old Stupid!" That's what she'd call me. "Old Stupid. Not to know how to keep my little girl pure! Spend your life making them behave, watching over them like a mother hen, running after them with mufflers and sweaters to keep them warm, and egg nogs to make them strong; and then at four o'clock in the morning, you who always complained you never could sleep a wink, snoring in your bed and letting them slip out into the bushes." That's what she'd say, your mother. And I'd stand there, dying of shame if I wasn't dead already. And all I could do would be not to dare look her in the face; and "That's true," I'd say. "That's all true what you say, Your Majesty."

ANTIGONE   Nanny, dear. Dear Nanny. Don't cry. You'll be able to look Mamma in the face when it's your time to see her. And she'll say, "Good morning, Nanny. Thank you for my little Antigone. You did look after her so well." She knows why I went out this morning.

NURSE   Not to meet a lover?

ANTIGONE   No. Not to meet a lover.

NURSE   Well, you've a queer way of teasing me, I must say! Not to know when she's teasing me! (*Rises to stand behind* ANTIGONE) I must be getting awfully old, that's what it is. But if you loved me, you'd tell me the truth. You'd tell me why your bed was empty when I went along to tuck you in. Wouldn't you?

ANTIGONE   Please, Nanny, don't cry any more. (ANTI-GONE *turns partly toward* NURSE, *puts an arm up to* NURSE's *shoulder. With her other hand,* ANTIGONE *caresses* NURSE's *face*).   There now, my sweet red apple. Do you remember how I used to rub your cheeks to make them shine? My dear, wrinkled red apple! I didn't do anything tonight that was worth sending tears down the little gullies of your dear face. I am pure, and I swear that I have no other lover than Haemon. If you like, I'll swear that I shall never have any other lover than Haemon. Save your tears, Nanny, save them, Nanny dear; you may still need them. When you cry like that, I become a little girl again; and I mustn't be a little girl today. (ANTIGONE *rises and moves upstage*)

(ISMENE *enters through arch, left. She pauses in front of arch*)

ISMENE  Antigone! What are you doing up at this hour? I've just been to your room.

NURSE  The two of you, now! You're both going mad, to be up before the kitchen fire has been started. Do you like running about without a mouthful of breakfast? Do you think it's decent for the daughters of a king? (*She turns to* ISMENE) And look at you, with nothing on, and the sun not up! I'll have you both on my hands with colds before I know it.

ANTIGONE  Nanny dear, go away now. It's not chilly, really. Summer's here. Go and make us some coffee. Please, Nanny, I'd love some coffee. It would do me so much good.

NURSE  My poor baby! Her head's swimming, what with nothing on her stomach, and me standing here like an idiot when I could be getting her something hot to drink.

(NURSE *exits*)

(*A pause*)

ISMENE  Aren't you well?

ANTIGONE  Of course I am. Just a little tired. I got up too early. (ANTIGONE *sits on a chair, suddenly tired*)

ISMENE  I couldn't sleep, either.

ANTIGONE  Ismene, you ought not to go without your beauty sleep.

ISMENE  Don't make fun of me.

ANTIGONE  I'm not, Ismene, truly. This particular morning, seeing how beautiful you are makes everything easier for me. Wasn't I a miserable little beast when we were small? I used to fling mud at you, and put worms down your neck. I remember tying you to a tree and cutting off your hair. Your beautiful hair! How easy it must be never to be unreasonable with all that smooth silken hair so beautifully set round your head.

ISMENE (*Abruptly*)  Why do you insist upon talking about other things?

ANTIGONE (*Gently*)   I am not talking about other things.

ISMENE   Antigone, I've thought about it a lot.

ANTIGONE   Have you?

ISMENE   I thought about it all night long. Antigone, you're mad.

ANTIGONE   Am I?

ISMENE   We cannot do it.

ANTIGONE   Why not?

ISMENE   Creon will have us put to death.

ANTIGONE   Of course he will. That's what he's here for. He will do what he has to do, and we will do what we have to do. He is bound to put us to death. We are bound to go out and bury our brother. That's the way it is. What do you think we can do to change it?

ISMENE (*Releases* ANTIGONE's *hand; draws back a step*) I don't want to die.

ANTIGONE   I'd prefer not to die, myself.

ISMENE   Listen to me, Antigone. I thought about it all night. I'm older than you are. I always think things over, and you don't. You are impulsive. You get a notion in your head and you jump up and do the thing straight off. And if it's silly, well, so much the worse for you. Whereas, *I* think things out.

ANTIGONE   Sometimes it is better not to think too much.

ISMENE   I don't agree with you! (ANTIGONE *looks at* ISMENE, *then turns and moves to chair behind table.* ISMENE *leans on end of table top, toward* ANTIGONE) Oh, I know it's horrible. And I pity Polynices just as much as you do. But all the same, I sort of see what Uncle Creon means.

ANTIGONE   I don't want to "sort of see" anything.

ISMENE   Uncle Creon is the king. He has to set an example!

ANTIGONE   But I am not the king; and I don't have to set people examples. Little Antigone gets a notion in her head—the nasty brat, the wilful, wicked girl; and they put her in a corner all day, or they lock her up in the cellar. And she deserves it. She shouldn't have disobeyed!

ISMENE There you go, frowning, glowering, wanting your own stubborn way in everything. Listen to me. I'm right oftener than you are.

ANTIGONE I don't want to be right!

ISMENE At least you can try to understand.

ANTIGONE Understand! The first word I ever heard out of any of you was that word "understand." Why didn't I "understand" that I must not play with water—cold, black, beautiful flowing water—because I'd spill it on the palace tiles. Or with earth, because earth dirties a little girl's frock. Why didn't I "understand" that nice children don't eat out of every dish at once; or give everything in their pockets to beggars; or run in the wind so fast that they fall down; or ask for a drink when they're perspiring; or want to go swimming when it's either too early or too late, merely because they happen to feel like swimming. Understand! I don't want to understand. There'll be time enough to understand when I'm old. . . . If I ever *am* old. But not now.

ISMENE He is stronger than we are, Antigone. He is the king. And the whole city is with him. Thousands and thousands of them, swarming through all the streets of Thebes.

ANTIGONE I am not listening to you.

ISMENE His mob will come running, howling at it runs. A thousand arms will seize our arms. A thousand breaths will breathe into our faces. Like one single pair of eyes, a thousand eyes will stare at us. We'll be driven in a tumbrel through their hatred, through the smell of them and their cruel, roaring laughter. We'll be dragged to the scaffold for torture, surrounded by guards with their idiot faces all bloated, their animal hands clean-washed for the sacrifice, their beefy eyes squinting as they stare at us. And we'll know that no shrieking and no begging will make them understand that we want to live, for they are like slaves who do exactly as they've been told, without caring about right or wrong. And we shall suffer, we shall feel pain rising in us until it becomes so unbearable that we *know* it must stop. But it won't stop; it will go on rising and rising, like a screaming voice. Oh, I can't, I can't, Antigone!

(*A pause*)

ANTIGONE   How well you have thought it all out.

ISMENE   I thought of it all night long. Didn't you?

ANTIGONE   Oh, yes.

ISMENE   I'm an awful coward, Antigone.

ANTIGONE   So am I. But what has that to do with it?

ISMENE   But, Antigone! Don't you want to go on living?

ANTIGONE   Go on living! Who was it that was always the first out of bed because she loved the touch of the cold morning air on her bare skin? Who was always the last to bed because nothing less than infinite weariness could wean her from the lingering night? Who wept when she was little because there were too many grasses in the meadow, too many creatures in the field, for her to know and touch them all?

ISMENE (*Clasps* ANTIGONE's *hands, in a sudden rush of tenderness*)   Darling little sister!

ANTIGONE (*Repulsing her*)   No! For heaven's sake! Don't paw me! And don't let us start sniveling! You say you've thought it all out. The howling mob—the torture—the fear of death. . . . They've made up your mind for you. Is that it?

ISMENE   Yes.

ANTIGONE   All right. They're as good excuses as any.

ISMENE   Antigone, be sensible. It's all very well for men to believe in ideas and die for them. But you are a girl!

ANTIGONE  Don't I know I'm a girl? Haven't I spent my life cursing the fact that I was a girl?

ISMENE (*With spirit*)  Antigone! You have everything in the world to make you happy. All you have to do is reach out for it. You are going to be married; you are young; you are beautiful—

ANTIGONE  I am not beautiful.

ISMENE  Yes, you are! Not the way other girls are. But it's always you that the little boys turn to look back at when they pass us in the street. And when you go by, the little girls stop talking. They stare and stare at you, until we've turned a corner.

ANTIGONE (*A faint smile*)  "Little boys—little girls."

ISMENE (*Challengingly*)  And what about Haemon?
(*A pause*)

ANTIGONE  I shall see Haemon this morning. I'll take care of Haemon. You always said I was mad; and it didn't matter how little I was or what I wanted to do. Go back to bed now, Ismene. The sun is coming up, and, as you see, there is nothing I can do today. Our brother Polynices is as well guarded as if he had won the war and were sitting on his throne. Go along. You are pale with weariness.

ISMENE  What are you going to do?

NURSE (*Calls from off-stage*)  Come along, my dove. Come to breakfast.

ANTIGONE  I don't feel like going to bed. However, if you like, I'll promise not to leave the house till you wake up. Nurse is getting me breakfast. Go and sleep. The sun is just up. Look at you: you can't keep your eyes open. Go.

ISMENE  And you will listen to reason, won't you? You'll let me talk to you about this again? Promise?

ANTIGONE  I promise. I'll let you talk. I'll let all of you talk. Go to bed, now. (ISMENE *goes to arch and exits*) Poor Ismene!

NURSE (*Enters through arch, speaking as she enters*)

Come along, my dove. I've made you some coffee
and toast and jam. (*She turns toward arch as if to
exit*)

ANTIGONE    I'm not really hungry, Nurse.

> (NURSE *stops, looks at* ANTIGONE, *then moves be-
> hind her*)

NURSE (*Very tenderly*)    Where is your pain?

ANTIGONE    Nowhere, Nanny dear. But you must keep
me warm and safe, the way you used to do when I
was little. Nanny! Stronger than all fever, stronger
than any nightmare, stronger than the shadow of the
cupboard that used to snarl at me and turn into
a dragon on the bedroom wall. Stronger than the
thousand insects gnawing and nibbling in the silence
of the night. Stronger than the night itself, with the
weird hooting of the nightbirds that frightened me
even when I couldn't hear them. Nanny, stronger
than death, give me your hand, Nanny, as if I were
ill in bed, and you sitting beside me.

NURSE    My sparrow, my lamb! What is it that's eating
your heart out?

ANTIGONE    Oh, it's just that I'm a little young still for
what I have to go through. But nobody but you
must know that.

NURSE (*Places her other arm round* ANTIGONE's *shoulder*)
A little young for what, my kitten?

ANTIGONE    Nothing in particular, Nanny. Just—all this.
Oh, it's so good that you are here. I can hold your
callused hand, your hand that is so prompt to ward
off evil. You are very powerful, Nanny.

NURSE    What is it you want me to do for you, my baby?

ANTIGONE    There isn't anything to do, except put your
hand like this against my cheek. (*She places the
NURSE's hand against her cheek. A pause, then, as
ANTIGONE leans back, her eyes shut*) There! I'm not
afraid any more. Not afraid of the wicked ogre, nor
of the sandman, nor of the dwarf who steals little

children. (*A pause,* ANTIGONE *resumes on another note*) Nanny . . .

NURSE  Yes?

ANTIGONE  My dog, Puff . . .

NURSE (*Straightens up, draws her hand away*)  Well?

ANTIGONE  Promise me that you will never scold her again.

NURSE  Dogs that dirty up a house with their filthy paws deserve to be scolded.

ANTIGONE  I know. Just the same, promise me.

NURSE  You mean you want me to let her make a mess all over the place and not say a thing?

ANTIGONE  Yes, Nanny.

NURSE  You're asking a lot. The next time she wets my living-room carpet, I'll—

ANTIGONE  Please, Nanny, I beg of you!

NURSE  It isn't fair to take me on my weak side, just because you look a little peaked today. . . . Well, have it your own way. We'll mop up and keep our mouth shut. You're making a fool of me, though.

ANTIGONE  And promise me that you will talk to her. That you will talk to her often.

NURSE (*Turns and looks at* ANTIGONE)  Me, talk to a dog!

ANTIGONE  Yes. But mind you: you are not to talk to her the way people usually talk to dogs. You're to talk to her the way I talk to her.

NURSE  I don't see why both of us have to make fools of ourselves. So long as you're here, one ought to be enough.

ANTIGONE  But if there was a reason why I couldn't go on talking to her—

NURSE (*Interrupting*)  Couldn't go on talking to her! And why couldn't you go on talking to her? What kind of poppycock—?

ANTIGONE  And if she got too unhappy, if she moaned and moaned, waiting for me with her nose under the door as she does when I'm out all day, then the best thing, Nanny, might be to have her mercifully put to sleep.

NURSE   Now what *has* got into you this morning? (HAEMON *enters through arch*) Running round in the darkness, won't sleep, won't eat—(ANTIGONE *sees* HAEMON)—and now it's her dog she wants killed. I never—

ANTIGONE (*Interrupting*)   Nanny! Haemon is here. Go inside, please, And don't forget that you've promised me. (NURSE *goes to arch and exits.* ANTIGONE *rises*) Haemon, Haemon! Forgive me for quarreling with you last night. (*She crosses quickly to* HAEMON *and they embrace*) Forgive me for everything. It was all my fault. I beg you to forgive me.

HAEMON   You know that I've forgiven you. You had hardly slammed the door, your perfume still hung in the room, when I had already forgiven you. (*He holds her in his arms and smiles at her. Then draws slightly back*) You stole that perfume. From whom?

ANTIGONE   Ismene.

HAEMON   And the rouge? and the face powder? and the frock? Whom did you steal them from?

ANTIGONE   Ismene.

HAEMON   And in whose honor did you get yourself up so elegantly?

ANTIGONE   I'll tell you everything. (*She draws him closer*) Oh, darling, what a fool I was! To waste a whole evening! A whole, beautiful evening!

HAEMON   We'll have other evenings, my sweet.

ANTIGONE   Perhaps we won't.

HAEMON   And other quarrels, too. A happy love is full of quarrels, you know.

ANTIGONE   A happy love, yes. Haemon, listen to me.

HAEMON   Yes?

ANTIGONE   Don't laugh at me this morning. Be serious.

HAEMON   I am serious.

ANTIGONE   And hold me tight. Tighter than you have ever held me. I want all your strength to flow into me.

HAEMON   There! With all my strength.

(*A pause*)

ANTIGONE (*Breathless*)   That's good. (*They stand for a moment, silent and motionless*) Haemon! I wanted to tell you. You know—the little boy we were going to have when we were married?

HAEMON   Yes?

ANTIGONE   I'd have protected him against everything in the world.

HAEMON   Yes, dearest.

ANTIGONE   Oh, you don't know how I should have held him in my arms and given him my strength. He wouldn't have been afraid of anything, I swear he wouldn't. Not of the falling night, nor of the terrible noonday sun, nor of all the shadows or all the walls in the world. Our little boy, Haemon! His mother wouldn't have been very imposing: her hair wouldn't always have been brushed; but she would have been strong where he was concerned, so much stronger than all those real mothers with their real bosoms and their aprons round their middle. You believe that, don't you, Haemon?

HAEMON (*Soothingly*)   Yes, yes, my darling.

ANTIGONE   And you believe me when I say that you would have had a real wife?

HAEMON   Darling, you are my real wife.

ANTIGONE (*Pressing against him and crying out*)   Haemon, you loved me! You did love me that night, didn't you? You're sure of it!

HAEMON (*Rocking her gently*)   What night, my sweet?

ANTIGONE   And you are very sure, aren't you, that night, at the dance, when you came to the corner where I was sitting, there was no mistake? It was me you were looking for? It wasn't another girl? And you're sure that never, not in your most secret

heart of hearts, have you said to yourself that it was
Ismene you ought to have asked to marry you?

HAEMON (*Reproachfully*) Antigone, you are idiotic.
You might give me credit for knowing my own mind.
It's you I love, and no one else.

ANTIGONE　But you love me as a woman—as a woman
wants to be loved, don't you? Your arms round me
aren't lying, are they? Your hands, so warm against
my back—they're not lying? This warmth that's in
me; this confidence, this sense that I am safe, secure,
that flows through me as I stand here with my cheek
in the hollow of your shoulder: they are not lies, are
they?

HAEMON　Antigone, darling, I love you exactly as you
love me. With all of myself.

　　(*They kiss*)

ANTIGONE　I'm sallow, and I'm scrawny. Ismene is
pink and golden. She's like a fruit.

HAEMON　Look here, Antigone—

ANTIGONE　Ah, dearest, I am ashamed of myself. But
this morning, this special morning, I must know.
Tell me the truth! I beg you to tell me the truth!
When you think about me, when it strikes you suddenly that I am going to belong to you—do you have
the feeling that—that a great empty space is being
hollowed out inside you, that there is something inside you that is just—dying?

HAEMON　Yes, I do, I do.

　　(*A pause*)

ANTIGONE　That's the way I feel. And another thing.
I wanted you to know that I should have been very
proud to be your wife—the woman whose shoulder
you would put your hand on as you sat down to table,
absentmindedly, as upon a thing that belonged to
you. (*After a moment, draws away from him. Her
tone changes*) There! Now I have two things more
to tell you. And when I have told them to you, you

must go away instantly, without asking any questions. However strange they may seem to you. However much they may hurt you. Swear that you will!

HAEMON (*Beginning to be troubled*) What are these things that you are going to tell me?

ANTIGONE Swear, first, that you will go away without one word. Without so much as looking at me. (*She looks at him, wretchedness in her face*) You hear me, Haemon. Swear it, please. This is the last mad wish that you will ever have to grant me.

(*A pause*)

HAEMON I swear it, since you insist. But I must tell you that I don't like this at all.

ANTIGONE Please, Haemon. It's very serious. You must listen to me and do as I ask. First, about last night, when I came to your house. You asked me a moment ago why I wore Ismene's dress and rouge. It was because I was stupid. I wasn't very sure that you loved me as a woman; and I did it—because I wanted you to want me. I was trying to be more like other girls.

HAEMON Was *that* the reason? My poor—

ANTIGONE Yes. And you laughed at me. And we quarreled; and my awful temper got the better of me and I flung out of the house. . . . The real reason was that I wanted you to take me; I wanted to be your wife before—

HAEMON Oh, my darling—

ANTIGONE (*Shuts him off*) You swore you wouldn't ask any questions. You swore, Haemon. (*Turns her face away and goes on in a hard voice*) As a matter of fact, I'll tell you why. I wanted to be your wife last night because I love you that way very—very strongly. And also because— Oh, my darling, my darling, forgive me; I'm going to cause you quite a lot of pain. (*She draws away from him*) I wanted it also because I shall never, never be able to marry you, never! (HAEMON *is stupefied and mute; then he moves a step toward her*) Haemon! You look a solemn oath! You swore! Leave me quickly! Tomorrow the whole thing will be clear to you. Even before tomorrow: this afternoon. If you please, Haemon, go now. It is the only thing left that you can do for me if you still love me. (*A pause as* HAEMON *stares at her. Then he turns and goes out through the arch.* ANTIGONE *stands motionless, then moves to chair at end of table and lets herself gently down on it. In a mild voice, as of calm after storm*) Well, it's over for Haemon, Antigone.

>       (ISMENE *enters through arch, pauses for a moment in front of it when she sees* ANTIGONE, *then crosses behind table*)

ISMENE   I can't sleep. I'm terrified. I'm so afraid that even though it is daylight, you'll still try to bury Polynices. Antigone, little sister, we all want to make you happy—Haemon, and Nurse, and I, and Puff whom you love. We love you, we are alive, we need you. And you remember what Polynices was like. He was our brother, of course. But he's dead; and he never loved you. He was a bad brother. He was like an enemy in the house. He never thought of you. Why should you think of him? What if his soul does have to wander through endless time without rest or peace? Don't try something that is beyond your strength. You are always defying the world, but you're only a girl, after all. Stay at home tonight. Don't try to do it. I beg you. It's Creon's doing, not ours.

ANTIGONE   You are too late, Ismene. When you first saw me this morning, I had just come in from burying him.

>       (ANTIGONE *exits through arch*)
>       (*The lighting, which by this time has reached a point of early morning sun, is quickly dimmed out, leaving the stage bathed in a light blue color*)
>       (ISMENE *runs out after* ANTIGONE)
>       (*On* ISMENE'S *exit the lights are brought up suddenly to suggest a later period of the day*)

(CREON *and* PAGE *enter through curtain upstage.*
CREON *stands on the top step; his* PAGE *stands at
his right side*)

CREON   A private of the guards, you say? One of those
standing watch over the body? Show him in.

(*The* PAGE *crosses to arch and exits.* CREON *moves
down to end of table.*

PAGE *re-enters, preceded by the* FIRST GUARD, *livid
with fear.* PAGE *remains on upstage side of arch.*
GUARD *salutes*)

GUARD   Private Jonas, Second Battalion.

CREON   What are you doing here?

GUARD   It's like this, sir. Soon as it happened, we said:
"Got to tell the chief about this before anybody else
spills it. He'll want to know right away." So we tossed
a coin to see which one would come up and tell you
about it. You see, sir, we thought only one man had
better come because, after all, you don't want to leave
the body without a guard. Right? I mean, there's
three of us on duty, guarding the body.

CREON   What's wrong about the body?

GUARD   Sir, I've been seventeen years in the service.
Volunteer. Wounded three times. Two mentions. My
record's clean. I know my business and I know my
place. I carry out orders. Sir, ask any officer in the
battalion; they'll tell you. "Leave it to Jonas. Give
him an order: he'll carry it out." That's what they'll
tell you, sir. Jonas, that's me—that's my name.

CREON   What's the matter with you, man? What are
you shaking for?

GUARD   By rights it's the corporal's job, sir. I've been
recommended for a corporal but they haven't put it
through yet. June, it was supposed to go through.

CREON (*Interrupts*)   Stop chattering and tell me why
you are here. If anything has gone wrong, I'll break
all three of you.

GUARD   Nobody can say we didn't keep our eye on that
body. We had the two o'clock watch—the tough one.

You know how it is, sir. It's nearly the end of the night. Your eyes are like lead. You've got a crick in the back of your neck. There's shadows, and the fog is beginning to roll in. A fine watch they give us! And me, seventeen years in the service. But we was doing our duty all right. On our feet, all of us. Anybody says we were sleeping is a liar. First place, it was too cold. Second place—(CREON *makes a gesture of impatience*) Yes, sir. Well, I turned round and looked at the body. We wasn't only ten feet away from it, but that's how I am. I was keeping my eye on it. (*Shouts*) Listen, sir, I was the first man to see it! Me! They'll tell you. I was the one let out that yell!

CREON   What for? What was the matter?

GUARD   Sir, the body! Somebody had been there and buried it. (CREON *comes down a step on the stair. The* GUARD *becomes more frightened*) It wasn't much, you understand. With us three there, it couldn't have been. Just covered over with a little dirt, that's all. But enough to hide it from the buzzards.

CREON   By God, I'll—! (*He looks intently at the* GUARD) You are sure that it couldn't have been a dog, scratching up the earth?

GUARD   Not a chance, sir. That's kind of what we hoped it was. But the earth was scattered over the body just like the priests tell you you should do it. Whoever did that job knew what he was doing all right.

CREON   Who could have dared? (*He turns and looks at the* GUARD) Was there anything to indicate who might have done it?

GUARD   Not a thing, sir. Maybe we heard a footstep— I can't swear to it. Of course we started right in to search, and the corporal found a shovel, a kid's shovel no bigger than that, all rusty and everything. Corporal's got the shovel for you. We thought maybe a kid did it.

CREON (*To himself*)   A kid! (*He looks away from the*

GUARD) I broke the back of the rebellion; but like a
snake, it is coming together again. Polynices' friends,
with their gold, blocked by my orders in the banks
of Thebes. The leaders of the mob, stinking of garlic
and allied to envious princes. And the temple priests,
always ready for a bit of fishing in troubled waters.
A kid! I can imagine what he is like, their kid: a
baby-faced killer, creeping in the night with a toy
shovel under his jacket. (*He looks at his* PAGE) Though
why shouldn't they have corrupted a real child? Very
touching! Very useful to the party, an innocent child.
A martyr. A real white-faced baby of fourteen who
will spit with contempt at the guards who kill him.
A free gift to their cause: the precious, innocent blood
of a child on my hands. (*He turns to the* GUARD) They
must have accomplices in the Guard itself. Look here,
you. Who knows about this?

GUARD   Only us three, sir. We flipped a coin, and I
came right over.

CREON   Right. Listen, now. You will continue on duty.
When the relief squad comes up, you will tell them
to return to barracks. You will uncover the body. If
another attempt is made to bury it, I shall expect
you to make an arrest and bring the person straight
to me. And you will keep your mouths shut. Not one
word of this to a human soul. You are all guilty of
neglect of duty, and you will be punished; but if the
rumor spreads through Thebes that the body received
burial, you will be shot—all three of you.

GUARD (*excitedly*)   Sir, we never told nobody, I swear
we didn't! Anyhow, I've been up here. Suppose my
pals spilled it to the relief; I couldn't have been with
them and here too. That wouldn't be my fault if they
talked. Sir, I've got two kids. You're my witness, sir,
it couldn't have been me. I was here with you. I've got
a witness! If anybody talked, it couldn't have been
me! I was—

CREON (*Interrupting*) Clear out! If the story doesn't get round, you won't be shot. (*The* GUARD *salutes, turns and exits, at the double.* CREON *turns and paces upstage, then comes down to end of the table*) A child! (*He looks at* PAGE) Come along, my lad. Since we can't hope to keep this to ourselves, we shall have to be the first to give out the news. And after that, we shall have to clean up the mess. (PAGE *crosses to side of* CREON. CREON *puts his hands on* PAGE'S *shoulder*) Would you be willing to die for me? Would you defy the Guard with your little shovel? (PAGE *looks up at* CREON) Of course you would. You would do it, too. (*A pause.* CREON *looks away from* PAGE *and murmurs*) A child! (CREON *and* PAGE *go slowly upstage center to top step.* PAGE *draws aside the curtain, through which* CREON *exits with* PAGE *behind him*)

> (*As soon as* CREON *and* PAGE *have disappeared,* CHORUS *enters and leans against the upstage portal of arch, left. The lighting is brought up to its brightest point to suggest midafternoon.* CHORUS *allows a pause to indicate that a crucial moment has been reached in the play, then moves slowly downstage, center. He stands for a moment silent, reflecting, and then smiles faintly*)

CHORUS   The spring is wound up tight. It will uncoil of itself. That is what is so convenient in tragedy. The least little turn of the wrist will do the job. Anything will set it going: a glance at a girl who happens to be lifting her arms to her hair as you go by; a feeling when you wake up on a fine morning that you'd like a little respect paid to you today, as if it were as easy to order as a second cup of coffee; one question too many, idly thrown out over a friendly drink— and the tragedy is on.

The rest is automatic. You don't need to lift a finger. The machine is in perfect order; it has been oiled ever since time began, and it runs without friction. Death, treason, and sorrow are on the march; and they move in the wake of storm, of tears, of stillness. Every kind of stillness. The hush when the executioner's ax goes up at the end of the last act. The unbreathable silence when, at the beginning of the play, the two lovers, their hearts bared, their bodies naked, stand for the first time face to face in the darkened room, afraid to stir. The silence inside you when the roaring crowd acclaims the winner—so that you think of a film without a sound-track, mouths agape and no sound coming out of them, a clamor that is no more than a picture; and you, the victor, already vanquished, alone in the desert of your silence. That is tragedy.

Tragedy is clean, it is restful, it is flawless. It has nothing to do with melodrama—with wicked villains, persecuted maidens, avengers, sudden revelations, and eleventh-hour repentances. Death, in a melodrama, is really horrible because it is never inevitable. The dear old father might so easily have been saved; the honest young man might so easily have brought in the police five minutes earlier.

In a tragedy, nothing is in doubt and everyone's destiny is known. That makes for tranquillity. There is a sort of fellow-feeling among characters in a tragedy: he who kills is as innocent as he who gets killed: it's all a matter of what part you are playing. Tragedy is restful; and the reason is that hope, that foul, deceitful thing, has no part in it. There isn't any hope. You're trapped. The whole sky has fallen on you, and all you can do about it is to shout.

Don't mistake me: I said "shout": I did not say groan, whimper, complain. That, you cannot do. But you can shout aloud; you can get all those things said that you never thought you'd be able to say—or never even knew you had it in you to say. And you don't say these things because it will do any good to say them: you know better than that. You say them for their own sake; you say them because you learn a lot from them.

In melodrama, you argue and struggle in the hope of escape. That is vulgar; it's practical. But in tragedy, where there is no temptation to try to escape, argument is gratuitous: it's kingly.

(*Voices of the* GUARDS *and scuffling sounds heard through the archway.* CHORUS *looks in that direction, in a changed tone*)

The play is on. Antigone has been caught. For the first time in her life, little Antigone is going to be able to be herself.

(CHORUS *exits through arch*)

(*A pause, while the offstage voices rise in volume, then the* FIRST GUARD *enters, followed by* SECOND *and* THIRD GUARDS, *holding the arms of* ANTIGONE *and dragging her along. The* FIRST GUARD, *speaking as he enters, crosses swiftly to end of the table. The* TWO GUARDS *and* ANTIGONE *stop downstage*)

FIRST GUARD (*Recovered from his fright*) Come on, now, Miss, give it a rest. The chief will be here in a minute and you can tell him about it. All I know is my orders. I don't want to know what you were doing there. People always have excuses; but I can't afford to listen to them, see. Why, if we had to listen to all the people who want to tell us what's the matter with this country, we'd never get our work done. (*To the* GUARDS) You keep hold of her and I'll see that she keeps her face shut.

ANTIGONE   They are hurting me. Tell them to take their dirty hands off me.

FIRST GUARD   Dirty hands, eh? The least you can do is try to be polite, Miss. Look at me: I'm polite.

ANTIGONE   Tell them to let me go. I shan't run away. My father was King Oedipus. I am Antigone.

FIRST GUARD   King Oedipus' little girl! Well, well, well! Listen, Miss, the night watch never picks up a lady but they say, you better be careful: I'm sleeping with the police commissioner.

    (*The* GUARDS *laugh*)

ANTIGONE   I don't mind being killed, but I don't want them to touch me.

FIRST GUARD   And what about stiffs, and dirt, and such like? You wasn't afraid to touch them, was you? "Their dirty hands!" Take a look at your own hands. (ANTIGONE, *handcuffed, smiles despite herself as she looks down at her hands. They are grubby*) You must have lost your shovel, didn't you? Had to go at it with your fingernails the second time, I'll bet. By God, I never saw such nerve! I turn my back for about five seconds; I ask a pal for a chew; I say "thanks"; I get the tobacco stowed away in my cheek—the whole thing don't take ten seconds; and there she is, clawing away like a hyena. Right out in broad daylight; And did she scratch and kick when I grabbed her! Straight for my eyes with them nails she went. And yelling something fierce about, "I haven't finished yet; let me finish!" She ain't got all her marbles!

SECOND GUARD   I pinched a nut like that the other day. Right on the main square she was, hoisting up her skirts and showing her behind to anybody that wanted to take a look.

FIRST GUARD   Listen, we're going to get a bonus out of this. What do you say we throw a party, the three of us?

SECOND GUARD   At the old woman's? Behind Market Street?

THIRD GUARD   Suits me. Sunday would be a good day. We're off duty Sunday. What do you say we bring our wives?

FIRST GUARD   No. Let's have some fun this time. Bring your wife, there's always something goes wrong. First place, what do you do with the kids? Bring them, they always want to go to the can just when you're right in the middle of a game of cards or something. Listen, who would have thought an hour ago that us three would be talking about throwing a party now? The way I felt when the old man was interrogating me, we'd be lucky if we got off with being docked a month's pay. I want to tell you, I was scared.

SECOND GUARD  You sure we're going to get a bonus?

FIRST GUARD  Yes. Something tells me this is big stuff.

THIRD GUARD (*To* SECOND GUARD)  What's-his-name, you know—in the Third Battalion? He got an extra month's pay for catching a fire-bug.

SECOND GUARD  If we get an extra month's pay, I vote we throw the party at the Arabian's.

FIRST GUARD  You're crazy! He charges twice as much for liquor as anybody else in town. Unless you want to go upstairs, of course. Can't do that at the old woman's.

THIRD GUARD  Well, we can't keep this from our wives, no matter how you work it out. You get an extra month's pay, and what happens? Everybody in the battalion knows it, and your wife knows it too. They might even line up the battalion and give it to you in front of everybody, so how could you keep your wife from finding out?

FIRST GUARD  Well, we'll see about that. If they do the job out in the barrack-yard—of course that means women, kids, everything.

ANTIGONE  I should like to sit down, if you please.

(*A pause, as the* FIRST GUARD *thinks it over*)

FIRST GUARD  Let her sit down. But keep hold of her. (*The two* GUARDS *start to lead her toward the chair at end of table. The curtain upstage opens, and* CREON *enters, followed by his* PAGE. FIRST GUARD *turns and moves upstage a few steps, sees* CREON) 'Tenshun! (*The three* GUARDS *salute.* CREON, *seeing* ANTIGONE *handcuffed to* THIRD GUARD, *stops on the top step, astonished*)

CREON  Antigone! (*To the* FIRST GUARD) Take off those

handcuffs! (FIRST GUARD *crosses above table to left of* ANTIGONE) What is this? (CREON *and his* PAGE *come down off the steps*)

> (FIRST GUARD *takes key from his pocket and unlocks the cuff on* ANTIGONE'S *hand.* ANTIGONE *rubs her wrist as she crosses below table toward chair at end of table.* SECOND *and* THIRD GUARDS *step back to front of arch.* FIRST GUARD *turns upstage toward* CREON)

FIRST GUARD  The watch, sir. We all came this time.

CREON  Who is guarding the body?

FIRST GUARD  We sent for the relief.

> (CREON *comes down*)

CREON  But I gave orders that the relief was to go back to barracks and stay there! (ANTIGONE *sits on chair at left of table*) I told you not to open your mouth about this!

FIRST GUARD  Nobody's said anything, sir. We made this arrest, and brought the party in, the way you said we should.

CREON  Fools! (*To* ANTIGONE) Where did these men find you?

FIRST GUARD  Right by the body.

CREON  What were you doing near your brother's body? You knew what my orders were.

FIRST GUARD  What was she doing? Sir, that's why we brought her in. She was digging up the dirt with her nails. She was trying to cover up the body all over again.

CREON  Do you realize what you are saying?

FIRST GUARD  Sir, ask these men here. After I reported to you, I went back, and first thing we did, we uncovered the body. The sun was coming up and it was beginning to smell, so we moved it up on a little rise to get him in the wind. Of course, you wouldn't expect any trouble in broad daylight. But just the same, we decided one of us had better keep his eye peeled all the time. About noon, what with the sun and the smell, and as the wind dropped and I wasn't feeling none too good, I went over to my pal to get a chew. I just had time to say "thanks" and stick it in my mouth, when I turned round and there she was, clawing away at the dirt with both hands. Right out in broad daylight! Wouldn't you think when she saw me come running she'd stop and leg it out of there? Not her! She went right on digging as fast as she could, as if I wasn't there at all. And when I grabbed her, she scratched and bit and yelled to leave her alone, she hadn't finished yet, the body wasn't all covered yet, and the like of that.

CREON (*To* ANTIGONE)   Is this true?

ANTIGONE   Yes, it is true.

FIRST GUARD   We scraped the dirt off as fast as we could, then we sent for the relief and we posted them. But we didn't tell them a thing, sir. And we brought in the party so's you could see her. And that's the truth, so help me God.

CREON (*To* ANTIGONE)   And was it you who covered the body the first time? In the night?

ANTIGONE   Yes, it was. With a toy shovel we used to take to the seashore when we were children. It was Polynices' own shovel; he had cut his name in the handle. That was why I left it with him. But these men took it away; so the next time, I had to do it with my hands.

FIRST GUARD   Sir, she was clawing away like a wild animal. Matter of fact, first minute we saw her, what with the heat haze and everything, my pal says, "That must be a dog," he says. "Dog!" I says, "That's a girl, that is!" And it was.

CREON   Very well. (*Turns to the* PAGE) Show these men to the ante-room. (*The* PAGE *crosses to the arch, stands there, waiting.* CREON *moves behind the table. To the* FIRST GUARD) You three men will wait outside. I may want a report from you later.

FIRST GUARD   Do I put the cuffs back on her, sir?

CREON   No. (*The three* GUARDS *salute, do an about-turn and exit through arch, right.* PAGE *follows them out. A pause*) Had you told anybody what you meant to do?

ANTIGONE   No.

CREON   Did you meet anyone on your way—coming or going?

ANTIGONE   No, nobody.

CREON   Sure of that, are you?

ANTIGONE   Perfectly sure.

CREON   Very well. Now listen to me. You will go straight to your room. When you get there, you will go to bed. You will say that you are not well and that you have not been out since yesterday. Your nurse will tell the same story. (*He looks toward arch, through which the* GUARDS *have exited*) And I'll get rid of those three men.

ANTIGONE   Uncle Creon, you are going to a lot of trouble for no good reason. You must know that I'll do it all over again tonight.

(*A pause. They look one another in the eye*)

CREON   Why did you try to bury your brother?

ANTIGONE   I owed it to him.

CREON   I had forbidden it.

ANTIGONE   I owed it to him. Those who are not buried wander eternally and find no rest. If my brother were alive, and he came home weary after a long day's hunting, I should kneel down and unlace his boots, I should fetch him food and drink, I should see that his bed was ready for him. Polynices is home from the hunt. I owe it to him to unlock the house of the dead in which my father and my mother are waiting to welcome him. Polynices has earned his rest.

CREON   Polynices was a rebel and a traitor, and you know it.

ANTIGONE   He was my brother.

CREON    You heard my edict. It was proclaimed throughout Thebes. You read my edict. It was posted up on
the city walls.

ANTIGONE    Of course I did.

CREON    You knew the punishment I decreed for any
person who attempted to give him burial.

ANTIGONE    Yes, I knew the punishment.

CREON    Did you by any chance act on the assumption
that a daughter of Oedipus, a daughter of Oedipus'
stubborn pride, was above the law?

ANTIGONE    No, I did not act on that assumption.

CREON    Because if you had acted on that assumption,
Antigone, you would have been deeply wrong. Nobody has a more sacred obligation to obey the law
than those who make the law. You are a daughter
of law-makers, a daughter of kings, Antigone. You
must observe the law.

ANTIGONE    Had I been a scullery maid washing my
dishes when that law was read aloud to me, I should
have scrubbed the greasy water from my arms and
gone out in my apron to bury my brother.

CREON    What nonsense! If you had been a scullery maid,
there would have been no doubt in your mind about
the seriousness of that edict. You would have known
that it meant death; and you would have been satisfied to weep for your brother in your kitchen. But
you! You thought that because you come of the royal
line, because you were my niece and were going to
marry my son, I shouldn't dare have you killed.

ANTIGONE    You are mistaken. Quite the contrary. I
never doubted for an instant that you would have me
put to death.

(*A pause, as* CREON *stares fixedly at her*)

CREON    The pride of Oedipus! Oedipus and his head-
strong pride all over again. I can see your father in
you—and I believe you. Of course you thought that I
should have you killed! Proud as you are, it seemed

to you a natural climax in your existence. Your father was like that. For him as for you human happiness was meaningless; and mere human misery was not enough to satisfy his passion for torment. (*He sits on a stool behind the table*) You come of people for whom the human vestment is a kind of strait jacket: it cracks at the seams. You spend your lives wriggling to get out of it. Nothing less than a cosy tea party with death and destiny will quench your thirst. The happiest hour of your father's life came when he listened greedily to the story of how, unknown to himself, he had killed his own father and dishonored the bed of his own mother. Drop by drop, word by word, he drank in the dark story that the gods had destined him, first to live and then to hear. How avidly men and women drink the brew of such a tale when their names are Oedipus—and Antigone! And it is so simple, afterward, to do what your father did, to put out one's eyes and take one's daughter begging on the highways.

Let me tell you, Antigone: those days are over for Thebes. Thebes has a right to a king without a past. My name, thank God, is only Creon. I stand here with both feet firm on the ground; with both hands in my pockets; and I have decided that so long as I am king—being less ambitious than your father was—I shall merely devote myself to introducing a little order into this absurd kingdom; if that is possible.

Don't think that being a king seems to me romantic. It is my trade; a trade a man has to work at every day; and like every other trade, it isn't all beer and skittles. But since it is my trade, I take it seriously. And if, tomorrow, some wild and bearded messenger walks in from some wild and distant valley—which is what happened to your dad—and tells me that he's not quite sure who my parents were, but thinks that my wife Eurydice is actually my mother, I shall ask him to do me the kindness to go back where he came from; and I shan't let a little matter like that persuade me to order my wife to take a blood test and the police to let me know whether or not my birth certificate was forged. Kings, my girl, have other things to do than to surrender themselves to their private feelings. (*He looks at her and smiles*) Hand *you* over to be killed! (*He rises, moves to end of table and sits on the top of table*) I have other plans for you. You're going to marry Haemon; and I want you to fatten up a bit so that you can give him a sturdy boy. Let me assure you that Thebes needs that boy a good deal more than it needs your death. You will go to your room, now, and do as you have been told; and you won't say a word about this to anybody. Don't fret about the guards: I'll see that their mouths are shut. And don't annihilate me with those eyes. I know that you think I am a brute, and I'm sure you must consider me very prosaic. But the fact is, I have always been fond of you, stubborn though you always were. Don't forget that the first doll you ever had came from me. (*A pause.* ANTIGONE *says nothing, rises and crosses slowly below the table toward the arch.* CREON *turns and watches her; then*) Where are you going?

ANTIGONE (*Stops downstage. Without any show of rebellion*)  You know very well where I am going.

CREON (*After a pause*)  What sort of game are you playing?

ANTIGONE   I am not playing games.

CREON   Antigone, do you realize that if, apart from those three guards, a single soul finds out what you have tried to do, it will be impossible for me to avoid putting you to death? There is still a chance that I can save you; but only if you keep this to yourself and give up your crazy purpose. Five minutes more, and it will be too late. You understand that?

ANTIGONE   I must go and bury my brother. Those men uncovered him.

CREON   What good will it do? You know that there are other men standing guard over Polynices. And even if you did cover him over with earth again, the earth would again be removed.

ANTIGONE   I know all that. I know it. But that much, at least, I can do. And what a person can do, a person ought to do.

(*Pause*)

CREON   Tell me, Antigone, do you believe all that flummery about religious burial? Do you really believe that a so-called shade of your brother is condemned to wander for ever homeless if a little earth is not flung on his corpse to the accompaniment of some priestly abracadabra? Have you ever listened to the priests of Thebes when they were mumbling their formula? Have you ever watched those dreary bureaucrats while they were preparing the dead for burial—skipping half the gestures required by the ritual, swallowing half their words, hustling the dead into their graves out of fear that they might be late for lunch?

ANTIGONE   Yes, I have seen all that.

CREON   And did you never say to yourself as you watched them, that if someone you really loved lay dead under the shuffling, mumbling ministrations of the priests, you would scream aloud and beg the priests to leave the dead in peace?

ANTIGONE   Yes, I've thought all that.

CREON   And you still insist upon being put to death—merely because I refuse to let your brother go out with that grotesque passport; because I refuse his body the wretched consolation of that mass-production jibber-jabber, which you would have been the first to be embarrassed by if I had allowed it. The whole thing is absurd!

ANTIGONE   Yes, it's absurd.

CREON   Then why, Antigone, why? For whose sake? For the sake of them that believe in it? To raise them against me?

ANTIGONE　No.

CREON　For whom then if not for them and not for Polynices either?

ANTIGONE　For nobody. For myself.

　　　(*A pause as they stand looking at one another*)

CREON　You must want very much to die. You look like a trapped animal.

ANTIGONE　Stop feeling sorry for me. Do as I do. Do your job. But if you are a human being, do it quickly. That is all I ask of you. I'm not going to be able to hold out for ever.

CREON (*Takes a step toward her*)　I want to save you, Antigone.

ANTIGONE　You are the king, and you are all-powerful. But that you cannot do.

CREON　You think not?

ANTIGONE　Neither save me nor stop me.

CREON　Prideful Antigone! Little Oedipus!

ANTIGONE　Only this can you do: have me put to death.

CREON　Have you tortured, perhaps?

ANTIGONE　Why would you do that? To see me cry? To hear me beg for mercy? Or swear whatever you wish, and then begin over again?

　　　(*A pause*)

CREON　You listen to me. You have cast me for the villain in this little play of yours, and yourself for the heroine. And you know it, you damned little mischief-maker! But don't you drive me too far! If I were one of your preposterous little tyrants that Greece is full of, you would be lying in a ditch this minute with your tongue pulled out and your body drawn and quartered. But you can see something in my face that makes me hesitate to send for the guards and turn you over to them. Instead, I let you go on arguing; and you taunt me, you take the offensive. (*He grasps her left wrist*) What are you driving at, you she-devil?

ANTIGONE　Let me go. You are hurting my arm.

CREON (*Gripping her tighter*)    I will not let you go.

ANTIGONE (*Moans*)    Oh!

CREON    I was a fool to waste words. I should have done this from the beginning. (*He looks at her*) I may be your uncle—but we are not a particularly affectionate family. Are we, eh? (*Through his teeth, as he twists*) Are we? (CREON *propels* ANTIGONE *round below him to his side*) What fun for you, eh? To be able to spit in the face of a king who has all the power in the world; a man who has done his own killing in his day; who has killed people just as pitiable as you are—and who is still soft enough to go to all this trouble in order to keep you from being killed.

(*A pause*)

ANTIGONE    Now you are squeezing my arm too tightly. It doesn't hurt any more.

(CREON *stares at her, then drops her arm*)

CREON    I shall save you yet. (*He goes below the table to the chair at end of table, takes off his coat and places it on the chair*) God knows, I have things enough to do today without wasting my time on an insect like you. There's plenty to do, I assure you, when you've just put down a revolution. But urgent things can wait. I am not going to let politics be the cause of your death. For it is a fact that this whole business is nothing but politics: the mournful shade of Polynices, the decomposing corpse, the sentimental weeping and the hysteria that you mistake for heroism —nothing but politics.

Look here. I may not be soft, but I'm fastidious. I like things clean, ship-shape, well scrubbed. Don't think that I am not just as offended as you are by the thought of that meat rotting in the sun. In the evening, when the breeze comes in off the sea, you can smell it in the palace, and it nauseates me. But I refuse even to shut my window. It's vile; and I can tell you what I wouldn't tell anybody else: it's stupid, monstrously stupid. But the people of Thebes have got to have their noses rubbed into it a little longer. My God! If it was up to me, I should have had them bury your brother long ago as a mere matter of public hygiene. I admit that what I am doing is childish. But if the featherheaded rabble I govern are to understand what's what, that stench has got to fill the town for a month!

ANTIGONE (*Turns to him*)   You are a loathsome man!

CREON   I agree. My trade forces me to be. We could argue whether I ought or ought not to follow my trade; but once I take on the job, I must do it properly.

ANTIGONE   Why do you do it at all?

CREON   My dear, I woke up one morning and found myself King of Thebes. God knows, there were other things I loved in life more than power.

ANTIGONE   Then you should have said no.

CREON   Yes, I could have done that. Only, I felt that it would have been cowardly. I should have been like a workman who turns down a job that has to be done. So I said yes.

ANTIGONE   So much the worse for you, then. I didn't say yes. I can say no to anything I think vile, and I don't have to count the cost. But because you said yes, all that you can do, for all your crown and your trappings, and your guards—all that you can do is to have me killed.

CREON   Listen to me.

ANTIGONE   If I want to. I don't have to listen to you if I don't want to. You've said your *yes*. There is nothing more you can tell me that I don't know. You stand there, drinking in my words. (*She moves behind chair*) Why is it that you don't call your guards? I'll tell you why. You want to hear me out to the end; that's why.

CREON   You amuse me.

ANTIGONE  Oh, no, I don't. I frighten you. That is why you talk about saving me. Everything would be so much easier if you had a docile, tongue-tied little Antigone living in the palace. I'll tell you something, Uncle Creon: I'll give you back one of your own words. You are too fastidious to make a good tyrant. But you are going to have to put me to death today, and you know it. And that's what frightens you. God! Is there anything uglier than a frightened man!

CREON  Very well. I am afraid, then. Does that satisfy you? I am afraid that if you insist upon it, I shall have to have you killed. And I don't want to.

ANTIGONE  I don't have to do things that I think are wrong. If it comes to that, you didn't really want to leave my brother's body unburied, did you? Say it! Admit that you didn't.

CREON  I have said it already.

ANTIGONE  But you did it just the same. And now, though you don't want to do it, you are going to have me killed. And you call that being a king!

CREON  Yes, I call that being a king.

ANTIGONE  Poor Creon! My nails are broken, my fingers are bleeding, my arms are covered with the welts left by the paws of your guards—but I am a queen!

CREON  Then why not have pity on me, and live? Isn't your brother's corpse, rotting there under my windows, payment enough for peace and order in Thebes? My son loves you. Don't make me add your life to the payment. I've paid enough.

ANTIGONE  No, Creon! You said yes, and made yourself king. Now you will never stop paying.

CREON  But God in Heaven! Won't you try to understand me! I'm trying hard enough to understand you! There had to be one man who said yes. Somebody had to agree to captain the ship. She had sprung a hundred leaks; she was loaded to the water-line with crime, ignorance, poverty. The wheel was swinging with the wind. The crew refused to work and were looting the cargo. The officers were building a raft, ready to slip overboard and desert the ship. The mast was splitting, the wind was howling, the sails were beginning to rip. Every man jack on board was about to drown—and only because the only thing they thought of was their own skins and their cheap little day-to-day traffic. Was that a time, do you think, for playing with words like yes and no? Was that a time for a man to be weighing the pros and cons, wondering if he wasn't going to pay too dearly later on; if he wasn't going to lose his life, or his family, or his touch with other men? You grab the wheel, you right the ship in the face of a mountain of water. You shout an order, and if one man refuses to obey, you shoot straight into the mob. Into the mob, I say! The beast as nameless as the wave that crashes down upon your deck; as nameless as the whipping wind. The thing that drops when you shoot may be someone who poured you a drink the night before; but it has no name. And you, braced at the wheel, you have no name, either. Nothing has a name—except the ship, and the storm. (*A pause as he looks at her*) Now do you understand?

ANTIGONE   I am not here to understand. That's all very well for you. I am here to say no to you, and die.

CREON   It is easy to say no.

ANTIGONE   Not always.

CREON   It is easy to say no. To say yes, you have to sweat and roll up your sleeves and plunge both hands into life up to the elbows. It is easy to say no, even if saying no means death. All you have to do is to sit still and wait. Wait to go on living; wait to be killed. That is the coward's part. *No* is one of your man-made words. Can you imagine a world in which trees say *no* to the sap? In which beasts say *no* to hunger or to propagation? Animals are good, simple, tough. They move in droves, nudging one another onward, all traveling the same road. Some of them keel over; but the rest go on; and no matter how many may fall by the wayside, there are always those few left which go on bringing their young into the world, traveling the same road with the same obstinate will, unchanged from those who went before.

ANTIGONE   Animals, eh, Creon! What a king you could be if only men were animals!

(*A pause.* CREON *turns and looks at her*)

CREON   You despise me, don't you? (ANTIGONE *is silent.* CREON *goes on, as if to himself*) Strange. Again and again, I have imagined myself holding this conversation with a pale young man I have never seen in the flesh. He would have come to assassinate me, and would have failed. I would be trying to find out from him why he wanted to kill me. But with all my logic and all my powers of debate, the only thing I could get out of him would be that he despised me. Who would have thought that the white-faced boy would turn out to be you? And that the debate would arise out of something so meaningless as the burial of your brother?

ANTIGONE (*Repeats contemptuously*)   Meaningless!

CREON (*Earnestly, almost desperately*)   And yet, you must hear me out. My part is not an heroic one, but I shall play my part. I shall have you put to death. Only, before I do, I want to make one last appeal. I want to be sure that you know what you are doing as well as I know what I am doing. Antigone, do you know what you are dying for? Do you know the sordid story to which you are going to sign your name in blood, for all time to come?

ANTIGONE   What story?

CREON   The story of Eteocles and Polynices, the story of your brothers. You think you know it, but you don't. Nobody in Thebes knows that story but me. And it seems to me, this afternoon, that you have a right to know it too. (*A pause as* ANTIGONE *moves to chair and sits*) It's not a pretty story. (*He turns, gets stool from behind the table and places it between the the table and the chair*) You'll see. (*He looks at her for a moment*) Tell me, first. What do you remember about your brothers? They were older than you, so they must have looked down on you. And I imagine that they tormented you—pulled your pigtails, broke your dolls, whispered secrets to each other to put you in a rage.

ANTIGONE    They were big and I was little.

CREON    And later on, when they came home wearing evening clothes, smoking cigarettes, they would have nothing to do with you; and you thought they were wonderful.

ANTIGONE    They were boys and I was a girl.

CREON    You didn't know why, exactly, but you knew that they were making your mother unhappy. You saw her in tears over them; and your father would fly into a rage because of them. You heard them come in, slamming doors, laughing noisily in the corridors—insolent, spineless, unruly, smelling of drink.

ANTIGONE    (*Staring outward*) Once, it was very early and we had just got up. I saw them coming home, and hid behind a door. Polynices was very pale and his eyes were shining. He was so handsome in his evening clothes. He saw me, and said: "Here, this is for you"; and he gave me a big paper flower that he had brought home from his night out.

CREON    And of course you still have that flower. Last night, before you crept out, you opened a drawer and looked at it for a time, to give yourself courage.

ANTIGONE    Who told you so?

CREON    Poor Antigone! With her night-club flower. Do you know what your brother was?

ANTIGONE    Whatever he was, I know that you will say vile things about him.

CREON  A cheap, idiotic bounder, that is what he was. A cruel, vicious little voluptuary. A little beast with just wit enough to drive a car faster and throw more money away than any of his pals. I was with your father one day when Polynices, having lost a lot of money gambling, asked him to settle the debt; and when your father refused, the boy raised his hand against him and called him a vile name.

ANTIGONE  That's a lie!

CREON  He struck your father in the face with his fist. It was pitiful. Your father sat at his desk with his head in his hands. His nose was bleeding. He was weeping with anguish. And in a corner of your father's study, Polynices stood sneering and lighting a cigarette.

ANTIGONE  That's a lie.

(*A pause*)

CREON  When did you last see Polynices alive? When you were twelve years old. *That's* true, isn't it?

ANTIGONE  Yes, that's true.

CREON  Now you know why. Oedipus was too chicken-hearted to have the boy locked up. Polynices was allowed to go off and join the Argive army. And as soon as he reached Argos, the attempts upon your father's life began—upon the life of an old man who couldn't make up his mind to die, couldn't bear to be parted from his kingship. One after another, men slipped into Thebes from Argos for the purpose of assassinating him, and every killer we caught always ended by confessing who had put him up to it, who had paid him to try it. And it wasn't only Polynices. That is really what I am trying to tell you. I want you to know what went on in the back room, in the kitchen of politics; I want you to know what took place in the wings of this drama in which you are burning to play a part.

Yesterday, I gave Eteocles a State funeral, with pomp

and honors. Today, Eteocles is a saint and a hero in the eyes of all Thebes. The whole city turned out to bury him. The schoolchildren emptied their savings-boxes to buy wreaths for him. Old men, orating in quavering, hypocritical voices, glorified the virtues of the great-hearted brother, the devoted son, the loyal prince. I made a speech myself; and every temple priest was present with an appropriate show of sorrow and solemnity in his stupid face. And military honors were accorded the dead hero.

Well, what else could I have done? People had taken sides in the civil war. Both sides couldn't be wrong; that would be too much. I couldn't have made them swallow the truth. Two gangsters was more of a luxury than I could afford. (*He pauses for a moment*) And this is the whole point of my story. Eteocles, that virtuous brother, was just as rotten as Polynices. That great-hearted son had done his best, too, to procure the assassination of his father. That loyal prince had also offered to sell out Thebes to the highest bidder. Funny, isn't it? Polynices lies rotting in the sun while Eteocles is given a hero's funeral and will be housed in a marble vault. Yet I have absolute proof that everything that Polynices did, Eteocles had plotted to do. They were a pair of blackguards—both engaged in selling out Thebes, and both engaged in selling out each other; and they died like the cheap gangsters they were, over a division of the spoils.

But, as I told you a moment ago, I had to make a martyr of one of them. I sent out to the holocaust for their bodies; they were found clasped in one another's arms—for the first time in their lives, I imagine. Each had been spitted on the other's sword, and the Argive cavalry had trampled them down. They were mashed to a pulp, Antigone. I had the prettier of the two carcases brought in, and gave it a State funeral; and I left the other to rot. I don't know which was which.

And I assure you, I don't care. (*Long silence, neither looking at the other*)

ANTIGONE (*In a mild voice*) Why do you tell me all this?

CREON Would it have been better to let you die a victim to that obscene story?

ANTIGONE It might have been. I had my faith.

CREON What are you going to do now?

ANTIGONE (*Rises to her feet in a daze*) I shall go up to my room.

CREON Don't stay alone. Go and find Haemon. And get married quickly.

ANTIGONE (*In a whisper*) Yes.

CREON All this is really beside the point. You have your whole life ahead of you—and life is a treasure.

ANTIGONE Yes.

CREON And you were about to throw it away. Don't think me fatuous if I say that I understand you; and that at your age I should have done the same thing. A moment ago, when we were quarreling, you said I was drinking in your words. I was. But it wasn't you I was listening to; it was a lad named Creon who lived here in Thebes many years ago. He was thin and pale, as you are. His mind, too, was filled with thoughts of self-sacrifice. Go and find Haemon. And get married quickly, Antigone. Be happy. Life flows like water, and you young people let it run away through your fingers. Shut your hands; hold on to it, Antigone. Life is not what you think it is. Life is a child playing round your feet, a tool you hold firmly in your grip, a bench you sit down upon in the evening, in your garden. People will tell you that that's not life, that life is something else. They will tell you that because they need your strength and your fire, and they will want to make use of you. Don't listen to them. Believe me, the only poor consolation that we have in our old age is to discover

that what I have said to you is true. Life is nothing
more than the happiness that you get out of it.

ANTIGONE (*Murmurs, lost in thought*)  Happiness . . .

CREON (*Suddenly a little self-conscious*)  Not much of
a word, is it?

ANTIGONE (*Quietly*)  What kind of happiness do you
foresee for me? Paint me the picture of your happy
Antigone. What are the unimportant little sins that
I shall have to commit before I am allowed to sink
my teeth into life and tear happiness from it? Tell
me: to whom shall I have to lie? Upon whom shall
I have to fawn? To whom must I sell myself? Whom
do you want me to leave dying, while I turn away
my eyes?

CREON  Antigone, be quiet.

ANTIGONE  Why do you tell me to be quiet when all
I want to know is what I have to do to be happy?
This minute; since it is this very minute that I must
make my choice. You tell me that life is so wonderful.
I want to know what I have to do in order to be able
to say that myself.

CREON  Do you love Haemon?

ANTIGONE  Yes, I love Haemon. The Haemon I love
is hard and young, faithful and difficult to satisfy,
just as I am. But if what I love in Haemon is to be
worn away like a stone step by the tread of the thing
you call life, the thing you call happiness; if Haemon
reaches the point where he stops growing pale with
fear when I grow pale, stops thinking that I must
have been killed in an accident when I am five
minutes late, stops feeling that he is alone on earth
when I laugh and he doesn't know why—if he too
has to learn to say yes to everything—why, no, then,
no! I do not love Haemon!

CREON  You don't know what you are talking about!

ANTIGONE  I do know what I am talking about! Now
it is you who have stopped understanding. I am too

far away from you now, talking to you from a kingdom you can't get into, with your quick tongue and
your hollow heart. (*Laughs*) I laugh, Creon, because
I see you suddenly as you must have been at fifteen:
the same look of impotence in your face and the
same inner conviction that there was nothing you
couldn't do. What has life added to you, except those
lines in your face, and that fat on your stomach?

CREON  Be quiet, I tell you!

ANTIGONE  Why do you want me to be quiet? Because
you know that I am right? Do you think I can't see
in your face that what I am saying is true? You can't
admit it, of course; you have to go on growling and
defending the bone you call happiness.

CREON  It is your happiness, too, you little fool!

ANTIGONE  I spit on your happiness! I spit on your idea
of life—that life that must go on, come what may.
You are all like dogs that lick everything they smell.
You with your promise of a humdrum happiness—
provided a person doesn't ask too much of life. I want
everything of life, I do; and I want it now! I want
it total, complete: otherwise I reject it! I will *not* be
moderate. I will *not* be satisfied with the bit of cake
you offer me if I promise to be a good little girl.
I want to be sure of everything this very day; sure
that everything will be as beautiful as when I was
a little girl. If not, I want to die!

CREON  Scream on, daughter of Oedipus! Scream on,
in your father's own voice!

ANTIGONE  In my father's own voice, yes! We are of
the tribe that asks questions, and we ask them to the
bitter end. Until no tiniest chance of hope remains
to be strangled by our hands. We are of the tribe
that hates your filthy hope, your docile, female hope;
hope, your whore—

CREON  (*Grasps her by her arms*) Shut up! If you
could see how ugly you are, shrieking those words!

ANTIGONE　Yes, I am ugly! Father was ugly, too. (CREON *releases her arms, turns and moves away. Stands with his back to* ANTIGONE) But Father became beautiful. And do you know when? (*She follows him to behind the table*) At the very end. When all his questions had been answered. When he could no longer doubt that he *had* killed his own father; that he *had* gone to bed with his own mother. When all hope was gone, stamped out like a beetle. When it was absolutely certain that nothing, nothing could save him. Then he was at peace; then he could smile, almost; then he became beautiful. . . . Whereas you! Ah, those faces of yours, you candidates for election to happiness! It's you who are the ugly ones, even the handsomest of you—with that ugly glint in the corner of your eyes, that ugly crease at the corner of your mouths. Creon, you spoke the word a moment ago: the kitchen of politics. You look it and you smell of it.

CREON　(*Struggles to put hand over her mouth*) I order you to shut up! Do you hear me!

ANTIGONE　*You* order me? Cook! Do you really believe that you can give me orders?

CREON　Antigone! The ante-room is full of people! Do you want them to hear you?

ANTIGONE　Open the doors! Let us make sure that they can hear me!

CREON　By God! You shut up, I tell you!

　　　(ISMENE *enters through arch*)

ISMENE　(*Distraught*) Antigone!

ANTIGONE　(*Turns to* ISMENE) You, too? What do you want?

ISMENE　Oh, forgive me, Antigone. I've come back. I'll be brave. I'll go with you now.

ANTIGONE　Where will you go with me?

ISMENE　(*To* CREON) Creon! If you kill her, you'll have to kill me too.

ANTIGONE  Oh, no, Ismene. Not a bit of it. I die alone. You don't think I'm going to let you die with me after what I've been through? You don't deserve it.

ISMENE  If you die, I don't want to live. I don't want to be left behind, alone.

ANTIGONE  You chose life and I chose death. Now stop blubbering. You had your chance to come with me in the black night, creeping on your hands and knees. You had your chance to claw up the earth with your nails, as I did; to get yourself caught like a thief, as I did. And you refused it.

ISMENE  Not any more. I'll do it alone tonight.

ANTIGONE (*Turns round toward* CREON)  You hear that, Creon? The thing is catching! Who knows but that lots of people will catch the disease from me! What are you waiting for? Call in your guards! Come on, Creon! Show a little courage! It only hurts for a minute! Come on, cook!

CREON (*Turns toward arch and calls*)  Guard!
      (GUARDS *enter through arch*)

ANTIGONE (*In a great cry of relief*)  At last, Creon!
      (CHORUS *enters through left arch*)

CREON (*To the* GUARDS)  Take her away! (CREON *goes up on top step*)
      (GUARDS *grasp* ANTIGONE *by her arms, turn and hustle her toward the arch, right, and exit*)
      (ISMENE *mimes horror, backs away toward the arch, left, then turns and runs out through the arch. A long pause, as* CREON *moves slowly downstage*)

CHORUS (*Behind* CREON. *Speaks in a deliberate voice*)  You are out of your mind, Creon. What have you done?

CREON (*His back to* CHORUS)  She has to die.

CHORUS  You must not let Antigone die. We shall carry the scar of her death for centuries.

CREON  No man on earth was strong enough to dissuade

her. Death was her purpose, whether she knew it or not. Polynices was a mere pretext. When she had to give up that pretext, she found another one. She was bent upon only one thing: to reject life and to die.

CHORUS  She is a mere child, Creon.

CREON  What do you want me to do for her? Condemn her to live?

HAEMON  (*Calls from offstage*)  Father! (HAEMON *enters through arch, right.* CREON *turns toward him*)

CREON  Haemon, forget Antigone. Forget her, my dearest boy.

HAEMON  How can you talk like that?

CREON  (*Grasps* HAEMON *by the hands*)  I did everything I could to save her, Haemon. I used every argument. I swear I did. The girl doesn't love you. She could have gone on living for you; but she refused. She wanted it this way; she wanted to die.

HAEMON  Father! The guards are dragging Antigone away! You've got to stop them! (*He breaks away from* CREON)

CREON  (*Looks away from* HAEMON)  I can't stop them. It's too late. Antigone has spoken. The story is all over Thebes. I cannot save her now.

CHORUS  Creon, you must find a way. Lock her up. Say that she has gone out of her mind.

CREON  Everybody will know it isn't so. The nation will say that I am making an exception of her because my son loves her. I cannot.

CHORUS  You can still gain time, and get her out of Thebes.

CREON  The mob already knows the truth. It is howling for her blood. I can do nothing.

HAEMON  But, Father, you are master in Thebes!

CREON  I am master under the law. Not above the law.

HAEMON  You cannot let Antigone be taken from me. I am your son!

CREON  I cannot do anything else, my poor boy. She must die and you must live.

HAEMON  Live, you say! Live a life without Antigone? A life in which I am to go on admiring you as you busy yourself about your kingdom, make your persuasive speeches, strike your attitudes? Not without Antigone. I love Antigone. I will not live without Antigone!

CREON  Haemon—you will have to resign yourself to life without Antigone. (*He moves to left of* HAEMON) Sooner or later there comes a day of sorrow in each man's life when he must cease to be a child and take up the burden of manhood. That day has come for you.

HAEMON  (*Backs away a step*)  That giant strength, that courage. That massive god who used to pick me up in his arms and shelter me from shadows and monsters—was that you, Father? Was it of you I stood in awe? Was that man you?

CREON  For God's sake, Haemon, do not judge me! Not you, too!

HAEMON  (*Pleading now*)  This is all a bad dream, Father. You are not yourself. It isn't true that we have been backed up against a wall, forced to surrender. We don't have to say *yes* to this terrible thing. You are still king. You are still the father I revered. You have no right to desert me, to shrink into nothingness. The world will be too bare, I shall be too alone in the world, if you force me to disown you.

CREON  The world *is* bare, Haemon, and you *are* alone. You must cease to think your father all-powerful. Look straight at me. See your father as he is. That is what it means to grow up and be a man.

HAEMON  (*Stares at* CREON *for a moment*)  I tell you that I will not live without Antigone. (*Turns and goes quickly out through arch*)

CHORUS  Creon, the boy will go mad.

CREON  Poor boy! He loves her.

CHORUS  Creon, the boy is wounded to death.

CREON  We are all wounded to death.

(FIRST GUARD *enters through arch, right, followed by* SECOND *and* THIRD GUARDS *pulling* ANTIGONE *along with them*)

FIRST GUARD   Sir, the people are crowding into the palace!

ANTIGONE   Creon, I don't want to see their faces. I don't want to hear them howl. You are going to kill me; let that be enough. I want to be alone until it is over.

CREON   Empty the palace! Guards at the gates! (CREON *quickly crosses toward the arch and exits. Two* GUARDS *release* ANTIGONE *and exit behind* CREON. CHORUS *goes out through arch, left*)

(*The lighting dims so that only the area about the table is lighted. The cyclorama is covered with a dark blue color. The scene is intended to suggest a prison cell, filled with shadows and dimly lit.* ANTIGONE *moves to stool and sits. The* FIRST GUARD *stands upstage. He watches* ANTIGONE, *and as she sits, he begins pacing slowly downstage, then upstage*)

(*A pause*)

ANTIGONE   (*Turns and looks at the* GUARD)   It's you, is it?

GUARD   What do you mean, me?

ANTIGONE   The last human face that I shall see. (*A pause as they look at each other, then* GUARD *paces upstage; turns and crosses behind table*) Was it you that arrested me this morning?

GUARD   Yes, that was me.

ANTIGONE   You hurt me. There was no need for you to hurt me. Did I act as if I was trying to escape?

GUARD   Come on now, Miss. It was my business to bring you in. I did it. (*A pause. He paces to and fro upstage. Only the sound of his boots is heard*)

ANTIGONE   How old are you?

GUARD   Thirty-nine.

ANTIGONE   Have you any children?

GUARD   Yes. Two.

ANTIGONE   Do you love your children?

GUARD   What's that got to do with you? (*A pause. He paces upstage and downstage*)

ANTIGONE   How long have you been in the Guard?

GUARD   Since the war. I was in the army. Sergeant. Then I joined the Guard.

ANTIGONE   Does one have to have been an army sergeant to get into the Guard?

GUARD   Supposed to be. Either that or on special detail. But when they make you a guard, you lose your stripes.

ANTIGONE (*Murmurs*)   I see.

GUARD   Yes. Of course, if you're a guard, everybody knows you're something special; they know you're an old N.C.O. Take pay, for instance. When you're a guard you get your pay, and on top of that you get six months' extra pay, to make sure you don't lose anything by not being a sergeant any more. And of course you do better than that. You get a house, coal, rations, extras for the wife and kids. If you've got two kids, like me, you draw better than a sergeant.

ANTIGONE (*Barely audible*)   I see.

GUARD   That's why sergeants, now, they don't like guards. Maybe you noticed they try to make out they're better than us? Promotion, that's what it is. In the army, anybody can get promoted. All you need is good conduct. Now in the Guard, it's slow, and you have to know your business—like how to make out a report and the like of that. But when you're an N.C.O. in the Guard, you've got something that even a sergeant-major ain't got. For instance—

ANTIGONE (*Breaking him off*)   Listen.

GUARD   Yes, Miss.

ANTIGONE   I'm going to die soon.

(*The* GUARD *looks at her for a moment, then turns and moves away*)

GUARD　For instance, people have a lot of respect for guards, they have. A guard may be a soldier, but he's kind of in the civil service, too.

ANTIGONE　Do you think it hurts to die?

GUARD　How would I know? Of course, if somebody sticks a saber in your guts and turns it round, it hurts.

ANTIGONE　How are they going to put me to death?

GUARD　Well, I'll tell you. I heard the proclamation all right. Wait a minute. How did it go now? (*He stares into space and recites from memory*) "In order that our fair city shall not be pol-luted with her sin-ful blood, she shall be im-mured—immured." That means, they shove you in a cave and wall up the cave.

ANTIGONE　Alive?

GUARD　Yes. . . . (*He moves away a few steps*)

ANTIGONE (*Murmurs*)　O tomb! O bridal bed! Alone! (ANTIGONE *sits there, a tiny figure in the middle of the stage. You would say she felt a little chilly. She wraps her arms round herself*)

GUARD　Yes! Outside the south-east gate of the town. In the Cave of Hades. In broad daylight. Some detail, eh, for them that's on the job! First they thought maybe it was a job for the army. Now it looks like it's going to be the Guard. There's an outfit for you! Nothing the Guard can't do. No wonder the army's jealous.

ANTIGONE　A pair of animals.

GUARD　What do you mean, a pair of animals?

ANTIGONE　When the winds blow cold, all they need do is to press close against one another. I am all alone.

GUARD　Is there anything you want? I can send out for it, you know.

ANTIGONE　You are very kind. (*A pause.* ANTIGONE *looks up at the* GUARD) Yes, there is something I want. I want you to give someone a letter from me, when I am dead.

GUARD   How's that again? A letter?

ANTIGONE   Yes, I want to write a letter; and I want you to give it to someone for me.

GUARD   (*Straightens up*)   Now, wait a minute. Take it easy. It's as much as my job is worth to go handing out letters from prisoners.

ANTIGONE   (*Removes a ring from her finger and holds it out toward him*)   I'll give you this ring if you will do it.

GUARD   Is it gold? (*He takes the ring from her*)

ANTIGONE   Yes, it is gold.

GUARD   (*Shakes his head*)   Uh-uh. No can do. Suppose they go through my pockets. I might get six months for a thing like that. (*He stares at the ring, then glances off right to make sure that he is not being watched*) Listen, tell you what I'll do. You tell me what you want to say, and I'll write it down in my book. Then, afterward, I'll tear out the pages and give them to the party, see? If it's in my handwriting, it's all right.

ANTIGONE   (*Winces*)   In your handwriting? (*She shudders slightly*) No. that would be awful. The poor darling! In your handwriting.

GUARD   (*Offers back the ring*)   O.K. It's no skin off my nose.

ANTIGONE   (*Quickly*)   Of course, of course. No, keep the ring. But hurry. Time is getting short. Where is your notebook? (*The GUARD pockets the ring, takes his notebook and pencil from his pocket, puts his foot up on chair, and rests the notebook on his knee, licks his pencil*) Ready? (*He nods*) Write, now. "My darling . . ."

GUARD   (*Writes as he mutters*)   The boy friend, eh?

ANTIGONE   "My darling. I wanted to die, and perhaps you will not love me any more . . ."

GUARD   (*Mutters as he writes*)   ". . . will not love me any more."

ANTIGONE   "Creon was right, it's terrible; now, beside this man, I no longer know why I am dying. I am afraid . . ."

GUARD (*Repeats as he writes*)  "Creon was right, it's terrible . . ."

ANTIGONE   "Oh, Haemon, our little boy. Only now do I understand how easy it was to live."

GUARD (*Looks at her*)  Wait a minute! How fast do you think I can write?

ANTIGONE (*Takes hold of herself*)  Where are you?

GUARD (*Reads from his notebook*)  "It's terrible now beside this man . . ."

ANTIGONE   "I no longer know why I am dying."

GUARD (*Writing*)  "I no longer know why I am dying." You never know why you're dying.

ANTIGONE (*Continuing*)  "I'm afraid. . . ." No. Scratch that out. Nobody must know that. It's as if they saw me naked and touched me, after I was dead. Scratch it all out. Just write: "Forgive me."

GUARD (*Looks at* ANTIGONE)  I cut out everything you said there at the end, and I put down, "Forgive me"?

ANTIGONE   Yes. "Forgive me, my darling. You would all have been so happy except for Antigone. I love you."

GUARD (*Finishes the letter*)  ". . . I love you." (*He looks at her*)  Is that all?

ANTIGONE   That's all.

GUARD (*Straightens up, looks at notebook*)  Damn funny letter.

ANTIGONE   I know.

GUARD (*Looks at her*)  Who is it to? (*A sudden roll of drums begins and continues until after* ANTIGONE *exits. The* FIRST GUARD *pockets the notebook and shouts at* ANTIGONE)  O.K. That's enough out of you! Come on!
    (*At the sound of the drum roll,* SECOND *and* THIRD GUARDS *enter through the right arch.* ANTIGONE *rises.* GUARDS *seize her and exit with her*)

(*The lighting moves up to suggest late afternoon*)
(CHORUS *enters*)

CHORUS    And now it is Creon's turn.

(MESSENGER *runs through the arch, right*)

MESSENGER    The Queen . . . the Queen! Where is the Queen?

CHORUS    What do you want with the Queen? What have you to tell the Queen?

MESSENGER    News to break her heart. Antigone had just been thrust into the cave. They hadn't finished heaving the last blocks of stone into place when Creon and the rest heard a sudden moaning from the tomb. A hush fell over us all, for it was not the voice of Antigone. It was Haemon's voice that came forth from the tomb. Everybody looked at Creon; and he howled like a man demented: "Take away the stones! Take away the stones!" The slaves leaped at the wall of stones, and Creon worked with them, sweating and tearing at the blocks with his bleeding hands. Finally a narrow opening was forced, and into it slipped the smallest guard.

Antigone had hanged herself by the cord of her robe, by the red and golden twisted cord of her robe. The cord was round her neck like a child's collar. Haemon was on his knees, holding her in his arms and moaning, his face buried in her robe. More stones were removed, and Creon went into the tomb. He tried to raise Haemon to his feet. I could hear him begging Haemon to rise to his feet. Haemon was deaf to his father's voice, till suddenly he stood up of his own accord, his eyes dark and burning. Anguish was in his face, but it was the face of a little boy. He stared at his father. Then suddenly he struck him—hard; and he drew his sword. Creon leaped out of range. Haemon went on staring at him, his eyes full of contempt—a glance that was like a knife, and that Creon couldn't escape. The King stood trembling in the far corner of the tomb, and Haemon went on staring. Then, without a word, he stabbed himself and lay down beside Antigone, embracing her in a great pool of blood.

> (*A pause as* CREON *and* PAGE *enter through arch on the* MESSENGER's *last words.* CHORUS *and the* MESSENGER *both turn to look at* CREON, *then the* MESSENGER *exits through curtain*)

CREON    I have had them laid out side by side. They are together at last, and at peace. Two lovers on the morrow of their bridal. Their work is done.

CHORUS    But not yours, Creon. You have still one thing to learn. Eurydice, the Queen, your wife—

CREON    A good woman. Always busy with her garden, her preserves, her jerseys—those jerseys she never stopped knitting for the poor. Strange, how the poor never stop needing jerseys. One would almost think that was all they needed.

CHORUS    The poor in Thebes are going to be cold this winter, Creon. When the Queen was told of her son's death, she waited carefully until she had finished her row, then put down her knitting calmly—as she did everything. She went up to her room, her lavender-scented room, with its embroidered doilies and its pictures framed in plush; and there, Creon, she cut her throat. She is laid out now in one of those two old-fashioned twin beds, exactly where you went to her one night when she was still a maiden. Her smile is still the same, scarcely a shade more melancholy. And if it were not for that great red blot on the bed linen by her neck, one might think she was asleep.

CREON (*In a dull voice*)    She, too. They are all asleep. (*Pause*) It must be good to sleep.

CHORUS    And now you are alone, Creon.

CREON    Yes, all alone. (*To* PAGE) My lad.

PAGE    Sir?

CREON    Listen to me. They don't know it, but the truth

is the work is there to be done, and a man can't fold his arms and refuse to do it. They say it's dirty work. But if we didn't do it, who would?

PAGE   I don't know, sir.

CREON   Of course you don't. You'll be lucky if you never find out. In a hurry to grow up, aren't you?

PAGE   Oh yes, sir.

CREON   I shouldn't be if I were you. Never grow up if you can help it. (*He is lost in thought as the hour chimes*) What time is it?

PAGE   Five o'clock, sir.

CREON   What have we on at five o'clock?

PAGE   Cabinet meeting, sir.

CREON   Cabinet meeting. Then we had better go along to it.

(CREON *and* PAGE *exit slowly through arch, left, and* CHORUS *moves downstage*)

CHORUS   And there we are. It is quite true that if it had not been for Antigone they would all have been at peace. But that is over now. And they are all at peace. All those who were meant to die have died: those who believed one thing, those who believed the contrary thing, and even those who believed nothing at all, yet were caught up in the web without knowing why. All dead: stiff, useless, rotting. And those who have survived will now begin quietly to forget the dead: they won't remember who was who or which was which. It is all over. Antigone is calm tonight and we shall never know the name of the fever that consumed her. She has played her part.

(*Three* GUARDS *enter, resume their places on steps as at the rise of the curtain, and begin to play cards*)

A great melancholy wave of peace now settles down upon Thebes, upon the empty palace, upon Creon, who can now begin to wait for his own death.

Only the guards are left, and none of this matters to

them. It's no skin off their noses. They go on playing
cards.

> (CHORUS *walks toward the arch, left, as the curtain
> falls*)

# *No Exit*

by
# JEAN-PAUL SARTRE

A Play in One Act

*Translated by*
*STUART GILBERT*

## CHARACTERS

VALET
GARCIN
ESTELLE
INEZ

No Exit *was first presented at the Théâtre
du Vieux Colombier, Paris, in May, 1944.*

# Scene

*A drawing-room in Second Empire style. A massive bronze ornament stands on the mantelpiece.*

GARCIN (*Enters, accompanied by the* ROOM-VALET, *and glances around him*)  Hm! So here we are?

VALET  Yes, Mr. Garcin.

GARCIN  And this is what it looks like?

VALET  Yes.

GARCIN  Second Empire furniture, I observe. . . . Well, well, I dare say one gets used to it in time.

VALET  Some do. Some don't.

GARCIN  Are all the other rooms like this one?

VALET  How could they be? We cater for all sorts: Chinamen and Indians, for instance. What use would they have for a Second Empire chair?

GARCIN  And what use do you suppose *I* have for one? Do you know who I was? . . . Oh, well, it's no great matter. And, to tell the truth, I had quite a habit of living among furniture that I didn't relish, and in false positions. I'd even come to like it. A false position in a Louis-Philippe dining-room—you know the style?—well, that had its points, you know. Bogus in bogus, so to speak.

VALET  And you'll find that living in a Second Empire drawing-room has its points.

GARCIN  Really? . . . Yes, yes, I dare say. . . . (*He takes another look around*) Still, I certainly didn't expect—this! You know what they tell us down there?

VALET  What about?

GARCIN  About (*Makes a sweeping gesture*) this—er—residence.

VALET    Really, sir, how could you believe such cock-
and-bull stories? Told by people who'd never set foot
here. For, of course, if they had—

GARCIN    Quite so. (*Both laugh. Abruptly the laugh dies
from* GARCIN's *face*) But, I say, where are the instruments of torture?

VALET    The what?

GARCIN    The racks and red-hot pincers and all the other
paraphernalia?

VALET    Ah, you must have your little joke, sir!

GARCIN    My little joke? Oh, I see. No, I wasn't joking.
(*A short silence. He strolls round the room*) No
mirrors, I notice. No windows. Only to be expected.
And nothing breakable. (*Bursts out angrily*) But,
damn it all, they might have left me my toothbrush!

VALET    That's good! So you haven't yet got over your
—what-do-you-call-it?—sense of human dignity? Excuse my smiling.

GARCIN    (*Thumping ragefully the arm of an armchair*)
I'll ask you to be more polite. I quite realize the position I'm in, but I won't tolerate . . .

VALET    Sorry, sir. No offense meant. But all our guests
ask me the same questions. Silly questions, if you'll
pardon me saying so. Where's the torture-chamber?
That's the first thing they ask, all of them. They don't
bother their heads about the bathroom requisites, that
I can assure you. But after a bit, when they've got
their nerve back, they start in about their tooth-
brushes and what-not. Good heavens, Mr. Garcin,
can't you use your brains? What, I ask you, would be
the point of brushing your teeth?

GARCIN    (*More calmly*) Yes, of course you're right. (*He
looks around again*) And why should one want to see
oneself in a looking-glass? But that bronze contraption on the mantelpiece, that's another story. I suppose there will be times when I stare my eyes out
at it. Stare my eyes out—see what I mean? . . . All
right, let's put our cards on the table. I assure you

I'm quite conscious of my position. Shall I tell you what it feels like? A man's drowning, choking, sinking by inches, till only his eyes are just above water. And what does he see? A bronze atrocity by—what's the fellow's name?—Barbedienne. A collector's piece. As in a nightmare. That's their idea, isn't it? . . . No, I suppose you're under orders not to answer questions; and I won't insist. But don't forget, my man, I've a good notion of what's coming to me, so don't you boast you've caught me off my guard. I'm facing the situation, facing it. (*He starts pacing the room again*) So that's that; no toothbrush. And no bed, either. One never sleeps, I take it?

VALET  That's so.

GARCIN  Just as I expected. *Why* should one sleep? A sort of drowsiness steals on you, tickles you behind the ears, and you feel your eyes closing—but why sleep? You lie down on the sofa and—in a flash sleep flies away. Miles and miles away. So you rub your eyes, get up, and it starts all over again.

VALET  Romantic, that's what you are.

GARCIN  Will you keep quiet, please! . . . I won't make a scene, I shan't be sorry for myself, I'll face the situation, as I said just now. Face it fairly and squarely. I won't have it springing at me from behind, before I've time to size it up. And you call that being "romantic"! . . . So it comes to this; one doesn't need rest. Why bother about sleep if one isn't sleepy? That stands to reason, doesn't it? Wait a minute, there's a snag somewhere; something disagreeable. Why, now, should it be disagreeable? . . . Ah, I see; it's life without a break.

VALET  What do you mean by that?

GARCIN  What do I mean (*Eyes the* VALET *suspiciously*) I thought as much. That's why there's something so beastly, so damn bad-mannered, in the way you stare at me. They're paralyzed.

VALET  What are you talking about?

GARCIN  Your eyelids. We move ours up and down. Blinking, we call it. It's like a small black shutter that clicks down and makes a break. Everything goes black; one's eyes are moistened. You can't imagine how restful, refreshing, it is. Four thousand little rests per hour. Four thousand little respites—just think! . . . So that's the idea. I'm to live without eyelids. Don't act the fool, you know what I mean. No eyelids, no sleep; it follows, doesn't it? I shall never sleep again. But then—how shall I endure my own company? Try to understand. You see, I'm fond of teasing, it's a second nature with me—and I'm used to teasing myself. Plaguing myself, if you prefer; I don't tease nicely. But I can't go on doing that without a break. Down there I had my nights. I slept. I always had good nights. By way of compensation, I suppose. And happy little dreams. There was a green field. Just an ordinary field. I used to stroll in it. . . . Is it daytime now?

VALET  Can't you see? The lights are on.

GARCIN  Ah yes, I've got it. It's *your* daytime. And outside?

VALET  Outside?

GARCIN  Damn it, you know what I mean. Beyond that wall.

VALET  There's a passage.

GARCIN  And at the end of the passage?

VALET  There's more rooms, more passages, and stairs.

GARCIN  And what lies beyond them?

VALET  That's all.

GARCIN  But surely you have a day off sometimes. Where do you go?

VALET  To my uncle's place. He's the head valet here. He has a room on the third floor.

GARCIN  I should have guessed as much. Where's the light-switch?

VALET  There isn't any.

GARCIN   What? Can't one turn off the light?

VALET   Oh, the management can cut off the current if they want to. But I can't remember their having done so on this floor. We have all the electricity we want.

GARCIN   So one has to live with one's eyes open all the time?

VALET   To *live*, did you say?

GARCIN   Don't let's quibble over words. With one's eyes open. Forever. Always broad daylight in my eyes— and in my head. (*Short silence*) And suppose I took that contraption on the mantelpiece and dropped it on the lamp—wouldn't it go out?

VALET   You can't move it. It's too heavy.

GARCIN (*Seizing the bronze ornament and trying to lift it*)   You're right. It's too heavy.

(*A short silence follows*)

VALET   Very well, sir, if you don't need me any more, I'll be off.

GARCIN   What? You're going? (*The* VALET *goes up to the door*) Wait. (VALET *looks around*) That's a bell, isn't it? (VALET *nods*) And if I ring, you're bound to come?

VALET   Well, yes, that's so—in a way. But you can never be sure about that bell. There's something wrong with the wiring, and it doesn't always work. (GARCIN *goes to the bell-push and presses the button. A bell purrs outside*)

GARCIN   It's working all right.

VALET (*Looking surprised*)   So it is. (*He, too, presses the button*) But I shouldn't count on it too much if I were you. It's—capricious. Well, I really must go now. (GARCIN *makes a gesture to detain him*) Yes, sir?

GARCIN   No, never mind. (*He goes to the mantelpiece and picks up a paper-knife*) What's this?

VALET   Can't you see? An ordinary paper-knife.

GARCIN   Are there books here?

VALET   No.

GARCIN    Then what's the use of this? (VALET *shrugs his shoulders*) Very well. You can go. (VALET *goes out*) (GARCIN *is by himself. He goes to the bronze ornament and strokes it reflectively. He sits down; then gets up, goes to the bell-push, and presses the button. The bell remains silent. He tries two or three times, without success. Then he tries to open the door, also without success. He calls the* VALET *several times, but gets no result. He beats the door with his fists, still calling. Suddenly he grows calm and sits down again. At the same moment the door opens and* INEZ *enters, followed by the* VALET)

VALET    Did you call, sir?

GARCIN (*On the point of answering "Yes"—but then his eyes fall on* INEZ)    No.

VALET (*Turning to* INEZ)    This is your room, Madam. (INEZ *says nothing*) If there's any information you require—? (INEZ *still keeps silent, and the* VALET *looks slightly huffed*) Most of our guests have quite a lot to ask me. But I won't insist. Anyhow, as regards the toothbrush, and the electric bell, and that thing on the mantelshelf, this gentleman can tell you anything you want to know as well as I could. We've had a little chat, him and me. (VALET *goes out.* GARCIN *refrains from looking at* INEZ, *who is inspecting the room. Abruptly she turns to* GARCIN)

INEZ    Where's Florence? (GARCIN *does not reply*) Didn't you hear? I asked you about Florence. Where is she?

GARCIN    I haven't any idea.

INEZ    Ah, that's the way it works, is it? Torture by separation. Well, as far as I'm concerned, you won't get anywhere. Florence was a tiresome little fool, and I shan't miss her in the least.

GARCIN    I beg your pardon. Who do you suppose I am?

INEZ    You? Why, the torturer, of course.

GARCIN (*Looks startled, then bursts out laughing*)    Well,

that's a good one! Too comic for words. I the torturer! So you came in, had a look at me, and thought
I was—er—one of the staff. Of course, it's that silly
fellow's fault; he should have introduced us. A torturer indeed! I'm Joseph Garcin, journalist and man
of letters by profession. And as we're both in the
same boat, so to speak, might I ask you, Mrs.—?

INEZ (*Testily*)  Not "Mrs." I'm unmarried.

GARCIN  Right. That's a start, anyway. Well, now that
we've broken the ice, do you *really* think I look like
a torturer? And, by the way, how does one recognize
torturers when one sees them? Evidently you've ideas
on the subject.

INEZ  They look frightened.

GARCIN  Frightened! But how ridiculous! Of whom
should they be frightened? Of their victims?

INEZ  Laugh away, but I know what I'm talking about.
I've often watched my face in the glass.

GARCIN  In the glass? (*He looks around him*) How
beastly of them! They've removed everything in the
least resembling a glass. (*Short silence*) Anyhow, I
can assure you I'm not frightened. Not that I take
my position lightly; I realize its gravity only too well.
But I'm not afraid.

INEZ (*Shrugging her shoulders*)  That's your affair.
(*Silence*) Must you be here all the time, or do you
take a stroll outside, now and then?

GARCIN  The door's locked.

INEZ  Oh! . . . That's too bad.

GARCIN  I can understand that it bores you having me
here. And I, too—well, quite frankly, I'd rather be
alone. I want to think things out, you know; to set
my life in order, and one does that better by oneself.
But I'm sure we'll manage to pull along together
somehow. I'm no talker, I don't move much; in fact
I'm a peaceful sort of fellow. Only, if I may venture
on a suggestion, we should make a point of being

extremely courteous to each other. That will ease the
situation for us both.

INEZ   I'm not polite.

GARCIN   Then I must be polite for two.

>    (*A longish silence.* GARCIN *is sitting on a sofa,
>    while* INEZ *paces up and down the room*)

INEZ (*Fixing her eyes on him*)   Your mouth!

GARCIN (*As if waking from a dream*)   I beg your pardon.

INEZ   Can't you keep your mouth still? You keep twist-
ing it about all the time. It's grotesque.

GARCIN   So sorry. I wasn't aware of it.

INEZ   That's just what I reproach you with. (GARCIN's
*mouth twitches*) There you are! You talk about
politeness, and you don't even try to control your
face. Remember you're not alone; you've no right to
inflict the sight of your fear on me.

GARCIN (*Getting up and going toward her*)   How about
you? Aren't you afraid?

INEZ   What would be the use? There was some point
in being afraid *before;* while one still had hope.

GARCIN (*In a low voice*)   There's no more hope—but
it's still "before." We haven't yet begun to suffer.

INEZ   That's so. (*A short silence*) Well? What's going
to happen?

GARCIN   I don't know. I'm waiting.

>    (*Silence again.* GARCIN *sits down and* INEZ *resumes
>    her pacing up and down the room.* GARCIN's
>    *mouth twitches; after a glance at* INEZ *he buries
>    his face in his hands. Enter* ESTELLE *with the*
>    VALET. ESTELLE *looks at* GARCIN, *whose face is still
>    hidden by his hands.*)

ESTELLE (*to* GARCIN)   No! Don't look up. I know what
you're hiding with your hands. I know you've no face
left. (GARCIN *removes his hands*) What! (*A short pause.
Then, in a tone of surprise*) But I don't know you!

GARCIN   I'm not the torturer, Madam.

ESTELLE   I never thought you were. I—I thought someone was trying to play a rather nasty trick on me. (*To the* VALET) Is anyone else coming?

VALET   No, Madam. No one else is coming.

ESTELLE   Oh! Then we're to stay by ourselves, the three of us, this gentleman, this lady, and myself. (*She starts laughing*)

GARCIN (*Angrily*)   There's nothing to laugh about.

ESTELLE (*Still laughing*)   It's those sofas. They're so hideous. And just look how they've been arranged. It makes me think of New Year's Day—when I used to visit that boring old aunt of mine, Aunt Mary. Her house is full of horrors like that. . . . I suppose each of us has a sofa of his own. Is that one mine? (*To the* VALET) But you can't expect me to sit on that one. It would be too horrible for words. I'm in pale blue and it's vivid green.

INEZ   Would you prefer mine?

ESTELLE   That claret-colored one, you mean? That's very sweet of you, but really—no, I don't think it'd be so much better. What's the good of worrying, anyhow? We've got to take what comes to us, and I'll stick to the green one. (*Pauses*) The only one which might do, at a pinch, is that gentleman's. (*Another pause*)

INEZ   Did you hear, Mr. Garcin?

GARCIN (*With a slight start*)   Oh—the sofa, you mean. So sorry. (*He rises*) Please take it, Madam.

ESTELLE   Thanks. (*She takes off her coat and drops it on the sofa. A short silence*) Well, as we're to live together, I suppose we'd better introduce ourselves. My name's Rigault. Estelle Rigault. (GARCIN *bows and is going to announce his name, but* INEZ *steps in front of him*)

INEZ   And I'm Inez Serrano. Very pleased to meet you.

GARCIN (*Bowing again*)   Joseph Garcin.

VALET   Do you require me any longer?

ESTELLE   No, you can go. I'll ring when I want you.

(*Exit* VALET, *with polite bows to everyone*)

INEZ You're very pretty. I wish we'd had some flowers to welcome you with.

ESTELLE Flowers? Yes, I loved flowers. Only they'd fade so quickly here, wouldn't they? It's so stuffy. Oh, well, the great thing is to keep as cheerful as we can, don't you agree? Of course, you, too, are—

INEZ Yes. Last week. What about you?

ESTELLE I'm—quite recent. Yesterday. As a matter of fact, the ceremony's not quite over. (*Her tone is natural enough, but she seems to be seeing what she describes*) The wind's blowing my sister's veil all over the place. She's trying her best to cry. Come, dear! Make another effort. That's better. Two tears, two little tears are twinkling under the black veil. Oh dear! What a sight Olga looks this morning! She's holding my sister's arm, helping her along. She's not crying, and I don't blame her; tears always mess one's face up, don't they? Olga was my bosom friend, you know.

INEZ Did you suffer much?

ESTELLE No. I was only half conscious, mostly.

INEZ What was it?

ESTELLE Pneumonia. (*In the same tone as before*) It's over now, they're leaving the cemetery. Good-by. Good-by. Quite a crowd they are. My husband's stayed at home. Prostrated with grief, poor man. (*To* INEZ) How about you?

INEZ The gas stove.

ESTELLE And you, Mr. Garcin?

GARCIN Twelve bullets through my chest. (ESTELLE *makes a horrified gesture*) Sorry! I fear I'm not good company among the dead.

ESTELLE Please, please don't use that word. It's so—so crude. In terribly bad taste, really. It doesn't mean much, anyhow. Somehow I feel we've never been so much alive as now. If we've absolutely got to mention this—this state of things, I suggest we call ourselves—wait!—absentees. Have you been—been absent for long?

GARCIN   About a month.

ESTELLE   Where do you come from?

GARCIN   From Rio.

ESTELLE   I'm from Paris. Have you anyone left down there?

GARCIN   Yes, my wife. (*In the same tone as* ESTELLE *has been using*) She's waiting at the entrance of the barracks. She comes there every day. But they won't let her in. Now she's trying to peep between the bars. She doesn't yet know I'm—absent, but she suspects it. Now she's going away. She's wearing her black dress. So much the better, she won't need to change. She isn't crying, but she never did cry, anyhow. It's a bright sunny day and she's like a black shadow creeping down the empty street. Those big tragic eyes of hers—with that martyred look they always had. Oh, how she got on my nerves!

(*A short silence.* GARCIN *sits on the central sofa and buries his head in his hands*)

INEZ   Estelle!

ESTELLE   Please, Mr. Garcin!

GARCIN   What is it?

ESTELLE   You're sitting on my sofa.

GARCIN   I beg your pardon. (*He gets up*)

ESTELLE   You looked so—so far away. Sorry I disturbed you.

GARCIN   I was setting my life in order. (INEZ *starts laughing*) You may laugh, but you'd do better to follow my example.

INEZ   No need. My life's in perfect order. It tidied itself up nicely of its own accord. So I needn't bother about it now.

GARCIN   Really? You imagine it's so simple as that. (*He runs his hand over his forehead*) Whew! How hot it is here! Do you mind if—? (*He begins taking off his coat*)

ESTELLE   How dare you! (*More gently*) No, please don't. I loathe men in their shirt-sleeves.

GARCIN (*Putting on his coat again*)   All right. (*A short pause*) Of course, I used to spend my nights in the newspaper office, and it was a regular Black Hole, so we never kept our coats on. Stiflingly hot it could be. (*Short pause. In the same tone as previously*) Stifling, that it *is*. It's night now.

ESTELLE   That's so. Olga's undressing; it must be after midnight. How quickly the time passes, on earth!

INEZ   Yes, after midnight. They've sealed up my room. It's dark, pitch-dark, and empty.

GARCIN   They've slung their coats on the backs of the chairs and rolled up their shirt-sleeves above the elbow. The air stinks of men and cigar-smoke. (*A short silence*) I used to like living among men in their shirt-sleeves.

ESTELLE (*Aggressively*)   Well, in that case our tastes differ. That's all it proves. (*Turning to* INEZ) What about you? Do you like men in their shirt-sleeves?

INEZ   Oh, I don't care much for men any way.

ESTELLE (*Looking at the other two with a puzzled air*) Really I can't imagine why they put us three together. It doesn't make sense.

INEZ (*Stifling a laugh*)   What's that you said?

ESTELLE   I'm looking at you two and thinking that we're going to live together. . . . It's so absurd. I expected to meet old friends, or relatives.

INEZ   Yes, a charming old friend—with a hole in the middle of his face.

ESTELLE   Yes, him too. He danced the tango so divinely. Like a professional. . . . But why, why should we of all people be put together?

GARCIN   A pure fluke, I should say. They lodge folks as they can, in the order of their coming. (*To* INEZ) Why are you laughing?

INEZ  Because you amuse me, with your "flukes." As
if they left anything to chance! But I suppose you've
got to reassure yourself somehow.

ESTELLE (*Hesitantly*)  I wonder, now. Don't you think
we may have met each other at some time in our lives?

INEZ  Never. I shouldn't have forgotten you.

ESTELLE  Or perhaps we have friends in common. I
wonder if you know the Dubois-Seymours?

INEZ  Not likely.

ESTELLE  But *everyone* went to their parties.

INEZ  What's their job?

ESTELLE  Oh, they don't do anything. But they have a
lovely house in the country, and hosts of people visit
them.

INEZ  I didn't. I was a post-office clerk.

ESTELLE (*Recoiling a little*)  Ah, yes. . . . Of course,
in that case—(*A pause*) And you, Mr. Garcin?

GARCIN  We've never met. I always lived in Rio.

ESTELLE  Then you must be right. It's mere chance that
has brought us together.

INEZ  Mere chance? Then it's by chance this room is
furnished as we see it. It's an accident that the sofa
on the right is a livid green, and that one on the left's
wine-red. Mere chance? Well, just try to shift the
sofas and you'll see the difference quick enough. And
that statue on the mantelpiece, do you think it's there
by accident? And what about the heat here? How
about that? (*A short silence*) I tell you they've thought
it all out. Down to the last detail. Nothing was left to
chance. This room was all set for us.

ESTELLE  But really! Everything here's so hideous; all
in angles, so uncomfortable. I always loathed angles.

INEZ (*Shrugging her shoulders*)  And do you think *I*
lived in a Second Empire drawing-room?

ESTELLE  So it was all fixed up beforehand?

INEZ  Yes. And they've put us together deliberately.

ESTELLE  Then it's not mere chance that *you* precisely

are sitting opposite *me?* But what can be the idea behind it?

INEZ   Ask me another! I only know they're waiting.

ESTELLE   I never could bear the idea of anyone's expecting something from me. It always made me want to do just the opposite.

INEZ   Well, do it. Do it if you can. You don't even know what they expect.

ESTELLE (*Stamping her foot*)   It's outrageous! So something's coming to me from you two? (*She eyes each in turn*) Something nasty, I suppose. There are some faces that tell me everything at once. Yours don't convey anything.

GARCIN (*Turning abruptly toward* INEZ)   Look here! Why are we together? You've given us quite enough hints, you may as well come out with it.

INEZ (*In a surprised tone*)   But I know nothing, absolutely nothing about it. I'm as much in the dark as you are.

GARCIN   We've *got* to know. (*Ponders for a while*)

INEZ   If only each of us had the guts to tell—

GARCIN   Tell what?

INEZ   Estelle!

ESTELLE   Yes?

INEZ   What have you done? I mean, why have they sent you here?

ESTELLE (*Quickly*)   That's just it. I haven't a notion, not the foggiest. In fact, I'm wondering if there hasn't been some ghastly mistake. (*To* INEZ) Don't smile. Just think of the number of people who—who become absentees every day. There must be thousands and thousands, and probably they're sorted out by—by understrappers, you know what I mean. Stupid employees who don't know their job. So they're bound to make mistakes sometimes. . . . Do stop smiling. (*To* GARCIN) Why don't you speak? If they made a mistake in my case, they may have done the same about you. (*To* INEZ) And you, too. Anyhow, isn't it better to think we've got here by mistake?

INEZ Is that all you have to tell us?

ESTELLE What else should I tell? I've nothing to hide. I lost my parents when I was a kid, and I had my young brother to bring up. We were terribly poor and when an old friend of my people asked me to marry him I said yes. He was very well off, and quite nice. My brother was a very delicate child and needed all sorts of attention, so really that was the right thing for me to do, don't you agree? My husband was old enough to be my father, but for six years we had a happy married life. Then two years ago I met the man I was fated to love. We knew it the moment we set eyes on each other. He asked me to run away with him, and I refused. Then I got pneumonia and it finished me. That's the whole story. No doubt, by certain standards, I did wrong to sacrifice my youth to a man nearly three times my age. (*To* GARCIN) Do *you* think that could be called a sin?

GARCIN Certainly not. (*A short silence*) And now, tell me, do you think it's a crime to stand by one's principles?

ESTELLE Of course not. Surely no one could blame a man for that!

GARCIN Wait a bit! I ran a pacifist newspaper. Then war broke out. What was I to do? Everyone was watching me, wondering: "Will he dare?" Well, I dared. I folded my arms and they shot me. Had I done anything wrong?

ESTELLE (*Laying her hand on his arm*) Wrong? On the contrary. You were—

INEZ (*Breaks in ironically*) —a hero! And how about your wife, Mr. Garcin?

GARCIN That's simple. I'd rescued her from—from the gutter.

ESTELLE (*To* INEZ) You see! You see!

INEZ   Yes, I see. *(A pause)* Look here! What's the point of play-acting, trying to throw dust in each other's eyes? We're all tarred with the same brush.

ESTELLE *(Indignantly)*   How dare you!

INEZ   Yes, we are criminals—murderers—all three of us. We're in hell, my pets; they never make mistakes, and people aren't damned for nothing.

ESTELLE   Stop! For heaven's sake—

INEZ   In hell! Damned souls—that's us, all three!

ESTELLE   Keep quiet! I forbid you to use such disgusting words.

INEZ   A damned soul—that's you, my little plaster saint. And ditto our friend there, the noble pacifist. We've had our hour of pleasure, haven't we? There have been people who burned their lives out for our sakes —and we chuckled over it. So now we have to pay the reckoning.

GARCIN *(Raising his fist)*   Will you keep your mouth shut, damn it!

INEZ *(Confronting him fearlessly, but with a look of vast surprise)*   Well, well! *(A pause)* Ah, I understand now. I know why they've put us three together.

GARCIN   I advise you to—to think twice before you say any more.

INEZ   Wait! You'll see how simple it is. Childishly simple. Obviously there aren't any physical torments— you agree, don't you? And yet we're in hell. And no one else will come here. We'll stay in this room together, the three of us, for ever and ever. . . . In short, there's someone absent here, the official torturer.

GARCIN *(Sotto voce)*   I'd noticed that.

INEZ   It's obvious what they're after—an economy of man-power—or devil-power, if you prefer. The same idea as in the cafeteria, where customers serve themselves.

ESTELLE   What ever do you mean?

INEZ   I mean that each of us will act as torturer of the two others.

*(There is a short silence while they digest this information)*

GARCIN *(Gently)* No, I shall never be your torturer. I wish neither of you any harm, and I've no concern with you. None at all. So the solution's easy enough; each of us stays put in his or her corner and takes no notice of the others. You here, you here, and I there. Like soldiers at our posts. Also, we mustn't speak. Not one word. That won't be difficult; each of us has plenty of material for self-communings. I think I could stay ten thousand years with only my thoughts for company.

ESTELLE Have *I* got to keep silent, too?

GARCIN Yes. And that way we—we'll work out our salvation. Looking into ourselves, never raising our heads. Agreed?

INEZ Agreed.

ESTELLE *(After some hesitation)* I agree.

GARCIN Then—good-by.

*(He goes to his sofa and buries his head in his hands. There is a long silence; then* INEZ *begins singing to herself)*

INEZ *(Singing)*


What a crowd in Whitefriars Lane!
They've set trestles in a row,
With a scaffold and the knife,
And a pail of bran below.
Come, good folks, to Whitefriars Lane,
Come to see the merry show!


The headsman rose at crack of dawn,
He'd a long day's work in hand,
Chopping heads off generals,
Priests and peers and admirals,
All the highest in the land.
What a crowd in Whitefriars Lane!

See them standing in a line,
Ladies all dressed up so fine.
But their heads have got to go,
Heads and hats roll down below.
Come, good folks, to Whitefriars Lane,
Come to see the merry show!

(*Meanwhile* ESTELLE *has been plying her powder-puff and lipstick. She looks round for a mirror, fumbles in her bag, then turns toward* GARCIN)

ESTELLE   Excuse me, have you a glass? (GARCIN *does not answer*) Any sort of glass, a pocket-mirror will do. (GARCIN *remains silent*) Even if you won't speak to me, you might lend me a glass.

(*His head still buried in his hands,* GARCIN *ignores her*)

INEZ   (*Eagerly*)  Don't worry. I've a glass in my bag. (*She opens her bag. Angrily*) It's gone! They must have taken it from me at the entrance.

ESTELLE   How tiresome!

(*A short silence.* ESTELLE *shuts her eyes and sways, as if about to faint.* INEZ *runs forward and holds her up*)

INEZ   What's the matter?

ESTELLE   (*Opens her eyes and smiles*)  I feel so queer. (*She pats herself*) Don't you ever get taken that way? When I can't see myself I begin to wonder if I really and truly exist. I pat myself just to make sure, but it doesn't help much.

INEZ   You're lucky. I'm always conscious of myself—in my mind. Painfully conscious.

ESTELLE   Ah yes, in your mind. But everything that goes on in one's head is so vague, isn't it? It makes one want to sleep. (*She is silent for a while*) I've six big mirrors in my bedroom. There they are. I can see them. But they don't see me. They're reflecting the carpet, the settee, the window—but how empty it is, a glass in which I'm absent! When I talked to people

I always made sure there was one near by in which I could see myself. I watched myself talking. And somehow it kept me alert, seeing myself as the others saw me. . . . Oh dear! My lipstick! I'm sure I've put it on all crooked. No, I can't do without a looking-glass for ever and ever, I simply can't.

INEZ Suppose I try to be your glass? Come and pay me a visit, dear. Here's a place for you on my sofa.

ESTELLE But—(*Points to* GARCIN)

INEZ Oh, he doesn't count.

ESTELLE But we're going to—to hurt each other. You said it yourself.

INEZ Do I look as if I wanted to hurt you?

ESTELLE One never can tell.

INEZ Much more likely *you'll* hurt *me*. Still, what does it matter? If I've got to suffer, it may as well be at your hands, your pretty hands. Sit down. Come closer. Closer. Look into my eyes. What do you see?

ESTELLE Oh, I'm there! But so tiny I can't see myself properly.

INEZ But *I* can. Every inch of you. Now ask me questions. I'll be as candid as any looking-glass.

(ESTELLE *seems rather embarrassed and turns to* GARCIN, *as if appealing to him for help*)

ESTELLE Please, Mr. Garcin. Sure our chatter isn't bothering you?

(GARCIN *makes no reply*)

INEZ Don't worry about him. As I said, he doesn't count. We're by ourselves. . . . Ask away.

ESTELLE Are my lips all right?

INEZ Show! No, they're a bit smudgy.

ESTELLE I thought as much. Luckily (*Throws a quick glance at* GARCIN) no one's seen me. I'll try again.

INEZ That's better. No. Follow the line of your lips. Wait! I'll guide your hand. There. That's quite good.

ESTELLE As good as when I came in?

INEZ Far better. Crueler. Your mouth looks quite diabolical that way.

ESTELLE   Good gracious! And you say you like it! How maddening, not being able to see for myself! You're quite sure, Miss Serrano, that it's all right now?

INEZ   Won't you call me Inez?

ESTELLE   Are you sure it looks all right?

INEZ   You're lovely, Estelle.

ESTELLE   But how can I rely upon your taste? Is it the same as *my* taste? Oh, how sickening it all is, enough to drive one crazy!

INEZ   I *have* your taste, my dear, because I like you so much. Look at me. No, straight. Now smile. I'm not so ugly, either. Am I not nicer than your glass?

ESTELLE   Oh, I don't know. You scare me rather. My reflection in the glass never did that; of course, I knew it so well. Like something I had tamed. . . . I'm going to smile, and my smile will sink down into your pupils, and heaven knows what it will become.

INEZ   And why shouldn't you "tame" *me?* (*The women gaze at each other*, ESTELLE *with a sort of fearful fascination*) Listen! I want you to call me Inez. We must be great friends.

ESTELLE   I don't make friends with women very easily.

INEZ   Not with postal clerks, you mean? Hullo, what's that—that nasty red spot at the bottom of your cheek? A pimple?

ESTELLE   A pimple? Oh, how simply foul! Where?

INEZ   There. . . . You know the way they catch larks —with a mirror? I'm your lark-mirror, my dear, and you can't escape me. . . . There isn't any pimple, not a trace of one. So what about it? Suppose the mirror started telling lies? Or suppose I covered my eyes—as he is doing—and refused to look at you, all that loveliness of yours would be wasted on the desert air. No, don't be afraid, I can't help looking at you, I shan't turn my eyes away. And I'll be nice to you, ever so nice. Only you must be nice to me, too.

   (*A short silence*)

ESTELLE   Are you really—attracted by me?

INEZ   Very much indeed.

    (*Another short silence*)

ESTELLE  (*Indicating* GARCIN *by a slight movement of her head*)  But I wish he'd notice me, too.

INEZ   Of course! Because he's a Man! (*To* GARCIN) You've won. (GARCIN *says nothing*) But look at her, damn it! (*Still no reply from* GARCIN) Don't pretend. You haven't missed a word of what we've said.

GARCIN   Quite so; not a word. I stuck my fingers in my ears, but your voices thudded in my brain. Silly chatter. Now will you leave me in peace, you two? I'm not interested in you.

INEZ   Not in me, perhaps—but how about this child? Aren't you interested in her? Oh, I saw through your game; you got on your high horse just to impress her.

GARCIN   I asked you to leave me in peace. There's someone talking about me in the newspaper office and I want to listen. And, if it'll make you any happier, let me tell you that I've no use for the "child," as you call her.

ESTELLE   Thanks.

GARCIN   Oh, I didn't mean it rudely.

ESTELLE   You cad!

    (*They confront each other in silence for some moments*)

GARCIN   So's that's that. (*Pause*) You know I begged you not to speak.

ESTELLE   It's *her* fault; she started. I didn't ask anything of her and she came and offered me her—her glass.

INEZ   So you say. But all the time you were making up to him, trying every trick to catch his attention.

ESTELLE   Well, why shouldn't I?

GARCIN   You're crazy, both of you. Don't you see where this is leading us? For pity's sake, keep your mouths shut. (*Pause*) Now let's all sit down again quite quietly; we'll look at the floor and each must try to forget the others are there.

    (*A longish silence.* GARCIN *sits down. The women*

> *return hesitantly to their places. Suddenly* INEZ
> *swings round on him*)

INEZ   To forget about the others? How utterly absurd!
I *feel* you there, in every pore. Your silence clamors
in my ears. You can nail up your mouth, cut your
tongue out—but you can't prevent your *being there*.
Can you stop your thoughts? I hear them ticking away
like a clock tick-tock, tick-tock, and I'm certain you
hear mine. It's all very well skulking on your sofa, but
you're everywhere, and every sound comes to me
soiled, because you've intercepted it on its way. Why,
you've even stolen my face; you know it and I don't!
And what about her, about Estelle? You've stolen her
from me, too; if she and I were alone do you suppose
she'd treat me as she does? No, take your hands from
your face, I won't leave you in peace—that would suit
your book too well. You'd go on sitting there, in a
sort of trance, like a yogi, and even if I didn't see her
I'd feel it in my bones—that she was making every
sound, even the rustle of her dress, for your benefit,
throwing you smiles you didn't see. . . . Well, I
won't stand for that, I prefer to choose my hell; I
prefer to look you in the eyes and fight it out face to
face.

GARCIN   Have it your own way. I suppose we were
bound to come to this; they knew what they were
about, and we're easy game. If they'd put me in a
room with men—men can keep their mouths shut.
But it's no use wanting the impossible. (*He goes to*
ESTELLE *and lightly fondles her neck*) So I attract
you, little girl? It seems you were making eyes at me?

ESTELLE   Don't touch me.

GARCIN   Why not? We might, anyhow, be natural. . . .
Do you know, I used to be mad about women? And
some were fond of me. So we may as well stop posing,
we've nothing to lose. Why trouble about politeness,
and decorum, and the rest of it? We're between our-

selves. And presently we shall be naked as—as new-born babes.

ESTELLE Oh, let me be!

GARCIN As new-born babes. Well, I'd warned you, anyhow. I asked so little of you, nothing but peace and a little silence. I'd put my fingers in my ears. Gomez was spouting away as usual, standing in the center of the room, with all the pressmen listening. In their shirt-sleeves. I tried to hear, but it wasn't too easy. Things on earth move so quickly, you know. Couldn't you have held your tongues? Now it's over, he's stopped talking, and what he thinks of me has gone back into his head. Well, we've got to see it through somehow. . . . Naked as we were born. So much the better; I want to know whom I have to deal with.

INEZ You know already. There's nothing more to learn.

GARCIN You're wrong. So long as each of us hasn't made a clean breast of it—why they've damned him or her—we know nothing. Nothing that counts. You, young lady, you shall begin. Why? Tell us why. If you are frank, if we bring our specters into the open, it may save us from disaster. So—out with it! Why?

ESTELLE I tell you I haven't a notion. They wouldn't tell me why.

GARCIN That's so. They wouldn't tell me, either. But I've a pretty good idea. . . . Perhaps you're shy of speaking first? Right. I'll lead off. (*A short silence*) I'm not a very estimable person.

INEZ No need to tell us that. We know you were a deserter.

GARCIN Let that be. It's only a side-issue. I'm here because I treated my wife abominably. That's all. For five years. Naturally, she's suffering still. There she is: the moment I mention her, I see her. It's Gomez who interests me, and it's she I see. Where's Gomez got to? For five years. There! They've given her back my things; she's sitting by the window, with my coat on

her knees. The coat with the twelve bullet-holes. The
blood's like rust; a brown ring round each hole. It's
quite a museum-piece, that coat; scarred with history.
And I used to wear it, fancy! . . . Now, can't you
shed a tear, my love? Surely you'll squeeze one out—
at last? No? You can't manage it? . . . Night after
night I came home blind drunk, stinking of wine and
women. She'd sat up for me, of course. But she never
cried, never uttered a word of reproach. Only her eyes
spoke. Big, tragic eyes. I don't regret anything. I
must pay the price, but I shan't whine. . . . It's
snowing in the street. Won't you cry, confound you?
That woman was a born martyr, you know; a victim
by vocation.

INEZ (*Almost tenderly*) Why did you hurt her like
that?

GARCIN  It was so easy. A word was enough to make her
flinch. Like a sensitive-plant. But never, never a reproach. I'm fond of teasing. I watched and waited.
But no, not a tear, not a protest. I'd picked her up out
of the gutter, you understand. . . . Now she's stroking the coat. Her eyes are shut and she's feeling with
her fingers for the bullet-holes. What are you after?
What do you expect? I tell you I regret nothing. The
truth is, she admired me too much. Does that mean
anything to you?

INEZ  No. Nobody admired *me*.

GARCIN  So much the better. So much the better for
you. I suppose all this strikes you as very vague. Well,
here's something you can get your teeth into. I brought
a half-caste girl to stay in our house. My wife slept
upstairs; she must have heard—everything. She was
an early riser and, as I and the girl stayed in bed late,
she served us our morning coffee.

INEZ  You brute!

GARCIN  Yes, a brute, if you like. But a well-beloved
brute. (*A far-away look comes to his eyes*) No, it's

nothing. Only Gomez, and he's not talking about *me*.
. . . What were you saying? Yes, a brute. Certainly.
Else why should I be here? (*To* INEZ) Your turn.

INEZ  Well, I was what some people down there called
"a damned bitch." Damned already. So it's no surprise, being here.

GARCIN  Is that all you have to say?

INEZ  No. There was that affair with Florence. A dead
man's tale. With three corpses to it. He to start with;
then she and I. So there's no one left, I've nothing to
worry about; it was a clean sweep. Only that room.
I see it now and then. Empty, with the doors locked.
. . . No, they've just unlocked them. "To Let." It's
to let; there's a notice on the door. That's—too ridiculous.

GARCIN  Three. Three deaths, you said?

INEZ  Three.

GARCIN  One man and two women?

INEZ  Yes.

GARCIN  Well, well. (*A pause*) Did he kill himself?

INEZ  He? No, he hadn't the guts for that. Still, he'd
every reason; we led him a dog's life. As a matter of
fact, he was run over by a street car. A silly sort of
end. . . . I was living with them; he was my cousin.

GARCIN  Was Florence fair?

INEZ  Fair? (*Glances at* ESTELLE) You know, I don't
regret a thing; still, I'm not so very keen on telling
you the story.

GARCIN  That's all right. . . . So you got sick of him?

INEZ  Quite gradually. All sorts of little things got on
my nerves. For instance, he made a noise when he was
drinking—a sort of gurgle. Trifles like that. He was
rather pathetic really. Vulnerable. Why are you smiling?

GARCIN  Because I, anyhow, am *not* vulnerable.

INEZ  Don't be too sure. . . . I crept inside her skin,
she saw the world through my eyes. When she left

him, I had her on my hands. We shared a bed-sitting-room at the other end of the town.

GARCIN   And then?

INEZ   Then that street car did its job. I used to remind her every day: "Yes, my pet, we killed him between us." (*A pause*) I'm rather cruel, really.

GARCIN   So am I.

INEZ   No, you're not cruel. It's something else.

GARCIN   What?

INEZ   I'll tell you later. When I say I'm cruel, I mean I can't get on without making people suffer. Like a live coal. A live coal in others' hearts. When I'm alone I flicker out. For six months I flamed away in her heart, till there was nothing but a cinder. One night she got up and turned on the gas while I was asleep. Then she crept back into bed. So now you know.

GARCIN   Well! Well!

INEZ   Yes? What's in your mind?

GARCIN   Nothing. Only that it's not a pretty story.

INEZ   Obviously. But what matter?

GARCIN   As you say, what matter? (*To* ESTELLE) Your turn. What have you done?

ESTELLE   As I told you, I haven't a notion. I rack my brain, but it's no use.

GARCIN   Right. Then we'll give you a hand. That fellow with the smashed face, who was he?

ESTELLE   Who—who do you mean?

INEZ   You know quite well. The man you were so scared of seeing when you came in.

ESTELLE   Oh, him! A friend of mine.

GARCIN   Why were you afraid of him?

ESTELLE   That's my business, Mr. Garcin.

INEZ   Did he shoot himself on your account?

ESTELLE   Of course not. How absurd you are!

GARCIN   Then why should you have been so scared? He blew his brains out, didn't he? That's how his face got smashed.

ESTELLE   Don't! Please don't go on.

GARCIN   Because of you. Because of you.

INEZ   He shot himself because of you.

ESTELLE   Leave me alone! It's—it's not fair, bullying me like that. I want to go! I want to go!

(*She runs to the door and shakes it*)

GARCIN   Go if you can. Personally, I ask for nothing better. Unfortunately, the door's locked.

(ESTELLE *presses the bell-push, but the bell does not ring.* INEZ *and* GARCIN *laugh.* ESTELLE *swings round on them, her back to the door*)

ESTELLE   (*In a muffled voice*) You're hateful, both of you.

INEZ   Hateful? Yes, that's the word. Now get on with it. That fellow who killed himself on your account— you were his mistress, eh?

GARCIN   Of course she was. And he wanted to have her to himself alone. That's so, isn't it?

INEZ   He danced the tango like a professional, but he was poor as a church mouse—that's right, isn't it?

(*A short silence*)

GARCIN   Was he poor or not? Give a straight answer.

ESTELLE   Yes, he was poor.

GARCIN   And then you had your reputation to keep up. One day he came and implored you to run away with him, and you laughed in his face.

INEZ   That's it. You laughed at him. And so he killed himself.

ESTELLE   Did you use to look at Florence in that way?

INEZ   Yes.

(*A short pause, then* ESTELLE *bursts out laughing*)

ESTELLE   You've got it all wrong, you two. (*She stiffens her shoulders, still leaning against the door, and faces them. Her voice grows shrill, truculent*) He wanted me to have a baby. So there!

GARCIN   And you didn't want one?

ESTELLE   I certainly didn't. But the baby came, worse

luck. I went to Switzerland for five months. No one knew anything. It was a girl. Roger was with me when she was born. It pleased him no end, having a daughter. It didn't please *me!*

GARCIN   And then?

ESTELLE   There was a balcony overlooking the lake. I brought a big stone. He could see what I was up to and he kept on shouting: "Estelle, for God's sake, don't!" I hated him then. He saw it all. He was leaning over the balcony and he saw the rings spreading on the water—

GARCIN   Yes? And then?

ESTELLE   That's all. I came back to Paris—and he did as he wished.

GARCIN   You mean he blew his brains out?

ESTELLE   It was absurd of him, really, my husband never suspected anything. (*A pause*) Oh, how I loathe you! (*She sobs tearlessly*)

GARCIN   Nothing doing. Tears don't flow in this place.

ESTELLE   I'm a coward. A coward! (*Pause*) If you knew how I hate you!

INEZ (*Taking her in her arms*) Poor child! (*To* GARCIN) So the hearing's over. But there's no need to look like a hanging judge.

GARCIN   A hanging judge? (*He glances around him*) I'd give a lot to be able to see myself in a glass. (*Pause*) How hot it is! (*Unthinkingly he takes off his coat*) Oh, sorry! (*He starts putting it on again*)

ESTELLE   Don't bother. You can stay in your shirt-sleeves. As things are—

GARCIN   Just so. (*He drops his coat on the sofa*) You mustn't be angry with me, Estelle.

ESTELLE   I'm not angry with you.

INEZ   And what about me? Are you angry with me?

ESTELLE   Yes.

(*A short silence*)

INEZ   Well, Mr. Garcin, now you have us in the nude

all right. Do you understand things any better for
that?

GARCIN   I wonder. Yes, perhaps a trifle better. (*Timidly*)
And now suppose we start trying to help each other.

INEZ   I don't need help.

GARCIN   Inez, they've laid their snare damned cunningly
—like a cobweb. If you make any movement, if you
raise your hand to fan yourself, Estelle and I feel a
little tug. Alone, none of us can save himself or herself; we're linked together inextricably. So you can
take your choice. (*A pause*) Hullo? What's happening?

INEZ   They've let it. The windows are wide open, a man
is sitting on my bed. *My* bed, if you please! They've
let it, let it! Step in, step in, make yourself at home,
you brute! Ah, there's a woman, too. She's going up
to him, putting her hands on his shoulders. . . .
Damn it, why don't they turn the lights on? It's getting dark. Now he's going to kiss her. But that's my
room, *my* room! Pitch-dark now. I can't see anything,
but I hear them whispering, whispering. Is he going to
make love to her on *my* bed? What's that she said?
That it's noon and the sun is shining? I must be going
blind. (*A pause*) Blacked out. I can't see or hear a
thing. So I'm done with the earth, it seems. No more
alibis for me! (*She shudders*) I feel so empty, desic-
cated—really dead at last. All of me's here, in this
room. (*A pause*) What were you saying? Something
about helping me, wasn't it?

GARCIN   Yes.

INEZ   Helping me to do what?

GARCIN   To defeat their devilish tricks.

INEZ   And what do you expect me to do, in return?

GARCIN   To help *me*. It only needs a little effort, Inez;
just a spark of human feeling.

INEZ   Human feeling. That's beyond my range. I'm rotten to the core.

GARCIN　And how about me? (*A pause*) All the same, suppose we try?

INEZ　It's no use. I'm all dried up. I can't give and I can't receive. How could *I* help you? A dead twig, ready for the burning. (*She falls silent, gazing at* ESTELLE, *who has buried her head in her hands*) Florence was fair, a natural blonde.

GARCIN　Do you realize that this young woman's fated to be your torturer?

INEZ　Perhaps I've guessed it.

GARCIN　It's through her they'll get you. I, of course, I'm different—aloof. I take no notice of her. Suppose you had a try—

INEZ　Yes?

GARCIN　It's a trap. They're watching you, to see if you'll fall into it.

INEZ　I know. And you're another trap. Do you think they haven't foreknown every word you say? And of course there's a whole nest of pitfalls that we can't see. Everything here's a booby-trap. But what do I care? I'm a pitfall, too. For her, obviously. And perhaps I'll catch her.

GARCIN　You won't catch anything. We're chasing after each other, round and round in a vicious circle, like the horses on a merry-go-round. That's part of their plan, of course. . . . Drop it, Inez. Open your hands and let go of everything. Or else you'll bring disaster on all three of us.

INEZ　Do I look the sort of person who lets go? I know what's coming to me. I'm going to burn, and it's to last forever. Yes, I *know* everything. But do you think I'll let go? I'll catch her, she'll see you through my eyes, as Florence saw that other man. What's the good of trying to enlist my sympathy? I assure you I know everything, and I can't feel sorry even for myself. A trap! Don't I know it, and that I'm in a trap myself, up to the neck, and there's nothing to be done about it? And if it suits their book, so much the better!

GARCIN (*Gripping her shoulders*) Well, *I*, anyhow, can feel sorry for you, too. Look at me, we're naked, naked right through, and I can see into your heart. That's one link between us. Do you think I'd want to hurt you? I don't regret anything, I'm dried up, too. But for you I can still feel pity.

INEZ (*Who has let him keep his hands on her shoulders until now, shakes herself loose*) Don't. I hate being pawed about. And keep your pity for yourself. Don't forget, Garcin, that there are traps for you, too, in this room. All nicely set for you. You'd do better to watch your own interests. (*A pause*) But, if you will leave us in peace, this child and me, I'll see I don't do you any harm.

GARCIN (*Gazes at her for a moment, then shrugs his shoulders*) Very well.

ESTELLE (*Raising her head*) Please, Garcin.

GARCIN What do you want of me?

ESTELLE (*Rises and goes up to him*) You can help *me*, anyhow.

GARCIN If you want help, apply to her.

(INEZ *has come up and is standing behind* ESTELLE, *but without touching her. During the dialogue that follows she speaks almost in her ear. But* ESTELLE *keeps her eyes on* GARCIN, *who observes her without speaking, and she addresses her answers to him, as if it were he who is questioning her*)

ESTELLE I implore you, Garcin—you gave me your promise, didn't you? Help me quick. I don't want to be left alone. Olga's taken him to a cabaret.

INEZ Taken whom?

ESTELLE Peter. . . . Oh, now they're dancing together.

INEZ Who's Peter?

ESTELLE Such a silly boy. He called me his glancing stream—just fancy! He was terribly in love with me . . . She's persuaded him to come out with her to-night.

INEZ  Do you love him?

ESTELLE  They're sitting down now. She's puffing like a grampus. What a fool the girl is to insist on dancing! But I dare say she does it to reduce. . . . No, of course I don't love him; he's only eighteen, and I'm not a baby-snatcher.

INEZ  Then why bother about them? What difference can it make?

ESTELLE  He belonged to me.

INEZ  Nothing on earth belongs to you any more.

ESTELLE  I tell you he was mine. All mine.

INEZ  Yes, he *was* yours—once. But now—Try to make him hear, try to touch him. Olga can touch him, talk to him as much as she likes. That's so, isn't it? She can squeeze his hands, rub herself against him—

ESTELLE  Yes, look! She's pressing her great fat chest against him, puffing and blowing in his face. But, my poor little lamb, can't you see how ridiculous she is? Why don't you laugh at her? Oh, once I'd have only had to glance at them and she'd have slunk away. Is there really nothing, nothing left of me?

INEZ  Nothing whatever. Nothing of you's left on earth —not even a shadow. All you own is here. Would you like that paper-knife? Or that ornament on the mantelpiece? That blue sofa's yours. And I, my dear, am yours forever.

ESTELLE  You mine! That's good! Well, which of you two would dare to call me his glancing stream, his crystal girl? You know too much about me, you know I'm rotten through and through. . . . Peter dear, think of me, fix your thoughts on me, and save me. All the time you're thinking "my glancing stream, my crystal girl," I'm only half here, I'm only half wicked, and half of me is down there with you, clean and bright and crystal-clear as running water. . . . Oh, just look at her face, all scarlet, like a tomato. No, it's absurd, we've laughed at her together, you and I,

often and often. . . . What's that tune?—I always
loved it. Yes, the *St. Louis Blues.* . . . All right,
dance away, dance away. Garcin, I wish you could see
her, you'd die of laughing. Only—she'll never know
I *see* her. Yes, I see you, Olga, with your hair all anyhow, and you do look a dope, my dear. Oh, now
you're treading on his toes. It's a scream! Hurry up!
Quicker! Quicker! He's dragging her along, bundling
her round and round—it's too ghastly! He always
said I was so light, he loved to dance with me. (*She
is dancing as she speaks*) I tell you, Olga, I can see
you. No, she doesn't care, she's dancing through my
gaze. What's that? What's that you said? "Our poor
dear Estelle"? Oh, don't be such a humbug! You
didn't even shed a tear at the funeral. . . . And she
has the nerve to talk to him about her poor dear
friend Estelle! How dare she discuss me with Peter?
Now then, keep time. She never could dance and
talk at once. Oh, what's that? No, no. Don't tell him.
Please, please don't tell him. You can keep him, do
what you like with him, but please don't tell him
about—that! (*She has stopped dancing*) All right. You
can have him now. Isn't it *foul,* Garcin? She's told him
everything, about Roger, my trip to Switzerland, the
baby. "Poor Estelle wasn't exactly—" No, I wasn't
exactly— True enough. He's looking grave, shaking
his head, but he doesn't seem so very much surprised,
not what one would expect. Keep him, then—I won't
haggle with you over his long eyelashes, his pretty
girlish face. They're yours for the asking. His glancing stream, his crystal. Well, the crystal's shattered
into bits. "Poor Estelle!" Dance, dance, dance. On
with it. But do keep time. One, two. One, two. How
I'd love to go down to earth for just a moment, and
dance with him again. (*She dances again for some
moments*) The music's growing fainter. They've
turned down the lights, as they do for a tango. Why

are they playing so softly? Louder, please. I can't hear. It's so far away, so far away. I—I can't hear a sound. (*She stops dancing*) All over. It's the end. The earth has left me. (*To* GARCIN) Don't turn from me— please. Take me in your arms. (*Behind* ESTELLE's *back,* INEZ *signs to* GARCIN *to move away*)

INEZ (*Commandingly*)   Now then, Garcin!

> (GARCIN *moves back a step, and, glancing at* ESTELLE, *points to* INEZ)

GARCIN   It's to her you should say that.

ESTELLE (*Clinging to him*)   Don't turn away. You're a man, aren't you, and surely I'm not such a fright as all that! Everyone says I've lovely hair and, after all, a man killed himself on my account. You have to look at something, and there's nothing here to see except the sofas and that awful ornament and the table. Surely I'm better to look at than a lot of stupid furniture. Listen! I've dropped out of their hearts like a little sparrow fallen from its nest. So gather me up, dear, fold me to your heart—and you'll see how nice I can be.

GARCIN (*Freeing himself from her, after a short struggle*)   I tell you it's to that lady you should speak.

ESTELLE   To her? But she doesn't count, she's a woman.

INEZ   Oh, I don't count? Is that what you think? But, my poor little fallen nestling, you've been sheltering in my heart for ages, though you didn't realize it. Don't be afraid; I'll keep looking at you for ever and ever, without a flutter of my eyelids, and you'll live in my gaze like a mote in a sunbeam.

ESTELLE   A sunbeam indeed! Don't talk such rubbish! You've tried that trick already, and you should know it doesn't work.

INEZ   Estelle! My glancing stream! My crystal!

ESTELLE   *Your* crystal? It's grotesque. Do you think you can fool me with that sort of talk? Everyone knows by now what I did to my baby. The crystal's shattered, but I don't care. I'm just a hollow dummy, all that's left of me is the outside—but it's not for you.

INEZ   Come to me, Estelle. You shall be whatever you like: a glancing stream, a muddy stream. And deep down in my eyes you'll see yourself just as you want to be.

ESTELLE   Oh, leave me in peace. You haven't any eyes. Oh, damn it, isn't there anything I can do to get rid of you? I've an idea. (*She spits in* INEZ's *face*) There!

INEZ   Garcin, you shall pay for this.

(*A pause.* GARCIN *shrugs his shoulders and goes to* ESTELLE)

GARCIN   So it's a man you need?

ESTELLE   Not *any* man. You.

GARCIN   No humbug now. Any man would do your business. As I happen to be here, you want me. Right! (*He grips her shoulders*) Mind, I'm not your sort at all, really; I'm not a young nincompoop and I don't dance the tango.

ESTELLE   I'll take you as you are. And perhaps I shall change you.

GARCIN   I doubt it. I shan't pay much attention; I've other things to think about.

ESTELLE   What things?

GARCIN   They wouldn't interest you.

ESTELLE   I'll sit on your sofa and wait for you to take some notice of me. I promise not to bother you at all.

INEZ (*With a shrill laugh*)   That's right, fawn on him, like the silly bitch you are. Grovel and cringe! And he hasn't even good looks to commend him!

ESTELLE (*To* GARCIN)   Don't listen to her. She has no eyes, no ears. She's—nothing.

GARCIN   I'll give you what I can. It doesn't amount to much. I shan't love you; I know you too well.

ESTELLE   Do you want me, anyhow?

GARCIN   Yes.

ESTELLE   I ask no more.

GARCIN　In that case—(*He bends over her*)

INEZ　Estelle! Garcin! You must be going crazy. You're not alone. I'm here too.

GARCIN　Of course—but what does it matter?

INEZ　Under my eyes? You couldn't—couldn't do it.

ESTELLE　Why not? I often undressed with my maid looking on.

INEZ　(*Gripping* GARCIN's *arm*) Let her alone. Don't paw her with your dirty man's hands.

GARCIN　(*Thrusting her away roughly*) Take care. I'm no gentleman, and I'd have no compunction about striking a woman.

INEZ　But you promised me; you promised. I'm only asking you to keep your word.

GARCIN　Why should I, considering you were the first to break our agreement?

　　　(INEZ *turns her back on him and retreats to the far end of the room*)

INEZ　Very well, have it your own way. I'm the weaker party, one against two. But don't forget I'm here, and watching. I shan't take my eyes off you, Garcin; when you're kissing her, you'll feel them boring into you. Yes, have it your own way, make love and get it over. We're in hell; my turn will come.

　　　(*During the following scene she watches them without speaking*)

GARCIN　(*Coming back to* ESTELLE *and grasping her shoulders*) Now then. Your lips. Give me your lips.

　　　(*A pause. He bends to kiss her, then abruptly straightens up*)

ESTELLE　(*Indignantly*) Really! (*A pause*) Didn't I tell you not to pay any attention to her?

GARCIN　You've got it wrong. (*Short silence*) It's Gomez; he's back in the press-room. They've shut the windows; it must be winter down there. Six months since I—Well, I warned you I'd be absent-minded sometimes, didn't I? They're shivering, they've kept their coats on. Funny they should feel the cold like that,

when I'm feeling so hot. Ah, this time he's talking
about me.

ESTELLE    Is it going to last long? (*Short silence*) You
might at least tell me what he's saying.

GARCIN    Nothing. Nothing worth repeating. He's a
swine, that's all. (*He listens attentively*) A god-
damned bloody swine. (*He turns to* ESTELLE) Let's
come back to—to ourselves. Are you going to love
me?

ESTELLE (*Smiling*)    I wonder now!

GARCIN    Will you trust me?

ESTELLE    What a quaint thing to ask! Considering you'll
be under my eyes all the time, and I don't think I've
much to fear from Inez, so far as you're concerned.

GARCIN    Obviously. (*A pause. He takes his hands off*
ESTELLE's *shoulders*) I was thinking of another kind
of trust. (*Listens*) Talk away, talk away, you swine.
I'm not there to defend myself. (*To* ESTELLE) Estelle,
you *must* give me your trust.

ESTELLE    Oh, what a nuisance you are! I'm giving you
my mouth, my arms, my whole body—and everything
could be so simple. . . . My trust! I haven't any to
give, I'm afraid, and you're making me terribly embarrassed. You must have something pretty ghastly
on your conscience to make such a fuss about my
trusting you.

GARCIN    They shot me.

ESTELLE    I know. Because you refused to fight. Well,
why shouldn't you?

GARCIN    I—I didn't exactly refuse (*In a far-away voice*)
I must say he talks well, he makes out a good case
against me, but he never says what I should have done
instead. Should I have gone to the general and said:
"General, I decline to fight"? A mug's game; they'd
have promptly locked me up. But I wanted to show
my colors, my true colors, do you understand? I
wasn't going to be silenced. (*To* ESTELLE) So I—I took
the train. . . . They caught me at the frontier.

ESTELLE　Where were you trying to go?

GARCIN　To Mexico. I meant to launch a pacifist news-paper down there. (*A short silence*) Well, why don't you speak?

ESTELLE　What could I say? You acted quite rightly, as you didn't want to fight. (GARCIN *makes a fretful gesture*) But, darling, how on earth can I guess what you want me to answer?

INEZ　Can't you guess? Well, *I* can. He wants you to tell him that he bolted like a lion. For "bolt" he did, and that's what's biting him.

GARCIN　"Bolted," "went away"—we won't quarrel over words.

ESTELLE　But you *had* to run away. If you'd stayed they'd have sent you to jail, wouldn't they?

GARCIN　Of course. (*A pause*) Well, Estelle, am I a coward?

ESTELLE　How can I say? Don't be so unreasonable, darling. I can't put myself in your skin. You must decide that for yourself.

GARCIN (*Wearily*)　I can't decide.

ESTELLE　Anyhow, you must remember. You must have had reasons for acting as you did.

GARCIN　I had.

ESTELLE　Well?

GARCIN　But were they the real reasons?

ESTELLE　You've a twisted mind, that's your trouble. Plaguing yourself over such trifles!

GARCIN　I'd thought it all out, and I wanted to make a stand. But was that my real motive?

INEZ　Exactly. That's the question. Was that your real motive? No doubt you argued it out with yourself, you weighed the pros and cons, you found good reasons for what you did. But fear and hatred and all the dirty little instincts one keeps dark—they're motives too. So carry on, Mr. Garcin, and try to be honest with yourself—for once.

GARCIN   Do I need you to tell me that? Day and night
I paced my cell, from the window to the door, from
the door to the window. I pried into my heart, I
sleuthed myself like a detective. By the end of it I
felt as if I'd given my whole life to introspection.
But always I harked back to the one thing certain—
that I had acted as I did, I'd taken that train to the
frontier. But why? Why? Finally I thought: My death
will settle it. If I face death courageously, I'll prove
I am no coward.

INEZ   And how did you face death?

GARCIN   Miserably. Rottenly. (INEZ *laughs*) Oh, it was
only a physical lapse—that might happen to anyone;
I'm not ashamed of it. Only everything's been left in
suspense, forever. (*To* ESTELLE) Come here, Estelle.
Look at me. I want to feel someone looking at me
while they're talking about me on earth. . . . I like
green eyes.

INEZ   Green eyes! Just hark to him! And you, Estelle,
do you like cowards?

ESTELLE   If you knew how little I care! Coward or
hero, it's all one—provided he kisses well.

GARCIN   There they are, slumped in their chairs, suck-
ing at their cigars. Bored they look. Half-asleep.
They're thinking: "Garcin's a coward." But only
vaguely, dreamily. One's got to think of something.
"That chap Garcin was a coward." That's what they've
decided, those dear friends of mine. In six months'
time they'll be saying: "Cowardly as that skunk Garcin." You're lucky, you two; no one on earth is giving
you another thought. But I—I'm long in dying.

INEZ   What about your wife, Garcin?

GARCIN   Oh, didn't I tell you? She's dead.

INEZ   Dead?

GARCIN   Yes, she died just now. About two months ago.

INEZ   Of grief?

GARCIN   What else should she die of? So all is for the

best, you see; the war's over, my wife's dead, and I've
carved out my place in history.

    (*He gives a choking sob and passes his hand over
his face,* ESTELLE *catches his arm*)

ESTELLE  My poor darling! Look at me. Please look.
Touch me. Touch me. (*She takes his hand and puts it
on her neck*) There! Keep your hand there. (GARCIN
*makes a fretful movement*) No, don't move. Why
trouble what those men are thinking? They'll die off
one by one. Forget them. There's only me, now.

GARCIN  But *they* won't forget *me,* not they! They'll
die, but others will come after them to carry on the
legend. I've left my fate in their hands.

ESTELLE  You think too much, that's your trouble.

GARCIN  What else is there to do now? I was a man of
action once. . . . Oh, if only I could be with them
again, for just one day—I'd fling their lie in their
teeth. But I'm locked out; they're passing judgment
on my life without troubling about me, and they're
right, because I'm dead. Dead and done with. (*Laughs*)
A back number.

    (*A short pause*)

ESTELLE (*Gently*)  Garcin.

GARCIN  Still there? Now listen! I want you to do me
a service. No, don't shrink away. I know it must seem
strange to you, having someone asking you for help;
you're not used to that. But if you'll make the effort,
if you'll only *will* it hard enough, I dare say we can
really love each other. Look at it this way. A thousand
of them are proclaiming I'm a coward; but what do
numbers matter? If there's someone, just one person,
to say quite positively I did not run away, that I'm not
the sort who runs away, that I'm brave and decent
and the rest of it—well, that one person's faith would
save me. Will you have that faith in me? Then I shall
love you and cherish you for ever. Estelle—will you?

ESTELLE (*Laughing*)  Oh, you dear silly man, do you
think I could love a coward?

GARCIN  But just now you said—

ESTELLE  I was only teasing you. I like men, my dear, who're real men, with tough skin and strong hands. You haven't a coward's chin, or a coward's mouth, or a coward's voice, or a coward's hair. And it's for your mouth, your hair, your voice, I love you.

GARCIN  Do you mean this? *Really* mean it?

ESTELLE  Shall I swear it?

GARCIN  Then I snap my fingers at them all, those below and those in here. Estelle, we shall climb out of hell. (INEZ *gives a shrill laugh. He breaks off and stares at her*) What's that?

INEZ  (*Still laughing*)  But she doesn't mean a word of what she says. How can you be such a simpleton? "Estelle, am I a coward?" As if she cared a damn either way.

ESTELLE  Inez, how dare you? (*To* GARCIN) Don't listen to her. If you want me to have faith in you, you must begin by trusting me.

INEZ  That's right! That's right! Trust away! She wants a man—that far you can trust her—she wants a man's arm round her waist, a man's smell, a man's eyes glowing with desire. And that's all she wants. She'd assure you you were God Almighty if she thought it would give you pleasure.

GARCIN  Estelle, is this true? Answer me. Is it true?

ESTELLE  What do you expect me to say? Don't you realize how maddening it is to have to answer questions one can't make head or tail of? (*She stamps her foot*) You do make things difficult. . . . Anyhow, I'd love you just the same, even if you were a coward. Isn't that enough?

(*A short pause*)

GARCIN  (*To the two women*)  You disgust me, both of you.

(*He goes toward the door*)

ESTELLE  What are you up to?

GARCIN  I'm going.

INEZ (*Quickly*)　You won't get far. The door is locked.

GARCIN　I'll *make* them open it. (*He presses the bell-push. The bell does not ring*)

ESTELLE　Please! Please!

INEZ (*To* ESTELLE)　Don't worry, my pet. The bell doesn't work.

GARCIN　I tell you they shall open. (*Drums on the door*) I can't endure it any longer, I'm through with you both. (ESTELLE *runs to him; he pushes her away*) Go away. You're even fouler than she. I won't let myself get bogged in your eyes. You're soft and slimy. Ugh! (*Bangs on the door again*) Like an octopus. Like a quagmire.

ESTELLE　I beg you, oh, I beg you not to leave me. I'll promise not to speak again, I won't trouble you in any way—but don't go. I daren't be left alone with Inez, now she's shown her claws.

GARCIN　Look after yourself. I never asked you to come here.

ESTELLE　Oh, how mean you are! Yes, it's quite true you're a coward.

INEZ (*Going up to* ESTELLE)　Well, my little sparrow fallen from the nest, I hope you're satisfied now. You spat in my face—playing up to him, of course—and we had a tiff on his account. But he's going, and a good riddance it will be. We two women will have the place to ourselves.

ESTELLE　You won't gain anything. If that door opens, I'm going, too.

INEZ　Where?

ESTELLE　I don't care where. As far from you as I can.
　　　　(GARCIN *has been drumming on the door while they talk*)

GARCIN　Open the door! Open, blast you! I'll endure anything, your red-hot tongs and molten lead, your racks and prongs and garrotes—all your fiendish gadgets, everything that burns and flays and tears—

I'll put up with any torture you impose. Anything, anything would be better than this agony of mind, this creeping pain that gnaws and fumbles and caresses one and never hurts quite enough. (*He grips the door-knob and rattles it*) Now will you open? (*The door flies open with a jerk, and he just avoids falling*) Ah! (*A long silence*)

INEZ    Well, Garcin? You're free to go.

GARCIN  (*Meditatively*)  Now I wonder why that door opened.

INEZ    What are you waiting for? Hurry up and go.

GARCIN  I shall not go.

INEZ    And you, Estelle? (ESTELLE *does not move.* INEZ *bursts out laughing*) So what? Which shall it be? Which of the three of us will leave? The barrier's down, why are we waiting? . . . But what a situation! It's a scream! We're—inseparables!

(ESTELLE *springs at her from behind*)

ESTELLE  Inseparables? Garcin, come and lend a hand. Quickly. We'll push her out and slam the door on her. That'll teach her a lesson.

INEZ    (*Struggling with* ESTELLE)  Estelle! I beg you, let me stay. I won't go, I won't go! Not into the passage.

GARCIN  Let go of her.

ESTELLE  You're crazy. She hates you.

GARCIN  It's because of her I'm staying here.

(ESTELLE *releases* INEZ *and stares dumfoundedly at* GARCIN)

INEZ    Because of me? (*Pause*) All right, shut the door. It's ten times hotter here since it opened. (GARCIN *goes to the door and shuts it*) Because of me, you said?

GARCIN  Yes. *You,* anyhow, know what it means to be a coward.

INEZ    Yes, I know.

GARCIN  And you know what wickedness is, and shame, and fear. There were days when you peered into yourself, into the secret places of your heart, and what you saw there made you faint with horror. And then, next day, you didn't know what to make of it, you couldn't interpret the horror you had glimpsed the day before. Yes, you know what evil costs. And when you say I'm a coward, you know from experience what that means. Is that so?

INEZ  Yes.

GARCIN  So it's you whom I have to convince; you are of my kind. Did you suppose I meant to go? No, I couldn't leave you here, gloating over my defeat, with all those thoughts about me running in your head.

INEZ  Do you really wish to convince me?

GARCIN  That's the one and only thing I wish for now. I can't hear them any longer, you know. Probably that means they're through with me. For good and all. The curtain's down, nothing of me is left on earth— not even the name of coward. So, Inez, we're alone. Only you two remain to give a thought to me. She— she doesn't count. It's you who matter; you who hate me. If you'll have faith in me I'm saved.

INEZ  It won't be easy. Have a look at me. I'm a hard-headed woman.

GARCIN  I'll give you all the time that's needed.

INEZ  Yes, we've lots of time in hand. *All* time.

GARCIN  (*Putting his hands on her shoulders*)  Listen! Each man has an aim in life, a leading motive; that's so, isn't it? Well, I didn't give a damn for wealth, or for love. I aimed at being a real man. A tough, as they say. I staked everything on the same horse. . . . Can one possibly be a coward when one's deliberately courted danger at every turn? And can one judge a life by a single action?

INEZ  Why not? For thirty years you dreamt you were a hero, and condoned a thousand petty lapses—be-cause a hero, of course, can do no wrong. An easy method, obviously. Then a day came when you were up against it, the red light of real danger—and you took the train to Mexico.

GARCIN  I "dreamt," you say. It was no dream. When I chose the hardest path, I made my choice deliberately. A man is what he wills himself to be.

INEZ  Prove it. Prove it was no dream. It's what one does, and nothing else, that shows the stuff one's made of.

GARCIN  I died too soon. I wasn't allowed time to—to do my deeds.

INEZ  One always dies too soon—or too late. And yet one's whole life is complete at that moment, with a line drawn neatly under it, ready for the summing up. You are—your life, and nothing else.

GARCIN  What a poisonous woman you are! With an answer for everything.

INEZ  Now then! Don't lose heart. It shouldn't be so hard, convincing me. Pull yourself together, man, rake up some arguments. (GARCIN *shrugs his shoulders*) Ah, wasn't I right when I said you were vulnerable? Now you're going to pay the price, and what a price! You're a coward, Garcin, because I wish it. I wish it—do you hear?—I wish it. And yet, just look at me, see how weak I am, a mere breath on the air, a gaze observing you, a formless thought that thinks you. (*He walks toward her, opening his hands*) Ah, they're open now, those big hands, those coarse, man's hands! But what do you hope to do? You can't throttle thoughts with hands. So you've no choice, you must convince me, and you're at my mercy.

ESTELLE  Garcin!

GARCIN  What?

ESTELLE  Revenge yourself.

GARCIN  How?

ESTELLE  Kiss me, darling—then you'll hear her squeal.

GARCIN  That's true, Inez. I'm at your mercy, but you're at mine as well.

(*He bends over* ESTELLE. INEZ *gives a little cry*)

INEZ  Oh, you coward, you weakling, running to women to console you!

ESTELLE   That's right, Inez. Squeal away.

INEZ   What a lovely pair you make! If you could see
his big paw splayed out on your back, rucking up
your skin and creasing the silk. Be careful, though!
He's perspiring, his hand will leave a blue stain on
your dress.

ESTELLE   Squeal away, Inez, squeal away! . . . Hug
me tight, darling; tighter still—that'll finish her off,
and a good thing too!

INEZ   Yes, Garcin, she's right. Carry on with it, press
her to you till you feel your bodies melting into each
other; a lump of warm, throbbing flesh. . . . Love's
a grand solace, isn't it, my friend? Deep and dark as
sleep. But I'll see you don't sleep.

(GARCIN *makes a slight movement*)

ESTELLE   Don't listen to her. Press your lips to my
mouth. Oh, I'm yours, yours, yours.

INEZ   Well, what are you waiting for? Do as you're told.
What a lovely scene: coward Garcin holding baby-
killer Estelle in his manly arms! Make your stakes,
everyone. Will coward Garcin kiss the lady, or won't
he dare? What's the betting? I'm watching you, everybody's watching, I'm a crowd all by myself. Do you
hear the crowd? Do you hear them muttering, Garcin?
Mumbling and muttering. "Coward! Coward! Coward!
Coward!"—that's what they're saying. . . . It's no
use trying to escape, I'll never let you go. What do
you hope to get from her silly lips? Forgetfulness?
But I shan't forget you, not I! "It's I you must convince." So come to me. I'm waiting. Come along, now.
. . . Look how obedient he is, like a well-trained dog
who comes when his mistress calls. You can't hold
him, and you never will.

GARCIN   Will night never come?

INEZ   Never.

GARCIN   You will always see me?

INEZ   Always.

(GARCIN *moves away from* ESTELLE *and takes some steps across the room. He goes to the bronze ornament*)

GARCIN This bronze. (*Strokes it thoughtfully*) Yes. now's the moment; I'm looking at this thing on the mantelpiece, and I understand that I'm in hell. I tell you, everything's been thought out beforehand. They knew I'd stand at the fireplace stroking this thing of bronze, with all those eyes intent on me. Devouring me. (*He swings round abruptly*) What? Only two of you? I thought there were more; many more. (*Laughs*) So this is hell. I'd never have believed it. You remember all we were told about the torture-chambers, the fire and brimstone, the "burning marl." Old wives' tales! There's no need for red-hot pokers. Hell is— other people!

ESTELLE My darling! Please—

GARCIN (*Thrusting her away*) No, let me be. She is between us. I cannot love you when she's watching.

ESTELLE Right! In that case, I'll stop her watching.
(*She picks up the paper-knife from the table, rushes at* INEZ, *and stabs her several times*)

INEZ (*Struggling and laughing*) But, you crazy creature, what do you think you're doing? You know quite well I'm dead.

ESTELLE Dead?
(*She drops the knife. A pause.* INEZ *picks up the knife and jabs herself with it regretfully*)

INEZ Dead! Dead! Dead! Knives, poison, ropes—all useless. It has happened *already*, do you understand? Once and for all. So here we are, forever. (*Laughs*)

ESTELLE (*With a peal of laughter*) Forever. My God, how funny! Forever.

GARCIN (*Looks at the two women, and joins in the laughter*) For ever, and ever, and ever.
(*They slump onto their respective sofas. A long*

*silence. Their laughter dies away and they gaze at each other)*

GARCIN　Well, let's get on with it. . . .

*Curtain*

# *Caligula*

## by
## ALBERT CAMUS

A Play in Four Acts

*Translated by*
*STUART GILBERT*

## CHARACTERS IN THE PLAY

CALIGULA
CÆSONIA
HELICON
SCIPIO
CHEREA
THE OLD PATRICIAN
METELLUS
LEPIDUS
INTENDANT
MEREIA
MUCIUS
MUCIUS' WIFE
PATRICIANS, KNIGHTS,
POETS, GUARDS, SERVANTS

Caligula *was first presented at the Théâtre Hébertot, Paris, in 1945.*

# Act One

*A number of patricians, one a very old man, are gathered in a state room of the imperial palace. They are showing signs of nervousness.*

FIRST PATRICIAN    Still no news.

THE OLD PATRICIAN    None last night, none this morning.

SECOND PATRICIAN    Three days without news. Strange indeed!

THE OLD PATRICIAN    Our messengers go out, our messengers return. And always they shake their heads and say: "Nothing."

SECOND PATRICIAN    They've combed the whole countryside. What more can be done?

FIRST PATRICIAN    We can only wait. It's no use meeting trouble halfway. Perhaps he'll return as abruptly as he left us.

THE OLD PATRICIAN    When I saw him leaving the palace, I noticed a queer look in his eyes.

FIRST PATRICIAN    Yes, so did I. In fact I asked him what was amiss.

SECOND PATRICIAN    Did he answer?

FIRST PATRICIAN    One word: "Nothing."

*(A short silence.* HELICON *enters. He is munching onions)*

SECOND PATRICIAN *(In the same nervous tone)*    It's all very perturbing.

FIRST PATRICIAN    Oh, come now! All young fellows are like that.

THE OLD PATRICIAN    You're right there. They take things hard. But time smooths everything out.

SECOND PATRICIAN   Do you really think so?

THE OLD PATRICIAN   Of course. For one girl dead, a dozen living ones.

HELICON   Ah? So you think that there's a girl behind it?

FIRST PATRICIAN   What else should there be? Anyhow— thank goodness!—grief never lasts forever. Is any one of us here capable of mourning a loss for more than a year on end?

SECOND PATRICIAN   Not I, anyhow.

FIRST PATRICIAN   No one can do that.

THE OLD PATRICIAN   Life would be intolerable if one could.

FIRST PATRICIAN   Quite so. Take my case. I lost my wife last year. I shed many tears, and then I forgot. Even now I feel a pang of grief at times. But, happily, it doesn't amount to much.

THE OLD PATRICIAN   Yes, Nature's a great healer.

(CHEREA *enters*)

FIRST PATRICIAN   Well . . . ?

CHEREA   Still nothing.

HELICON   Come, gentlemen! There's no need for consternation.

FIRST PATRICIAN   I agree.

HELICON   Worrying won't mend matters—and it's lunchtime.

THE OLD PATRICIAN   That's so. We mustn't drop the prey for the shadow.

CHEREA   I don't like the look of things. But all was going too smoothly. As an emperor, he was perfection's self.

SECOND PATRICIAN   Yes, exactly the emperor we wanted; conscientious and inexperienced.

FIRST PATRICIAN   But what's come over you? There's no reason for all these lamentations. We've no ground for assuming he will change. Let's say he loved Drusilla. Only natural; she was his sister. Or say his love for her was something more than brotherly; shocking enough, I grant you. But it's really going too far, setting all Rome in a turmoil because the girl has died.

CHEREA Maybe. But, as I said, I don't like the look of things; this escapade alarms me.

THE OLD PATRICIAN Yes, there's never smoke without fire.

FIRST PATRICIAN In any case, the interests of the State should prevent his making a public tragedy of . . . of, let's say, a regrettable attachment. No doubt such things happen; but the less said the better.

HELICON How can you be sure Drusilla is the cause of all this trouble?

SECOND PATRICIAN Who else should it be?

HELICON Nobody at all, quite likely. When there's a host of explanations to choose from, why pick on the stupidest, most obvious one?

(*Young* SCIPIO *enters.* CHEREA *goes toward him*)

CHEREA Well?

SCIPIO Still nothing. Except that some peasants think they saw him last night not far from Rome, rushing through the storm.

(CHEREA *comes back to the patricians,* SCIPIO *following him*)

CHEREA That makes three days, Scipio, doesn't it?

SCIPIO Yes . . . I was there, following him as I usually do. He went up to Drusilla's body. He stroked it with two fingers, and seemed lost in thought for a long while. Then he swung round and walked out, calmly enough. . . . And ever since we've been hunting for him—in vain.

CHEREA (*Shaking his head*) That young man was too fond of literature.

SECOND PATRICIAN Oh, at his age, you know . . .

CHEREA At his age, perhaps; but not in his position. An artistic emperor is an anomaly. I grant you we've had one or two; misfits happen in the best of empires.

But the others had the good taste to remember they were public servants.

FIRST PATRICIAN    It made things run more smoothly.

THE OLD PATRICIAN    One man, one job—that's how it should be.

SCIPIO    What can we do, Cherea?

CHEREA    Nothing.

SECOND PATRICIAN    We can only wait. If he doesn't return, a successor will have to be found. Between ourselves—there's no shortage of candidates.

FIRST PATRICIAN    No, but there's a shortage of the right sort.

CHEREA    Suppose he comes back in an ugly mood?

FIRST PATRICIAN    Oh, he's a mere boy; we'll make him see reason.

CHEREA    And what if he declines to see it?

FIRST PATRICIAN (*Laughing*)    In that case, my friend, don't forget I once wrote a manual of revolutions. You'll find all the rules there.

CHEARA    I'll look it up—if things come to that. But I'd rather be left to my books.

SCIPIO    If you'll excuse me. . . .

(*Goes out*)

CHEREA    He's offended.

THE OLD PATRICIAN    Scipio is young, and young people always hang together.

HELICON    Scipio doesn't count, anyhow.

(*Enter a member of the imperial bodyguard*)

THE GUARDSMAN    Caligula has been seen in the palace gardens.

(*All leave the room. The stage is empty for some moments. Then* CALIGULA *enters stealthily from the left. His legs are caked with mud, his garments dirty; his hair is wet, his look distraught. He brings his hand to his mouth several times. Then he approaches a mirror, stopping abruptly when he catches sight of his reflected self. After muttering some unintelligible words, he sits down on the right, letting his arms hang limp between his knees.* HELICON *enters, left. On seeing* CALIGULA, *he stops at the far end of the stage and contemplates him in silence.* CALIGULA *turns and sees him. A short silence*)

HELICON (*Across the stage*)  Good morning, Caius.

CALIGULA (*In quite an ordinary tone*)  Good morning, Helicon.

(*A short silence*)

HELICON  You're looking tired.

CALIGULA  I've walked a lot.

HELICON  Yes, you've been away for quite a while.

(*Another short silence*)

CALIGULA  It was hard to find.

HELICON  What was hard to find?

CALIGULA  What I was after.

HELICON  Meaning?

CALIGULA (*In the same matter-of-fact tone*)  The moon.

HELICON  What?

CALIGULA  Yes, I wanted the moon.

HELICON  Ah. . . . (*Another silence.* HELICON *approaches* CALIGULA) And why did you want it?

CALIGULA  Well . . . it's one of the things I haven't got.

HELICON  I see. And now—have you fixed it up to your satisfaction?

CALIGULA  No. I couldn't get it.

HELICON  Too bad!

CALIGULA  Yes, and that's why I'm tired. (*Pauses. Then*) Helicon!

HELICON  Yes, Caius?

CALIGULA  No doubt, you think I'm crazy.

HELICON  As you know well, I never think.

CALIGULA  Ah, yes. . . . Now, listen! I'm not mad; in fact I've never felt so lucid. What happened to me is quite simple; I suddenly felt a desire for the impossible. That's all. (*Pauses*) Things as they are, in my opinion, are far from satisfactory.

HELICON  Many people share your opinion.

CALIGULA    That is so. But in the past I didn't realize it. *Now* I know. (*Still in the same matter-of-fact tone*) Really, this world of ours, the scheme of things as they call it, is quite intolerable. That's why I want the moon, or happiness, or eternal life—something, in fact, that may sound crazy, but which isn't of this world.

HELICON    That's sound enough in theory. Only, in practice one can't carry it through to its conclusion.

CALIGULA (*Rising to his feet, but still with perfect calmness*)    You're wrong there. It's just because no one *dares* to follow up his ideas to the end that nothing is achieved. All that's needed, I should say, is to be logical right through, at all costs. (*He studies* HELICON's *face*) I can see, too, what you're thinking. What a fuss over a woman's death! But that's not it. True enough, I seem to remember that a woman died some days ago; a woman whom I loved. But love, what is it? A side issue. And I swear to you her death is not the point; it's no more than the symbol of a truth that makes the moon essential to me. A childishly simple, obvious, almost silly truth, but one that's hard to come by and heavy to endure.

HELICON    May I know what it is, this truth that you've discovered?

CALIGULA (*His eyes averted, in a toneless voice*)    Men die; and they are not happy.

HELICON (*After a short pause*)    Anyhow, Caligula, it's a truth with which one comes to terms, without much trouble. Only look at the people over there. This truth of yours doesn't prevent them from enjoying their meal.

CALIGULA (*With sudden violence*)    All it proves is that I'm surrounded by lies and self-deception. But I've had enough of that; I wish men to live by the light of truth. And I've the power to make them do so. For I know what they need and haven't got. They're without understanding and they need a teacher; someone who knows what he's talking about.

HELICON  Don't take offense, Caius, if I give you a word of advice. . . . But that can wait. First, you should have some rest.

CALIGULA  (*Sitting down. His voice is gentle again*) That's not possible, Helicon. I shall never rest again.

HELICON  But—why?

CALIGULA  If I sleep, who'll give me the moon?

HELICON  (*After a short silence*)  That's true.

CALIGULA  (*Rising to his feet again, with an effort*)  Listen, Helicon . . . I hear footsteps, voices. Say nothing —and forget you've seen me.

HELICON  I understand.

CALIGULA  (*Looking back, as he moves toward the door*) And please help me, from now on.

HELICON  I've no reason not to do so, Caius. But I know very few things, and few things interest me. In what way can I help you?

CALIGULA  In the way of . . . the impossible.

HELICON  I'll do my best.

(CALIGULA *goes out.* SCIPIO *and* CÆSONIA *enter hurriedly*)

SCIPIO  No one! Haven't you seen him?

HELICON  No.

CÆSONIA  Tell me, Helicon. Are you quite sure he didn't say anything to you before he went away?

HELICON  I'm not a sharer of his secrets, I'm his public. A mere onlooker. It's more prudent.

CÆSONIA  Please don't talk like that.

HELICON  My dear Cæsonia, Caius is an idealist as we all know. He follows his bent, and no one can foresee where it will take him. . . . But, if you'll excuse me, I'll go to lunch.

(*Exit* HELICON)

CÆSONIA  (*Sinking wearily onto a divan*)  One of the palace guards saw him go by. But all Rome sees Caligula everywhere. And Caligula, of course, sees nothing but his own idea.

SCIPIO   What idea?

CÆSONIA   How can I tell, Scipio?

SCIPIO   Are you thinking of Drusillla?

CÆSONIA   Perhaps. One thing is sure; he loved her. And it's a cruel thing to have someone die today whom only yesterday you were holding in your arms.

SCIPIO (*Timidly*)   And you . . . ?

CÆSONIA   Oh, I'm the old, trusted mistress. That's my role.

SCIPIO   Cæsonia, we must save him.

CÆSONIA   So you, too, love him?

SCIPIO   Yes. He's been very good to me. He encouraged me; I shall never forget some of the things he said. He told me life isn't easy, but it has consolations: religion, art, and the love one inspires in others. He often told me that the only mistake one makes in life is to cause others suffering. He tried to be a just man.

CÆSONIA (*Rising*)   He's only a child. (*She goes to the glass and scans herself*) The only god I've ever had is my body, and now I shall pray this god of mine to give Caius back to me.

(CALIGULA *enters. On seeing* CÆSONIA *and* SCIPIO *he hesitates, and takes a backward step. At the same moment several men enter from the opposite side of the room: patricians and the* INTENDANT *of the palace. They stop short when they see* CALIGULA. CÆSONIA *turns. She and* SCIPIO *hurry toward* CALIGULA, *who checks them with a gesture*)

INTENDANT (*In a rather quavering voice*)   We . . . we've been looking for you, Cæsar, high and low.

CALIGULA (*In a changed, harsh tone*)   So I see.

INTENDANT   We . . . I mean . . .

CALIGULA (*Roughly*)   What do you want?

INTENDANT   We were feeling anxious, Cæsar.

CALIGULA (*Going toward him*)   What business had you to feel anxious?

INTENDANT  Well . . . er . . . (*He has an inspiration*)
Well, as you know, there are points to be settled in
connection with the Treasury.

CALIGULA (*Bursting into laughter*)  Ah, yes. The Treasury! That's so. The Treasury's of prime importance.

INTENDANT  Yes, indeed.

CALIGULA (*Still laughing, to* CÆSONIA)  Don't you agree,
my dear? The Treasury is all-important.

CÆSONIA  No, Caligula. It's a secondary matter.

CALIGULA  That only shows your ignorance. We are
extremely interested in our Treasury. Everything's
important: our fiscal system, public morals, foreign
policy, army equipment, and agrarian laws. Everything's of cardinal importance, I assure you. And
everything's on an equal footing: the grandeur of
Rome and your attacks of arthritis. . . . Well, well,
I'm going to apply my mind to all that. And, to begin
with . . . Now listen well, Intendant.

INTENDANT  We are listening, sir.
    (*The patricians come forward*)

CALIGULA  You're our loyal subjects, are you not?

INTENDANT (*In a reproachful tone* )  Oh, Cæsar . . . !

CALIGULA  Well, I've something to propose to you.
We're going to make a complete change in our eco-
nomic system. In two moves. Drastic and abrupt. I'll
explain, Intendant . . . when the patricians have
left. (*The patricians go out.* CALIGULA *seats himself
beside* CÆSONIA, *with his arm around her waist*) Now
mark my words. The first move's this. Every patrician,
everyone in the Empire who has any capital—small
or large, it's all the same thing—is ordered to dis-
inherit his children and make a new will leaving his
money to the State.

INTENDANT  But Cæsar . . .

CALIGULA  I've not yet given you leave to speak. As the
need arises, we shall have these people die; a list will
be drawn up by us fixing the order of their deaths.
When the fancy takes us, we may modify that order.

And, of course, we shall step into their money.

CÆSONIA (*Freeing herself*)　But—what's come over you?

CALIGULA (*Imperturbably*)　Obviously the order of their going has no importance. Or, rather, all these executions have an equal importance—from which it follows that none has any. Really all those fellows are on a par, one's as guilty as another. (*To the* INTENDANT, *peremptorily*) You are to promulgate this edict without a moment's delay and see it's carried out forthwith. The wills are to be signed by residents in Rome this evening; within a month at the latest by persons in the provinces. Send out your messengers.

INTENDANT　Cæsar, I wonder if you realize . . .

CALIGULA　Do I realize . . . ? Now, listen well, you fool! If the Treasury has paramount importance, human life has none. That should be obvious to you. People who think like you are bound to admit the logic of my edict, and since money is the only thing that counts, should set no value on their lives or anyone else's. I have resolved to be logical, and I have the power to enforce my will. Presently you'll see what logic's going to cost you! I shall eliminate contradictions and contradicters. If necessary, I'll begin with you.

INTENDANT　Cæsar, my good will can be relied on, that I swear.

CALIGULA　And mine, too; that I guarantee. Just see how ready I am to adopt your point of view, and give the Treasury the first place in my program. Really you should be grateful to me; I'm playing into your hand, and with your own cards. (*He pauses, before continuing in a flat, unemotional tone*) In any case there is a touch of genius in the simplicity of my plan—which clinches the matter. I give you three seconds in which to remove yourself. One . . .

(*The* INTENDANT *hurries out*)

CÆSONIA　I can't believe it's you! But it was just a joke, wasn't it?—all you said to him.

CALIGULA  Not quite that, Cæsonia. Let's say, a lesson in statesmanship.

SCIPIO  But, Caius, it's . . . it's impossible!

CALIGULA  That's the whole point.

SCIPIO  I don't follow.

CALIGULA  I repeat—that is my point. I'm exploiting the impossible. Or, more accurately, it's a question of making the impossible possible.

SCIPIO  But that game may lead to—to anything! It's a lunatic's pastime.

CALIGULA  No, Scipio. An emperor's vocation. (*He lets himself sink back wearily among the cushions*) Ah, my dears, at last I've come to see the uses of supremacy. It gives impossibilities a run. From this day on, so long as life is mine, my freedom has no frontier.

CÆSONIA  (*Sadly*)  I doubt if this discovery of yours will make us any happier.

CALIGULA  So do I. But, I suppose, we'll have to live it through.

> (CHEREA *enters*)

CHEREA  I have just heard of your return. I trust your health is all it should be.

CALIGULA  My health is duly grateful. (*A pause. Then, abruptly*) Leave us, Cherea. I don't want to see you.

CHEREA  Really, Caius, I'm amazed . . .

CALIGULA  There's nothing to be amazed at. I don't like literary men, and I can't bear lies.

CHEREA  If we lie, it's often without knowing it. I plead Not Guilty.

CALIGULA  Lies are never guiltless. And yours attribute importance to people and to things. That's what I cannot forgive you.

CHEREA  And yet—since this world is the only one we have, why not plead its cause?

CALIGULA  Your pleading comes too late, the verdict's given. . . . This world has no importance; once a man realizes that, he wins his freedom. (*He has risen to his feet*) And that is why I hate you, you and your kind; because you are not free. You see in me the one free man in the whole Roman Empire. You should be glad to have at last among you an emperor who points the way to freedom. Leave me, Cherea; and you, too, Scipio, go—for what is friendship? Go, both of you, and spread the news in Rome that freedom has been given her at last, and with the gift begins a great probation.

> (*They go out.* CALIGULA *has turned away, hiding his eyes*)

CÆSONIA   Crying?

CALIGULA   Yes, Cæsonia.

CÆSONIA   But, after all, what's changed in your life? You may have loved Drusilla, but you loved many others—myself included—at the same time. Surely that wasn't enough to set you roaming the country-side for three days and nights and bring you back with this . . . this cruel look on your face?

CALIGULA (*Swinging round on her*)   What nonsense is this? Why drag in Drusilla? Do you imagine love's the only thing that can make a man shed tears?

CÆSONIA   I'm sorry, Caius. Only I was trying to understand.

CALIGULA   Men weep because . . . the world's all wrong. (*She comes toward him*) No, Cæsonia. (*She draws back*) But stay beside me.

CÆSONIA   I'll do whatever you wish. (*Sits down*) At my age one knows that life's a sad business. But why deliberately set out to make it worse?

CALIGULA   No, it's no good; you can't understand. But what matter? Perhaps I'll find a way out. Only, I feel a curious stirring within me, as if undreamed of things were forcing their way up into the light—and I'm helpless against them. (*He moves closer to her*) Oh, Cæsonia, I knew that men felt anguish, but I didn't know what that word anguish meant. Like everyone else I fancied it was a sickness of the mind—no more.

But no, it's my body that's in pain. Pain everywhere, in my chest, in my legs and arms. Even my skin is raw, my head is buzzing, I feel like vomiting. But worst of all is this queer taste in my mouth. Not blood, or death, or fever, but a mixture of all three. I've only to stir my tongue, and the world goes black, and everyone looks . . . horrible. How hard, how cruel it is, this process of becoming a man!

CÆSONIA  What you need, my dear, is a good, long sleep. Let yourself relax and, above all stop thinking. I'll stay by you while you sleep. And when you wake, you'll find the world's got back its savor. Then you must use your power to good effect—for loving better what you still find lovable. For the possible, too, deserves to be given a chance.

CALIGULA  Ah but for that I'd need to sleep, to let myself go—and that's impossible.

CÆSONIA  So one always thinks when one is overtired. A time comes when one's hand is firm again.

CALIGULA  But one must know where to place it. And what's the use to me of a firm hand, what use is the amazing power that's mine, if I can't have the sun set in the east, if I can't reduce the sum of suffering and make an end of death? No, Cæsonia, it's all one whether I sleep or keep awake, if I've no power to tamper with the scheme of things.

CÆSONIA  But that's madness, sheer madness. It's wanting to be a god on earth.

CALIGULA  So you, too, think I'm mad. And yet—what is a god that I should wish to be his equal? No, it's something higher, far above the gods, that I'm aiming at, longing for with all my heart and soul. I am taking over a kingdom where the impossible is king.

CÆSONIA  You can't prevent the sky from being the sky, or a fresh young face from aging, or a man's heart from growing cold.

CALIGULA  (*With rising excitement*) I want . . . I want

to drown the sky in the sea, to infuse ugliness with beauty, to wring a laugh from pain.

CÆSONIA (*Facing him with an imploring gesture*) There's good and bad, high and low, justice and injustice. And I swear to you these will never change.

CALIGULA (*In the same tone*) And I'm resolved to change them . . . I shall make this age of ours a kingly gift—the gift of equality. And when all is leveled out, when the impossible has come to earth and the moon is in my hands—then, perhaps, I shall be transfigured and the world renewed; then men will die no more and at last be happy.

CÆSONIA (*With a little cry*)　And love? Surely you won't go back on love!

CALIGULA (*In a wild burst of anger*)　Love, Cæsonia! (*He grips her shoulders and shakes her*) I've learned the truth about love; it's nothing, nothing! That fellow was quite right—you heard what he said, didn't you?—it's only the Treasury that counts. The fountainhead of all. Ah, now at last I'm going to live, really *live*. And living, my dear, is the opposite of loving. I know what I'm talking about—and I invite you to the most gorgeous of shows, a sight for gods to gloat on, a whole world called to judgment. But for that I must have a crowd—spectators, victims, criminals, hundreds and thousands of them. (*He rushes to the gong and begins hammering on it, faster and faster*) Let the accused come forward. I want my criminals, and they all are criminals. (*Still striking the gong*) Bring in the condemned men. I must have my public. Judges, witnesses, accused—all sentenced to death without a hearing. Yes, Cæsonia, I'll show them something they have never seen before, the one free man in the Roman Empire. (*To the clangor of the gong the palace has been gradually filling with noises; the clash of arms, voices, footsteps slow or hurried, coming nearer, growing louder. Some soldiers enter, and leave hastily*) And you, Cæsonia, shall obey me. You must stand by me to the end. It will be marvelous, you'll see. Swear to stand by me, Cæsonia.

CÆSONIA (*Wildly, between two gong strokes*)   I needn't swear. You know I love you.

CALIGULA (*In the same tone*)   You'll do all I tell you.

CÆSONIA   All, all, Caligula—but do, please, stop. . . .

CALIGULA (*Still striking the gong*)   You will be cruel.

CÆSONIA (*Sobbing*)   Cruel.

CALIGULA (*Still beating the gong*)   Cold and ruthless.

CÆSONIA   Ruthless.

CALIGULA   And you will suffer, too.

CÆSONIA   Yes, yes—oh, no, please . . . I'm—I'm going mad, I think! (*Some patricians enter, followed by members of the palace staff. All look bewildered and perturbed.* CALIGULA *bangs the gong for the last time, raises his mallet, swings round and summons them in a shrill, half-crazy voice*)

CALIGULA   Come here. All of you. Nearer. Nearer still. (*He is quivering with impatience*) Your Emperor commands you to come nearer. (*They come forward, pale with terror*) Quickly. And you, Cæsonia, come beside me. (*He takes her hand, leads her to the mirror, and with a wild sweep of his mallet effaces a reflection on its surface. Then gives a sudden laugh*) All gone. You see, my dear? An end of memories; no more masks. Nothing, nobody left. Nobody? No, that's not true. Look, Cæsonia. Come here, all of you, and *look* . . . (*He plants himself in front of the mirror in a grotesque attitude*)

CÆSONIA (*Staring, horrified, at the mirror*)   Caligula! (CALIGULA *lays a finger on the glass. His gaze steadies abruptly and when he speaks his voice has a new, proud ardor*)

CALIGULA   Yes . . . Caligula.

*Curtain*

# Act Two

*Three years later.*

*A room in* CHEREA's *house, where the patricians have met in secret.*

FIRST PATRICIAN   It's outrageous, the way he's treating us.

THE OLD PATRICIAN   He calls me "darling"! In public, mind you—just to make a laughingstock of me. Death's too good for him.

FIRST PATRICIAN   And fancy making us run beside his litter when he goes into the country.

SECOND PATRICIAN   He says the exercise will do us good.

THE OLD PATRICIAN   Conduct like that is quite inexcusable.

THIRD PATRICIAN   You're right. That's precisely the sort of thing one can't forgive.

FIRST PATRICIAN   He confiscated your property, Patricius. He killed your father, Scipio. He's taken your wife from you, Octavius, and forced her to work in his public brothel. He has killed your son, Lepidus. I ask you, gentlemen, can you endure this? I, anyhow, have made up my mind. I know the risks, but I also know this life of abject fear is quite unbearable. Worse than death, in fact. Yes, as I said, my mind's made up.

SCIPIO   He made my mind up for me when he had my father put to death.

FIRST PATRICIAN   Well? Can you still hesitate?

A KNIGHT   No. We're with you. He's transferred our

stalls at the Circus to the public, and egged us on to fight with the rabble—just to have a pretext for punishing us, of course.

THE OLD PATRICIAN    He's a coward.

SECOND PATRICIAN    A bully.

THIRD PATRICIAN    A buffoon.

THE OLD PATRICIAN    He's impotent—that's his trouble, I should say.

> (*A scene of wild confusion follows, weapons are brandished, a table is overturned, and there is a general rush toward the door. Just at this moment* CHEREA *strolls in, composed as usual, and checks their onrush*)

CHEREA    What's all this about? Where are you going?

A PATRICIAN    To the palace.

CHEREA    Ah, yes. And I can guess why. But do you think you'll be allowed to enter?

THE PATRICIAN    There's no question of asking leave.

CHEREA    Lepidus, would you kindly shut that door? (*The door is shut.* CHEREA *goes to the overturned table and seats himself on a corner of it. The others turn toward him*) It's not so simple as you think, my friends. You're afraid, but fear can't take the place of courage and deliberation. In short, you're acting too hastily.

A KNIGHT    If you're not with us, go. But keep your mouth shut.

CHEREA    I suspect I'm with you. But make no mistake. Not for the same reasons.

A VOICE    That's enough idle talk.

CHEREA (*Standing up*)    I agree. Let's get down to facts. But, first, let me make myself clear. Though I am *with* you, I'm not *for* you. That, indeed, is why I think you're going about it the wrong way. You haven't taken your enemy's measure; that's obvious, since you attribute petty motives to him. But there's nothing petty about Caligula, and you're riding for a

fall. You'd be better placed to fight him if you would
try to see him as he really is.

A VOICE   We see him as he is—a crazy tyrant.

CHEREA   No. We've had experience of mad emperors.
But this one isn't mad enough. And what I loathe
in him is this: that he knows what he wants.

FIRST PATRICIAN   And we, too, know it; he wants to
murder us all.

CHEREA   You're wrong. Our deaths are only a side
issue. He's putting his power at the service of a
loftier, deadlier passion; and it imperils everything
we hold most sacred. True, it's not the first time
Rome has seen a man wielding unlimited power; but
it's the first time he sets no limit to his use of it, and
counts mankind, and the world we know, for nothing.
That's what appalls me in Caligula; that's what I want
to fight. To lose one's life is no great matter; when
the time comes I'll have the courage to lose mine.
But what's intolerable is to see one's life being drained
of meaning, to be told there's no reason for existing.
A man can't live without some reason for living.

FIRST PATRICIAN   Revenge is a good reason.

CHEREA   Yes, and I propose to share it with you. But
I'd have you know that it's not on your account, or
to help you to avenge your petty humiliations. No, if
I join forces with you, it's to combat a big idea—an
ideal, if you like—whose triumph would mean the
end of everything. I can endure your being made a
mock of, but I cannot endure Caligula's carrying
out his theories to the end. He is converting his
philosophy into corpses and—unfortunately for us
—it's a philosophy that's logical from start to finish.
And where one can't refute, one strikes.

A VOICE   Yes. We must *act*.

CHEREA   We must take action, I agree. But a frontal
attack's quite useless when one is fighting an imperial madman in the full flush of his power. You

can take arms against a vulgar tyrant, but cunning
is needed to fight down disinterested malice. You can
only urge it on to follow its bent, and bide your time
until its logic founders in sheer lunacy. As you see,
I prefer to be quite frank, and I warn you I'll be with
you only for a time. Afterward, I shall do nothing
to advance your interests; all I wish is to regain
some peace of mind in a world that has regained a
meaning. What spurs me on is not ambition but fear,
my very reasonable fear of that inhuman vision in
which my life means no more than a speck of dust.

FIRST PATRICIAN (*Approaching him*)  I have an ink-
ling of what you mean, Cherea. Anyhow, the great
thing is that you, too, feel that the whole fabric of
society is threatened. You, gentlemen, agree with me,
I take it, that our ruling motive is of a moral order.
Family life is breaking down, men are losing their
respect for honest work, a wave of immorality is
sweeping the country. Who of us can be deaf to the
appeal of our ancestral piety in its hour of danger?
Fellow conspirators, will you tolerate a state of things
in which patricians are forced to run, like slaves,
beside the Emperor's litter?

THE OLD PATRICIAN  Will you allow them to be addressed as "darling"?

A VOICE  And have their wives snatched from them?

ANOTHER VOICE  And their money?

ALL TOGETHER  No!

FIRST PATRICIAN  Cherea, your advice is good, and you
did well to calm our passion. The time is not yet
ripe for action; the masses would still be against us.
Will you join us in watching for the best moment
to strike—and strike hard?

CHEREA  Yes—and meanwhile let Caligula follow his
dream. Or, rather, let's actively encourage him to
carry out his wildest plans. Let's put method into
his madness. And then, at last, a day will come when

he's alone, a lonely man in an empire of the dead
and kinsmen of the dead.

> (*A general uproar. Trumpet calls outside. Then
> silence, but for whispers of a name: "*CALIGULA!*"
> *CALIGULA *enters with* CÆSONIA, *followed by* HELI-
> CON *and some soldiers. Pantomime.* CALIGULA
> *halts and gazes at the conspirators. Without a
> word he moves from one to the other, straightens
> a buckle on one man's shoulder, steps back to
> contemplate another, sweeps them with his gaze,
> then draws his hand over his eyes and walks out,
> still without a word.*)

CÆSONIA (*Ironically, pointing to the disorder of the
room*)  Were you having a fight?

CHEREA  Yes, we were fighting.

CÆSONIA (*In the same tone*)  Really? Might I know
what you were fighting about?

CHEREA  About . . . nothing in particular.

CÆSONIA  Ah? Then it isn't true.

CHEREA  What isn't true?

CÆSONIA  You were *not* fighting.

CHEREA  Have it your own way. We weren't fighting.

CÆSONIA (*Smiling*)  Perhaps you'd do better to tidy
up the place. Caligula hates untidiness.

HELICON (*To the* OLD PATRICIAN)  You'll end by making
him do something out of character.

THE OLD PATRICIAN  Pardon . . . I don't follow. What
have we done to him?

HELICON  Nothing. Just nothing. It's fantastic being
futile to that point; enough to get on anybody's nerves.
Try to put yourselves in Caligula's place. (*A short
pause*) I see; doing a bit of plotting, weren't you now?

THE OLD PATRICIAN  Really, that's too absurd. I hope
Caligula doesn't imagine . . .

HELICON  He doesn't imagine. He *knows.* But, I suppose, at bottom, he rather wants it. . . . Well, we'd
better set to tidying up.

*(All get busy.* CALIGULA *enters and watches them)*

CALIGULA *(To the* OLD PATRICIAN*)* Good day, darling. *(To the others)* Gentlemen, I'm on my way to an execution. But I thought I'd drop in at your place, Cherea, for a light meal. I've given orders to have food brought here for all of us. But send for your wives first. *(A short silence)* Rufius should thank his stars that I've been seized with hunger. *(Confidentially)* Rufius, I may tell you, is the knight who's going to be executed. *(Another short silence)* What's this? None of you asks me why I've sentenced him to death? *(No one speaks. Meanwhile slaves lay the table and bring food)* Good for you! I see you're growing quite intelligent. *(He nibbles an olive)* It has dawned on you that a man needn't have done anything for him to die. *(He stops eating and gazes at his guests with a twinkle in his eye)* Soldiers, I am proud of you. *(Three or four women enter)* Good! Let's take our places. Anyhow. No order of precedence today. *(All are seated)* There's no denying it, that fellow Rufius is in luck. But I wonder if he appreciates this short reprieve. A few hours gained on death, why, they're worth their weight in gold! *(He begins eating; the others follow suit. It becomes clear that* CALIGULA's *table manners are deplorable. There is no need for him to flick his olive stones onto his neighbors' plates, or to spit out bits of gristle over the dish, or to pick his teeth with his nails, or to scratch his head furiously. However, he indulges in these practices throughout the meal, without the least compunction. At one moment he stops eating, stares at* LEPIDUS, *one of the guests, and says roughly)* You're looking grumpy, Lepidus. I wonder, can it be because I had your son killed?

LEPIDUS *(Thickly)* Certainly not, Caius. Quite the contrary.

CALIGULA *(Beaming at him)* "Quite the contrary!" It's

always nice to see a face that hides the secrets of the heart. Your face is sad. But what about your heart? Quite the contrary—isn't that so, Lepidus?

LEPIDUS (*Doggedly*)   Quite the contrary, Cæsar.

CALIGULA (*More and more enjoying the situation*) Really, Lepidus, there's no one I like better than you. Now let's have a laugh together, my dear friend. Tell me a funny story.

LEPIDUS (*Who has overrated his endurance*)   Please . . .

CALIGULA   Good! Very good! Then it's I who'll tell the story. But you'll laugh, won't you, Lepidus? (*With a glint of malice*) If only for the sake of your other son. (*Smiling again*) In any case, as you've just told us, you're not in a bad humor. (*He takes a drink, then says in the tone of a teacher prompting a pupil*) Quite . . . quite the . . .

LEPIDUS (*Wearily*)   Quite the contrary, Cæsar.

CALIGULA   Splendid! (*Drinks again*) Now listen. (*In a gentle, faraway tone*) Once upon a time there was a poor young emperor whom nobody loved. He loved Lepidus, and to root out of his heart his love for Lepidus, he had his youngest son killed. (*In a brisker tone*) Needless to say, there's not a word of truth in it. Still it's a funny story, eh? But you're not laughing. Nobody's laughing. Now listen! (*In a burst of anger*) I insist on everybody's laughing. You, Lepidus, shall lead the chorus. Stand up, every one of you, and laugh. (*He thumps the table*) Do you hear what I say? I wish to see you laughing, all of you. (*All rise to their feet. During this scene all the players,* CALIGULA *and* CÆSONIA *excepted, behave like marionettes in a puppet play.* CALIGULA *sinks back on his couch, beaming with delight, and bursts into a fit of laughter*) Oh, Cæsonia! Just look at them! The game is up; honor, respectability, the wisdom of the nations, gone with the wind! The wind of fear has blown them all away. Fear, Cæsonia—don't you agree?—is a noble emotion, pure and simple, self-sufficient, like no other; it draws its patent of nobility straight from the guts. (*He strokes his forehead and drinks again. In a friendly tone*) Well, well, let's change the subject. What have you to say, Cherea? You've been very silent.

CHEREA  I'm quite ready to speak, Caius. When you give me leave.

CALIGULA  Excellent. Then—keep silent. I'd rather have a word from our friend Mucius.

MUCIUS (*Reluctantly*)  As you will, Caius.

CALIGULA  Then tell us something about your wife. And begin by sending her to this place, on my right. (MUCIUS' WIFE *seats herself beside* CALIGULA) Well, Mucius? We're waiting.

MUCIUS (*Hardly knowing what he says*)  My wife . . . but . . . I'm very fond of her.

(*General laughter*)

CALIGULA  Why, of course, my friend, of course. But how ordinary of you! So unoriginal! (*He is leaning toward her, tickling her shoulder playfully with his tongue*) By the way, when I came in just now, you were hatching a plot, weren't you? A nice bloody little plot?

OLD PATRICIAN  Oh, Caius, how can you . . . ?

CALIGULA  It doesn't matter in the least, my pet. Old age will be served. I won't take it seriously. Not one of you has the spunk for a heroic act. . . . Ah, it's just come to my mind, I have some affairs of state to settle. But, first, let the imperious desires that nature creates in us have their way.

(*He rises and leads* MUCIUS' WIFE *into an adjoining room.* MUCIUS *starts up from his seat*)

CÆSONIA (*Amiably*)  Please, Mucius. Will you pour me out another glass of this excellent wine. (MUCIUS *complies; his movement of revolt is quelled. Everyone looks embarrassed. Chairs creak noisily. The ensuing conversation is in a strained tone.* CÆSONIA *turns to* CHEREA) Now, Cherea, suppose you tell me why you people were fighting just now?

CHEREA (*Coolly*)   With pleasure, my dear Cæsonia. Our quarrel arose from a discussion whether poetry should be bloodthirsty or not.

CÆSONIA   An interesting problem. Somewhat beyond my feminine comprehension, of course. Still it surprises me that your passion for art should make you come to blows.

CHEREA (*In the same rather stilted tone*)   That I can well understand. But I remember Caligula's telling me the other day that all true passion has a spice of cruelty.

CÆSONIA (*Helping herself from the dish in front of her*) There's truth in that. Don't you agree, gentlemen?

THE OLD PATRICIAN   Ah, yes. Caligula has a rare insight into the secret places of the heart.

FIRST PATRICIAN   And how eloquently he spoke just now of courage!

SECOND PATRICIAN   Really, he should put his ideas into writing. They would be most instructive.

CHEREA   And, what's more, it would keep him busy. It's obvious he needs something to occupy his leisure.

CÆSONIA (*Still eating*)   You'll be pleased to hear that Caligula shares your views; he's working on a book. Quite a big one, I believe.

(CALIGULA *enters, accompanied by* MUCIUS' WIFE)

CALIGULA   Mucius, I return your wife, with many thanks. But excuse me, I've some orders to give.

(*He hurries out.* MUCIUS *has gone pale and risen to his feet*)

CÆSONIA (*To* MUCIUS, *who is standing*)   This book of his will certainly rank among our Latin Classics. Are you listening, Mucius?

MUCIUS (*His eyes still fixed on the door by which*

CALIGULA *went out*) Yes. And what's the book about, Cæsonia?

CÆSONIA (*Indifferently*) Oh, it's above my head, you know.

CHEREA May we assume it deals with the murderous power of poetry?

CÆSONIA Yes, something of that sort, I understand.

THE OLD PATRICIAN (*Cheerfully*) Well anyhow, as our friend Cherea said, it will keep him busy.

CÆSONIA Yes, my love. But I'm afraid there's one thing you won't like quite so much about this book, and that's its title.

CHEREA What is it?

CÆSONIA *Cold Steel.*

(CALIGULA *hurries in*)

CALIGULA Excuse me, but I've some urgent public work in hand. (*To the* INTENDANT) Intendant, you are to close the public granaries. I have signed a decree to that effect; you will find it in my study.

INTENDANT But, sire . . .

CALIGULA Famine begins tomorrow.

INTENDANT But . . . but heaven knows what may happen—perhaps a revolution.

CALIGULA (*firmly and deliberately*) I repeat; famine begins tomorrow. We all know what famine means —a national catastrophe. Well, tomorrow there will be a catastrophe, and I shall end it when I choose. After all, I haven't so many ways of proving I am free. One is always free at someone else's expense. Absurd perhaps, but so it is. (*With a keen glance at* MUCIUS) Apply this principle to your jealousy—and you'll understand better. (*In a meditative tone*) Still, what an ugly thing is jealousy! A disease of vanity and the imagination. One pictures one's wife . . . (MUCIUS *clenches his fists and opens his mouth to speak. Before he can get a word out,* CALIGULA *cuts in*) Now, gentlemen, let's go on with our meal. . . .

Do you know, we've been doing quite a lot of work, with Helicon's assistance? Putting the final touches to a little monograph on execution—about which you will have much to say.

HELICON   Assuming we ask your opinion.

CALIGULA   Why not be generous, Helicon, and let them into our little secrets? Come now, give them a sample. Section Three, first paragraph.

HELICON (*Standing, declaims in a droning voice*)   "Execution relieves and liberates. It is universal, tonic, just in precept and in practice. A man dies because he is guilty. A man is guilty because he is one of Caligula's subjects. Now all men are Caligula's subjects. *Ergo,* all men are guilty and shall die. It is only a matter of time and patience."

CALIGULA (*Laughing*)   There's logic for you, don't you agree? That bit about patience was rather neat, wasn't it? Allow me to tell you, that's the quality I most admire in you . . . your patience. Now, gentlemen, you can disperse. Cherea doesn't need your presence any longer. Cæsonia, I wish you to stay. You too, Lepidus. Also our old friend Mereia. I want to have a little talk with you about our National Brothel. It's not functioning too well; in fact, I'm quite concerned about it.

(*The others file out slowly.* CALIGULA *follows* MUCIUS *with his eyes*)

CHEREA   At your orders, Caius. But what's the trouble? Is the staff unsatisfactory?

CALIGULA   No, but the takings are falling off.

MEREIA   Then you should raise the entrance fee.

CALIGULA   There, Mereia, you missed a golden opportunity of keeping your mouth shut. You're too old to be interested in the subject, and I don't want your opinion.

MEREIA   Then why ask me to stay?

CALIGULA   Because, presently, I may require some cool, dispassionate advice.

(MEREIA *moves away*)

CHEREA  If you wish to hear my views on the subject, Caius, I'd say, neither coolly nor dispassionately, that it would be a blunder to raise the scale of charges.

CALIGULA  Obviously. What's needed is a bigger turn-over. I've explained my plan of campaign to Cæsonia, and she will tell you all about it. As for me, I've had too much wine, I'm feeling sleepy.

(*He lies down and closes his eyes*)

CÆSONIA  It's very simple. Caligula is creating a new order of merit.

CHEREA  Sorry, I don't see the connection.

CÆSONIA  No? But there is one. It will be called the Badge of Civic Merit and awarded to those who have patronized Caligula's National Brothel most assiduously.

CHEREA  A brilliant idea!

CÆSONIA  I agree. Oh, I forgot to mention that the badge will be conferred each month, after checking the admission tickets. Any citizen who has not obtained the badge within twelve months will be exiled, or executed.

CHEREA  Why "or executed"?

CÆSONIA  Because Caligula says it doesn't matter which —but it's important he should have the right of choosing.

CHEREA  Bravo! The Public Treasury will wipe out its deficit in no time.

(CALIGULA *has half opened his eyes and is watching old* MEREIA *who, standing in a corner, has produced a small flask and is sipping its contents*)

CALIGULA (*Still lying on the couch*)  What's that you're drinking, Mereia?

MEREIA  It's for my asthma, Caius.

CALIGULA (*Rises, and thrusting the others aside, goes up to* MEREIA *and sniffs his mouth*)  No, it's an antidote.

MEREIA  What an idea, Caius! You must be joking. I

have choking fits at night and I've been in the doctor's hands for months.

CALIGULA   So you're afraid of being poisoned?

MEREIA   My asthma . . .

CALIGULA   No. Why beat about the bush? You're afraid I'll poison you. You suspect me. You're keeping an eye on me.

MEREIA   Good heavens, no!

CALIGULA   You suspect me. I'm not to be trusted, eh?

MEREIA   Caius!

CALIGULA   (*Roughly*)   Answer! (*In a cool, judicial tone*) If you take an antidote, it follows that you credit me with the intention of poisoning you. Q.E.D.

MEREIA   Yes . . . I mean . . . no!

CALIGULA   And thinking I intend to poison you, you take steps to frustrate my plan. (*He falls silent. Meanwhile* CÆSONIA *and* CHEREA *have moved away, backstage.* LEPIDUS *is watching the speakers with an air of consternation*) That makes two crimes, Mereia, and a dilemma from which you can't escape. *Either* I have no wish to cause your death; in which case you are unjustly suspecting me, your emperor. *Or else* I desire your death; in which case, vermin that you are, you're trying to thwart my will. (*Another silence.* CALIGULA *contemplates the old man gloatingly*) Well, Mereia, what have you to say to my logic?

MEREIA   It . . . it's sound enough, Caius. Only it doesn't apply to the case.

CALIGULA   A third crime. You take me for a fool. Now sit down and listen carefully. (*To* LEPIDUS) Let everyone sit down. (*To* MEREIA) Of these three crimes only one does you honor; the second one—because by crediting me with a certain wish and presuming to oppose it you are deliberately defying me. You are a rebel, a leader of revolt. And that needs courage. (*Sadly*) I've a great liking for you, Mereia. And that is why you'll be condemned for crime number two, and not for either of the others. You shall die nobly, a rebel's death. (*While he talks* MEREIA *is shrinking together on his chair*) Don't thank me. It's quite natural. Here. (*Holds out a phial. His tone is amiable*) Drink this poison. (MEREIA *shakes his head. He is sobbing violently.* CALIGULA *shows signs of impatience*) Don't waste time. Take it. (MEREIA *makes a feeble attempt to escape. But* CALIGULA *with a wild leap is on him, catches him in the center of the stage and after a brief struggle pins him down on a low couch. He forces the phial between his lips and smashes it with a blow of his fist. After some convulsive movements* MEREIA *dies. His face is streaming with blood and tears.* CALIGULA *rises, wipes his hands absent-mindedly, then hands* MEREIA'S *flask to* CÆSONIA) What was it? An antidote?

CÆSONIA (*Calmly*)   No, Caligula. A remedy for asthma.
   (*A short silence*)

CALIGULA (*Gazing down at* MEREIA)   No matter. It all comes to the same thing in the end. A little sooner, a little later. . . .

   (*He goes out hurriedly, still wiping his hands*)

LEPIDUS (*In a horrified tone*)   What . . . what shall we do?

CÆSONIA (*Coolly*)   Remove that body to begin with, I should say. It's rather a beastly sight.

   (CHEREA *and* LEPIDUS *drag the body into the wings*)

LEPIDUS (*To* CHEREA)   We must act quickly.

CHEREA   We'll need to be two hundred.

   (*Young* SCIPIO *enters. Seeing* CÆSONIA, *he makes as if to leave*)

CÆSONIA   Come.

SCIPIO   What do you want?

CÆSONIA   Come nearer. (*She pushes up his chin and looks him in the eyes. A short silence. Then, in a calm, unemotional voice*) He killed your father, didn't he?

SCIPIO   Yes.

CÆSONIA　Do you hate him?

SCIPIO　Yes.

CÆSONIA　And you'd like to kill him?

SCIPIO　Yes.

CÆSONIA (*Withdrawing her hand*)　But—why tell me this?

SCIPIO　Because I fear nobody. Killing him or being killed—either way out will do. And anyhow you won't betray me.

CÆSONIA　That's so. I won't betray you. But I want to tell you something—or, rather, I'd like to speak to what is best in you.

SCIPIO　What's best in me is—my hatred.

CÆSONIA　Please listen carefully to what I'm going to say. It may sound hard to grasp, but it's as clear as daylight, really. And it's something that would bring about the one real revolution in this world of ours, if people would only take it in.

SCIPIO　Yes? What is it?

CÆSONIA　Wait! Try to call up a picture of your father's death, of the agony on his face as they were tearing out his tongue. Think of the blood streaming from his mouth, and recall his screams, like a tortured animal's.

SCIPIO　Yes.

CÆSONIA　And now think of Caligula.

SCIPIO (*His voice rough with hatred*)　Yes.

CÆSONIA　Now listen. *Try to understand him.*

　　　　(*She goes out, leaving* SCIPIO *gaping after her in bewilderment.* HELICON *enters*)

HELICON　Caligula will be here in a moment. Suppose you go for your meal, young poet?

SCIPIO　Helicon, help me.

HELICON　Too dangerous, my lamb. And poetry means nothing to me.

SCIPIO　You can help me. You know . . . so many things.

HELICON  I know that the days go by—and growing boys should have their meals on time . . . I know, too, that you could kill Caligula . . . and he wouldn't greatly mind it.

(HELICON *goes out.* CALIGULA *enters*)

CALIGULA  Ah, it's you, Scipio. (*He pauses. One has the impression that he is somewhat embarrassed*) It's quite a long time since I saw you last. (*Slowly approaches* SCIPIO) What have you been up to? Writing more poems, I suppose. Might I see your latest composition?

SCIPIO (*Likewise ill at ease, torn between hatred and some less defined emotion*)  Yes, Cæsar, I've written some more poems.

CALIGULA  On what subject?

SCIPIO  Oh, on nothing in particular. Well, on Nature in a way.

CALIGULA  A fine theme. And a vast one. And what has Nature done for you?

SCIPIO (*Pulling himself together, in a somewhat truculent tone*)  It consoles me for not being Cæsar.

CALIGULA  Really? And do you think Nature could console me for being Cæsar?

SCIPIO (*In the same tone*)  Why not? Nature has healed worse wounds than that.

CALIGULA (*In a curiously young, unaffected voice*) Wounds, you said? There was anger in your voice. Because I put your father to death? . . . That word you used—if you only knew how apt it is! My wounds! (*In a different tone*) Well, well, there's nothing like hatred for developing the intelligence.

SCIPIO (*Stiffly*)  I answered your question about Nature.

(CALIGULA *sits down, gazes at* SCIPIO, *then brusquely grips his wrists and forces him to stand up. He takes the young man's face between his hands*)

CALIGULA  Recite your poem to me, please.

SCIPIO    No, please, don't ask me that.

CALIGULA    Why not?

SCIPIO    I haven't got it on me.

CALIGULA    Can't you remember it?

SCIPIO    No.

CALIGULA    Anyhow you can tell me what it's about.

SCIPIO (*Still hostile; reluctantly*)    I spoke of a . . . a certain harmony . . .

CALIGULA (*Breaking in; in a pensive voice*) . . . between one's feet and the earth.

SCIPIO (*Looking surprised*)    Yes, it's almost that . . . and it tells of the wavy outline of the Roman hills and the sudden thrill of peace that twilight brings to them . . .

CALIGULA    And the cries of swifts winding through the green dusk.

SCIPIO (*Yielding more and more to his emotion*)    Yes, yes! And that fantastic moment when the sky all flushed with red and gold swings round and shows its other side, spangled with stars.

CALIGULA    And the faint smell of smoke and trees and streams that mingles with the rising mist.

SCIPIO (*In a sort of ecstasy*)    Yes, and the chirr of crickets, the coolness veining the warm air, the rumble of carts and the farmers' shouts, dogs barking . . .

CALIGULA    And the roads drowned in shadow winding through the olive groves . . .

SCIPIO    Yes, yes. That's it, exactly. . . . But how did you know?

CALIGULA (*Drawing SCIPIO to his breast*)    I wonder! Perhaps because the same eternal truths appeal to us both.

SCIPIO (*Quivering with excitement, burying his head on CALIGULA's breast*)    Anyhow, what does it matter! All I know is that everything I feel or think of turns to love.

CALIGULA (*Stroking his hair*)    That, Scipio, is a privi-

lege of noble hearts—and how I wish I could share
your . . . your limpidity! But my appetite for life's
too keen; Nature can never sate it. You belong to
quite another world, and you can't understand. You
are single-minded for good; and I am single-minded
—for evil.

SCIPIO  I *do* understand.

CALIGULA  No. There's something deep down in me—
an abyss of silence, a pool of stagnant water, rotting
weeds. (*With an abrupt change of manner*) Your
poem sounds very good indeed, but, if you really
want my opinion. . . .

SCIPIO (*His head on* CALIGULA's *breast, murmurs*) Yes?

CALIGULA  All that's a bit . . . anemic.

SCIPIO (*Recoiling abruptly, as if stung by a serpent, and
gazing, horrified, at* CALIGULA, *he cries hoarsely*) Oh,
you brute! You loathsome brute! You've fooled me
again. I know! You were playing a trick on me,
weren't you? And now you're gloating over your success.

CALIGULA (*With a hint of sadness*)  There's truth in
what you say. I *was* playing a part.

SCIPIO (*In the same indignant tone*)  What a foul, black
heart you have! And how all that wickedness and
hatred must make you suffer!

CALIGULA (*Gently*)  That's enough.

SCIPIO  How I loathe you! And how I pity you!

CALIGULA (*Angrily*)  Enough, I tell you.

SCIPIO  And how horrible a loneliness like yours must
be!

CALIGULA (*In a rush of anger, gripping the boy by the
collar, and shaking him*)  Loneliness! What do *you*
know of it? Only the loneliness of poets and weak-
lings. You prate of loneliness, but you don't realize
that one is *never* alone. Always we are attended by
the same load of the future and the past. Those we
have killed are always with us. But *they* are no great

trouble. It's those we have loved, those who loved us and whom we did not love; regrets, desires, bitterness and sweetness, whores and gods, the celestial gang! Always, always with us! (*He releases* SCIPIO *and moves back to his former place*) Alone! Ah, if only in this loneliness, this ghoul-haunted wilderness of mine, I could know, but for a moment, real solitude, real silence, the throbbing stillness of a tree! (*Sitting down, in an access of fatigue*) Solitude? No, Scipio, mine is full of gnashings of teeth, hideous with jarring sounds and voices. And when I am with the women I make mine and darkness falls on us and I think, now my body's had its fill, that I can feel myself my own at last, poised between death and life—ah, then my solitude is fouled by the stale smell of pleasure from the woman sprawling at my side.

(*A long silence.* CALIGULA *seems weary and despondent.* SCIPIO *moves behind him and approaches hesitantly. He slowly stretches out a hand toward him, from behind, and lays it on his shoulder. Without looking round,* CALIGULA *places his hand on* SCIPIO's)

SCIPIO　All men have a secret solace. It helps them to endure, and they turn to it when life has wearied them beyond enduring.

CALIGULA　Yes, Scipio.

SCIPIO　Have you nothing of the kind in your life, no refuge, no mood that makes the tears well up, no consolation?

CALIGULA　Yes, I have something of the kind.

SCIPIO　What is it?

CALIGULA (*Very quietly*)　Scorn.

*Curtain*

# Act Three

*A room in the imperial palace.*

*Before the curtain rises a rhythmic clash of cymbals and the thudding of a drum have been coming from the stage, and when it goes up we see a curtained-off booth, with a small proscenium in front, such as strolling players use at country fairs. On the little stage are* CÆSONIA *and* HELICON, *flanked by cymbal players. Seated on benches, with their backs to the audience, are some patricians and young* SCIPIO.

HELICON (*In the tone of a showman at a fair*)   Walk up! Walk up! (*A clash of cymbals*) Once more the gods have come to earth. They have assumed the human form of our heaven-born emperor, known to men as Caligula. Draw near, mortals of common clay; a holy miracle is taking place before your eyes. By a divine dispensation peculiar to Caligula's hallowed reign, the secrets of the gods will be revealed to you. (*Cymbals*)

CÆSONIA   Come, gentlemen. Come and adore him—and don't forget to give your alms. Today heaven and its mysteries are on show, at a price to suit every pocket.

HELICON   For all to see, the secrets of Olympus, revelations in high places, featuring gods in undress, their little plots and pranks. Step this way! The whole truth about your gods! (*Cymbals*)

CÆSONIA   Adore him, and give your alms. Come near, gentlemen. The show's beginning.

*(Cymbals. Slaves are placing various objects on the platform)*

HELICON    An epoch-making reproduction of the life celestial, warranted authentic in every detail. For the first time the pomp and splendor of the gods are presented to the Roman public. You will relish our novel, breathtaking effects: flashes of lightning (*Slaves light Greek fires*), peals of thunder (*They roll a barrel filled with stones*), the divine event on its triumphal way. Now watch with all your eyes.

*(He draws aside the curtain. Grotesquely attired as Venus,* CALIGULA *beams down on them from a pedestal)*

CALIGULA (*Amiably*)    I'm Venus today.

CÆSONIA    Now for the adoration. Bow down. (*All but* SCIPIO *bend their heads*) And repeat after me the litany of Venus called Caligula.

"Our Lady of pangs and pleasures . . ."

THE PATRICIANS    "Our Lady of pangs and pleasures . . ."

CÆSONIA    "Born of the waves, bitter and bright with seafoam . . ."

THE PATRICIANS    "Born of the waves, bitter and bright with seafoam . . ."

CÆSONIA    "O Queen whose gifts are laughter and regrets . . ."

THE PATRICIANS    "O Queen whose gifts are laughter and regrets . . ."

CÆSONIA    "Rancors and raptures . . ."

THE PATRICIANS    "Rancors and raptures . . ."

CÆSONIA    "Teach us the indifference that kindles love anew . . ."

THE PATRICIANS    "Teach us the indifference that kindles love anew . . ."

CÆSONIA    "Make known to us the truth about this world—which is that it has none . . ."

THE PATRICIANS    "Make known to us the truth about this world—which is that it has none . . ."

CÆSONIA "And grant us strength to live up to this verity of verities."

THE PATRICIANS "And grant us strength to live up to this verity of verities."

CÆSONIA Now, pause.

THE PATRICIANS Now, pause.

CÆSONIA (*After a short silence*) "Bestow your gifts on us, and shed on our faces the light of your impartial cruelty, your wanton hatred; unfold above our eyes your arms laden with flowers and murders . . ."

THE PATRICIANS ". . . your arms laden with flowers and murders."

CÆSONIA "Welcome your wandering children home, to the bleak sanctuary of your heartless, thankless love. Give us your passions without object, your griefs devoid of reason, your raptures that lead nowhere . . ."

THE PATRICIANS ". . . your raptures that lead nowhere . . ."

CÆSONIA (*Raising her voice*) "O Queen, so empty yet so ardent, inhuman yet so earthly, make us drunk with the wine of your equivalence, and surfeit us forever in the brackish darkness of your heart."

THE PATRICIANS "Make us drunk with the wine of your equivalence, and surfeit us forever in the brackish darkness of your heart." (*When the patricians have said the last response,* CALIGULA, *who until now has been quite motionless, snorts and rises*)

CALIGULA (*In a stentorian voice*) Granted, my children. Your prayer is heard. (*He squats cross-legged on the pedestal. One by one the patricians make obeisance, deposit their alms, and line up on the right. The last, in his flurry, forgets to make an offering.* CALIGULA *bounds to his feet*) Steady! Steady on! Come here, my lad. Worship's very well, but almsgiving is better. Thank you. We are appeased. Ah, if the gods had no wealth other than the love you mortals give them, they'd be as poor as poor Caligula. Now, gentlemen, you may go, and spread abroad the glad tidings of the miracle you've been allowed to witness. You have seen Venus, seen her godhead with your fleshly eyes, and Venus herself has spoken to you. Go, most favored gentlemen. (*The patricians begin to move away*) Just a moment. When you leave, mind you take the exit on your left. I have posted sentries in the others, with orders to kill you.

> (*The patricians file out hastily, in some disorder. The slaves and musicians leave the stage*)

HELICON (*Pointing a threatening finger at* SCIPIO) Naughty boy, you've been playing the anarchist again.

SCIPIO (*To* CALIGULA) You spoke blasphemy, Caius.

CALIGULA Blasphemy? What's that?

SCIPIO You're befouling heaven, after bloodying the earth.

HELICON How this youngster loves big words!

> (*He stretches himself on a couch*)

CÆSONIA (*Composedly*) You should watch your tongue, my lad. At this moment men are dying in Rome for saying much less.

SCIPIO Maybe—but I've resolved to tell Caligula the truth.

CÆSONIA Listen to him, Caligula! That was the one thing missing in your Empire—a bold young moralist.

CALIGULA (*Giving* SCIPIO *a curious glance*) Do you really believe in the gods, Scipio?

SCIPIO No.

CALIGULA Then I fail to follow. If you don't believe, why be so keen to scent out blasphemy?

SCIPIO One may deny something without feeling called on to besmirch it, or deprive others of the right of believing in it.

CALIGULA But that's humility, the real thing, unless I'm much mistaken. Ah, my dear Scipio, how glad I am on your behalf—and a trifle envious, too. Humility's the one emotion I may never feel.

SCIPIO  It's not I you're envious of; it's the gods.

CALIGULA  If you don't mind, that will remain our secret—the great enigma of our reign. Really, you know, there's only one thing for which I might be blamed today—and that's this small advance I've made upon the path of freedom. For someone who loves power the rivalry of the gods is rather irksome. Well, I've proved to these imaginary gods that any man, without previous training, if he applies his mind to it, can play their absurd parts to perfection.

SCIPIO  That, Caius, is what I meant by blasphemy.

CALIGULA  No, Scipio, it's clear-sightedness. I've merely realized that there's only one way of getting even with the gods. All that's needed is to be as cruel as they.

SCIPIO  All that's needed is to play the tyrant.

CALIGULA  Tell me, my young friend. What exactly *is* a tyrant?

SCIPIO  A blind soul.

CALIGULA  That's a moot point. I should say the real tyrant is a man who sacrifices a whole nation to his ideal or his ambition. But I have no ideal, and there's nothing left for me to covet by way of power or glory. If I use this power of mine, it's to compensate.

SCIPIO  For what?

CALIGULA  For the hatred and stupidity of the gods.

SCIPIO  Hatred does not compensate for hatred. Power is no solution. Personally I know only one way of countering the hostility of the world we live in.

CALIGULA  Yes? And what is it?

SCIPIO  Poverty.

CALIGULA  (*Bending over his feet and scrutinizing his toes*)  I must try that, too.

SCIPIO  Meanwhile many men round you are dying.

CALIGULA  Oh, come! Not so many as all that. Do you know how many wars I've refused to embark on?

SCIPIO  No.

CALIGULA    Three. And do you know why I refused?

SCIPIO    Because the grandeur of Rome means nothing to you.

CALIGULA    No. Because I respect human life.

SCIPIO    You're joking, Caius.

CALIGULA    Or, anyhow, I respect it more than I respect military triumphs. But it's a fact that I don't respect it more than I respect my own life. And if I find killing easy, it's because dying isn't hard for me. No, the more I think about it, the surer I feel that I'm no tyrant.

SCIPIO    What does it matter, if it costs us quite as dear as if you were one?

CALIGULA    (*With a hint of petulance*)    If you had the least head for figures you'd know that the smallest war a tyrant—however levelheaded he might be—indulged in would cost you a thousand times more than all my vagaries (shall we call them?) put together.

SCIPIO    Possibly. But at least there'd be *some* sense behind a war; it would be understandable—and to understand makes up for much.

CALIGULA    There's no understanding fate; therefore I choose to play the part of fate. I wear the foolish, unintelligible face of a professional god. And that is what the men who were here with you have learned to adore.

SCIPIO    That, too, Caius, is blasphemy.

CALIGULA    No, Scipio, it's dramatic art. The great mistake you people make is not to take the drama seriously enough. If you did, you'd know that any man can play lead in the divine comedy and become a god. All he needs do is to harden his heart.

SCIPIO    You may be right, Caius. But I rather think you've done everything that was needed to rouse up against you a legion of human gods, ruthless as yourself, who will drown in blood your godhead of a day.

CÆSONIA  Really, Scipio!

CALIGULA  (*Peremptorily*)  No, don't stop him, Cæsonia. Yes, Scipio, you spoke truer than you knew; I've done everything needed to that end. I find it hard to picture the event you speak of—but I sometimes dream it. And in all those faces surging up out of the angry darkness, convulsed with fear and hatred, I see, and I rejoice to see, the only god I've worshipped on this earth; foul and craven as the human heart. (*Irritably*) Now go. I've had enough of you, more than enough. (*In a different tone*) I really must attend to my toenails; they're not nearly red enough, and I've no time to waste. (*All go, with the exception of* HELICON. *He hovers round* CALIGULA, *who is busy examining his toes*) Helicon!

HELICON  Yes?

CALIGULA  Getting on with your task?

HELICON  What task?

CALIGULA  You know . . . the moon.

HELICON  Ah yes, the moon. . . . It's a matter of time and patience. But I'd like to have a word with you.

CALIGULA  I might have patience; only I have not much time. So you must make haste.

HELICON  I said I'd do my utmost. But, first, I have something to tell you. Very serious news.

CALIGULA  (*As if he has not heard*)  Mind you, I've had her already.

HELICON  Whom?

CALIGULA  The moon.

HELICON  Yes, yes. . . . Now listen, please. Do you know there's a plot being hatched against your life?

CALIGULA  What's more, I had her thoroughly. Only two or three times, to be sure. Still, I had her all right.

HELICON  For the last hour I've been trying to tell you about it, only—

CALIGULA  It was last summer. I'd been gazing at her so long, and stroking her so often on the marble pillars in the gardens that evidently she'd come to understand.

HELICON    Please stop trifling, Caius. Even if you refuse to listen, it's my duty to tell you this. And if you shut your ears, it can't be helped.

CALIGULA (*Applying red polish to his toenails*)    This varnish is no good at all. But, to come back to the moon—it was a cloudless August night. (HELICON *looks sulkily away, and keeps silence*) She was coy, to begin with. I'd gone to bed. First she was blood-red, low on the horizon. Then she began rising, quicker and quicker, growing brighter and brighter all the while. And the higher she climbed, the paler she grew, till she was like a milky pool in a dark wood rustling with stars. Slowly, shyly, she approached, through the warm night air, soft, light as gossamer, naked in beauty. She crossed the threshold of my room, glided to my bed, poured herself into it, and flooded me with her smiles and sheen. . . . No, really this new varnish is a failure. . . . So you see, Helicon, I can say, without boasting, that I've had her.

HELICON    Now will you listen, and learn the danger that's threatening you?

CALIGULA (*Ceasing to fiddle with his toes, and gazing at him fixedly*)    All I want, Helicon, is—the moon. For the rest, I've always known what will kill me. I haven't yet exhausted all that is to keep me living. That's why I want the moon. And you must not return till you have secured her for me.

HELICON    Very well. . . . Now I'll do my duty and tell you what I've learned. There's a plot against you. Cherea is the ringleader. I came across this tablet which tells you all you need to know. See, I put it here.

> (*He places the tablet on one of the seats and moves away*)

CALIGULA  Where are you off to, Helicon?

HELICON (*From the threshold*)  To get the moon for you.

> (*There is a mouselike scratching at the opposite door.* CALIGULA *swings round and sees the* OLD PATRICIAN)

THE OLD PATRICIAN (*Timidly*)  May I, Caius . . .

CALIGULA (*Impatiently*)  Come in! Come in! (*Gazes at him*) So, my pet, you've returned to have another look at Venus.

THE OLD PATRICIAN  Well . . . no. It's not quite that. Ssh! Oh, sorry, Caius! I only wanted to say . . . You know I'm very, very devoted to you—and my one desire is to end my days in peace.

CALIGULA  Be quick, man. Get it out!

THE OLD PATRICIAN  Well, it's . . . it's like this. (*Hurriedly*) It's terribly serious, that's what I meant to say.

CALIGULA  No, it isn't serious.

THE OLD PATRICIAN  But—I don't follow. *What* isn't serious?

CALIGULA  But what are we talking about, my love?

THE OLD PATRICIAN (*Glancing nervously round the room*) I mean to say . . . (*Wriggles, shuffles, then bursts out with it*) There's a plot afoot, against you.

CALIGULA  There! You see. Just as I said; it isn't serious.

THE OLD PATRICIAN  But, Caius, they mean to kill you.

CALIGULA (*Approaching him and grasping his shoulders*) Do you know why I can't believe you?

THE OLD PATRICIAN (*Raising an arm, as if to take an oath*)  The gods bear witness, Caius, that . . .

CALIGULA (*Gently but firmly pressing him back toward the door*)  Don't swear. I particularly ask you not to swear. Listen, instead. Suppose it were true, what you are telling me—I'd have to assume you were betraying your friends, isn't that so?

THE OLD PATRICIAN (*Flustered*)  Well, Caius, considering the deep affection I have for you . . .

CALIGULA (*In the same tone as before*)　And I cannot assume *that*. I've always loathed baseness of that sort so profoundly that I could never restrain myself from having a betrayer put to death. But I know the man you are, my worthy friend. And I'm convinced you neither wish to play the traitor nor to die.

THE OLD PATRICIAN　Certainly not, Caius. Most certainly not.

CALIGULA　So you see I was right in refusing to believe you. You wouldn't stoop to baseness, would you?

THE OLD PATRICIAN　Oh, no, indeed!

CALIGULA　Nor betray your friends?

THE OLD PATRICIAN　I need hardly tell you that, Caius.

CALIGULA　Therefore it follows that there isn't any plot. It was just a joke—between ourselves, rather a silly joke—what you've just been telling me, eh?

THE OLD PATRICIAN (*Feebly*)　Yes, yes. A joke, merely a joke.

CALIGULA　Good. So now we know where we are. Nobody wants to kill me.

THE OLD PATRICIAN　Nobody. That's it. Nobody at all.

CALIGULA (*Drawing a deep breath; in measured tones*) Then—leave me, sweetheart. A man of honor is an animal so rare in the present-day world that I couldn't bear the sight of one too long. I must be left alone to relish this unique experience. (*For some moments he gazes, without moving, at the tablet. He picks it up and reads it. Then, again, draws a deep breath. Then summons a palace guard*)

CALIGULA　Bring Cherea to me. (*The man starts to leave*) Wait! (*The man halts*) Treat him politely. (*The man goes out.* CALIGULA *falls to pacing the room. After a while he approaches the mirror*) You decided to be logical, didn't you, poor simpleton? Logic for ever! The question now is: Where will that take you? (*Ironically*) Suppose the moon were brought here, everything would be different. That was the idea, wasn't it? Then the impossible would become pos-

sible, in a flash the Great Change come, and all things
be transfigured. After all, why shouldn't Helicon
bring it off? One night, perhaps, he'll catch her sleeping in a lake, and carry her here, trapped in a glisten-
ing net, all slimy with weeds and water, like a pale
bloated fish drawn from the depths. Why not, Caligula? Why not, indeed? *(He casts a glance round the
room)* Fewer and fewer people round me; I wonder
why. *(Addressing the mirror, in a muffled voice)* Too
many dead, too many dead—that makes an emptiness.
. . . No, even if the moon were mine, I could not re-
trace my way. Even were those dead men thrilling
again under the sun's caress, the murders wouldn't
go back underground for that. *(Angrily)* Logic, Caligula; follow where logic leads. Power to the uttermost;
wilfulness without end. Ah, I'm the only man on
earth to know the secret—that power can never be
complete without a total self-surrender to the dark
impulse of one's destiny. No, there's no return. I must
go on and on, until the consummation.

> *(CHEREA enters. CALIGULA is slumped in his chair,
> the cloak drawn tightly round him)*

CHEREA   You sent for me, Caius?

CALIGULA *(Languidly)*   Yes, Cherea.

> *(A short silence)*

CHEREA   Have you anything particular to tell me?

CALIGULA   No, Cherea.

> *(Another silence)*

CHEREA *(With a hint of petulance)*   Are you sure you
really need my presence?

CALIGULA   Absolutely sure, Cherea. *(Another silence.
Then, as if suddenly recollecting himself)* I'm sorry
for seeming so inhospitable. I was following up my
thoughts, and—Now do sit down, we'll have a friendly
little chat. I'm in a mood for some intelligent conversation. *(CHEREA sits down. For the first time since
the play began, CALIGULA gives the impression of being his natural self)* Do you think, Cherea, that it's

possible for two men of much the same temperament and equal pride to talk to each other with complete frankness—if only once in their lives? Can they strip themselves naked, so to speak, and shed their prejudices, their private interests, the lies by which they live?

CHEREA  Yes, Caius, I think it possible. But I don't think you'd be capable of it.

CALIGULA  You're right. I only wished to know if you agreed with me. So let's wear our masks, and muster up our lies. And we'll talk as fencers fight, padded on all the vital parts. Tell me, Cherea, why don't you like me?

CHEREA  Because there's nothing likeable about you, Caius. Because such feelings can't be had to order. And because I understand you far too well. One cannot like an aspect of oneself which one always tries to keep concealed.

CALIGULA  But why is it you hate me?

CHEREA  There, Caius, you're mistaken. I do not hate you. I regard you as noxious and cruel, vain and selfish. But I cannot hate you, because I don't think you are happy. And I cannot scorn you, because I know you are no coward.

CALIGULA  Then why wish to kill me?

CHEREA  I've told you why; because I regard you as noxious, a constant menace. I like, and need, to feel secure. So do most men. They resent living in a world where the most preposterous fancy may at any moment become a reality, and the absurd transfix their lives, like a dagger in the heart. I feel as they do; I refuse to live in a topsy-turvy world. I want to know where I stand, and to stand secure.

CALIGULA  Security and logic don't go together.

CHEREA  Quite true. My plan of life may not be logical, but at least it's sound.

CALIGULA  Go on.

CHEREA  There's no more to say. I'll be no party to your

logic. I've a very different notion of my duties as a
man. And I know that the majority of your subjects
share my view. You outrage their deepest feelings. It's
only natural that you should . . . disappear.

CALIGULA  I see your point, and it's legitimate enough.
For most men, I grant you, it's obvious. But *you,* I
should have thought, would have known better.
You're an intelligent man, and given intelligence, one
has a choice: either to pay its price or to disown it.
Why do you shirk the issue and neither disown it nor
consent to pay its price?

CHEREA  Because what I want is to live, and to be
happy. Neither, to my mind, is possible if one pushes
the absurd to its logical conclusions. As you see, I'm
quite an ordinary sort of man. True, there are moments when, to feel free of them, I desire the death
of those I love, or I hanker after women from whom
the ties of family or friendship debar me. Were logic
everything, I'd kill or fornicate on such occasions.
But I consider that these passing fancies have no great
importance. If everyone set to gratifying them, the
world would be impossible to live in, and happiness,
too, would go by the board. And these, I repeat, are
the things that count, for me.

CALIGULA  So, I take it, you believe in some higher
principle?

CHEREA  Certainly I believe that some actions are—
shall I say?—more praiseworthy than others.

CALIGULA  And *I* believe that all are on an equal footing.

CHEREA  I know it, Caius, and that's why I don't hate
you. I understand, and, to a point, agree with you.
But you're pernicious, and you've got to go.

CALIGULA  True enough. But why risk your life by telling me this?

CHEREA  Because others will take my place, and because
I don't like lying.

   (*A short silence*)

CALIGULA   Cherea!

CHEREA   Yes, Caius?

CALIGULA   Do you think that two men of similar temperament and equal pride can, if only once in their lives, open their hearts to each other?

CHEREA   That, I believe, is what we've just been doing.

CALIGULA   Yes, Cherea. But you thought I was incapable of it.

CHEREA   I was wrong, Caius. I admit it, and I thank you. Now I await your sentence.

CALIGULA   My sentence? Ah, I see. (*Producing the tablet from under his cloak*) You know what this is, Cherea?

CHEREA   I knew you had it.

CALIGULA   (*Passionately*)   You knew I had it! So your frankness was all a piece of play acting. The two friends did *not* open their hearts to each other. Well, well! It's no great matter. Now we can stop playing at sincerity, and resume life on the old footing. But first I'll ask you to make just one more effort; to bear with my caprices and my tactlessness a little longer. Listen well, Cherea. This tablet is the one and only piece of evidence against you.

CHEREA   Caius, I'd rather go. I'm sick and tired of all these antics. I know them only too well, and I've had enough. Let me go, please.

CALIGULA   (*In the same tense, passionate voice*)   No, stay. This tablet is the only evidence. Is that clear?

CHEREA   Evidence? I never knew you needed evidence to send a man to his death.

CALIGULA   That's true. Still, for once I wish to contradict myself. Nobody can object to that. It's so pleasant to contradict oneself occasionally; so restful. And I need rest, Cherea.

CHEREA   I don't follow . . . and, frankly, I've no taste for these subtleties.

CALIGULA   I know, Cherea, I know. You're not like me; you're an ordinary man, sound in mind and body.

And naturally you've no desire for the extraordinary. (*With a burst of laughter*) You want to live and to be happy. That's all!

CHEREA   I think, Caius, we'd better leave it at that. . . . Can I go?

CALIGULA   Not yet. A little patience, if you don't mind —I shall not keep you long. You see this thing—this piece of evidence? I choose to assume that I can't sentence you to death without it. That's my idea . . . and my repose. Well! See what becomes of evidence in an emperor's hands. (*He holds the tablet to a torch.* CHEREA *approaches. The torch is between them. The tablet begins to melt*) You see, conspirator! The tablet's melting, and as it melts a look of innocence is dawning on your face. What a handsome forehead you have, Cherea! And how rare, how beautiful a sight is an innocent man! Admire my power. Even the gods cannot restore innocence without first punishing the culprit. But your emperor needs only a torch flame to absolve you and give you a new lease of hope. So carry on, Cherea; follow out the noble precepts we've been hearing, wherever they may take you. Meanwhile your emperor awaits his repose. It's his way of living and being happy.

(CHEREA *stares, dumfounded, at* CALIGULA. *He makes a vague gesture, seems to understand, opens his mouth to speak—and walks abruptly away. Smiling, holding the tablet to the flame,* CALIGULA *follows the receding figure with his gaze*)

*Curtain*

# Act Four

*A room in the imperial palace.*

*The stage is in semidarkness.* CHEREA *and* SCIPIO *enter.* CHEREA *crosses to the right, then comes back left to* SCIPIO.

SCIPIO (*Sulkily*)  What do you want of me?

CHEREA  There's no time to lose. And we must know our minds, we must be resolute.

SCIPIO  Who says I'm not resolute?

CHEREA  You didn't attend our meeting yesterday.

SCIPIO (*Looking away*)  That's so, Cherea.

CHEREA  Scipio, I am older than you, and I'm not in the habit of asking others' help. But, I won't deny it, I need you now. This murder needs honorable men to sponsor it. Among all these wounded vanities and sordid fears, our motives only, yours and mine, are disinterested. Of course I know that, if you leave us, we can count on your silence. But that is not the point. What I want is—for you to stay with us.

SCIPIO  I understand. But I can't, oh, no, I *cannot* do as you wish.

CHEREA  So you are with him?

SCIPIO  No. But I cannot be against him. (*Pauses; then in a muffled voice*) Even if I killed him, my heart would still be with him.

CHEREA  And yet—he killed your father!

SCIPIO  Yes—and that's how it all began. But that, too, is how it ends.

CHEREA  He denies what you believe in. He tramples on all that you hold sacred.

SCIPIO  I know, Cherea. And yet something inside me is
  akin to him. The same fire burns in both our hearts.
CHEREA  There are times when a man must make his
  choice. As for me, I have silenced in my heart all that
  might be akin to him.
SCIPIO  But—*I*—I cannot make a choice. I have my own
  sorrow, but I suffer with him, too; I share his pain.
  I understand all—that is my trouble.
CHEREA  So that's it. You have chosen to take his side.
SCIPIO  (*Passionately*)  No, Cherea. I beg you, don't
  think that. I can never, never again take anybody's
  side.
CHEREA  (*Affectionately; approaching* SCIPIO)  Do you
  know, I hate him even more for having made of you
  —what he has made.
SCIPIO  Yes, he has taught me to expect everything of
  life.
CHEREA  No, he has taught you despair. And to have
  instilled despair into a young heart is fouler than the
  foulest of the crimes he has committed up to now.
  I assure you, *that* alone would justify me in killing
  him out of hand.

      (*He goes toward the door.* HELICON *enters*)

HELICON  I've been hunting for you high and low,
  Cherea. Caligula's giving a little party here, for his
  personal friends only. Naturally he expects you to
  attend it. (*To* SCIPIO)  You, my boy, aren't wanted.
  Off you go!
SCIPIO  (*Looking back at* CHEREA *as he goes out*)  Cherea.
CHEREA  (*Gently*)  Yes, Scipio?
SCIPIO  Try to understand.
CHEREA  (*In the same gentle tone*)  No, Scipio.

      (SCIPIO *and* HELICON *go out. A clash of arms in
      the wings. Two soldiers enter at right, escorting
      the* OLD PATRICIAN *and the* FIRST PATRICIAN, *who
      show signs of alarm*)

FIRST PATRICIAN (*To one of the soldiers, in a tone which*

*he vainly tries to steady*)  But . . . but what *can* he
want with us at this hour of the night?

SOLDIER  Sit there. (*Points to the chairs on the right*)

FIRST PATRICIAN  If it's only to have us killed—like so
many others—why all these preliminaries?

SOLDIER  Sit down, you old mule.

THE OLD PATRICIAN  Better do as he says. It's clear he
doesn't know anything.

SOLDIER  Yes, darling, quite clear. (*Goes out*)

FIRST PATRICIAN  We should have acted sooner; I always
said so. Now we're in for the torture chamber.

> (*The* SOLDIER *comes back with* CHEREA, *then goes
> out*)

CHEREA (*Seating himself. He shows no sign of apprehen-
sion*)  Any idea what's happening?

FIRST PATRICIAN AND THE OLD PATRICIAN (*Speaking together*)  He's found out about the conspiracy.

CHEREA  Yes? And then?

THE OLD PATRICIAN (*Shuddering*)  The torture chamber
for us all.

CHEREA (*Still unperturbed*)  I remember that Caligula
once gave eighty-one thousand sesterces to a slave
who, though he was tortured nearly to death, wouldn't
confess to a theft he had committed.

FIRST PATRICIAN  A lot of consolation that is—for us!

CHEREA  Anyhow, it shows that he appreciates courage.
You ought to keep that in mind. (*To the* OLD PATRI-
CIAN) Would you very much mind not chattering with
your teeth? It's a noise I particularly dislike.

THE OLD PATRICIAN  I'm sorry, but—

FIRST PATRICIAN  Enough trifling! Our lives are at stake.

CHEREA (*Coolly*)  Do you know Caligula's favorite remark?

THE OLD PATRICIAN (*On the verge of tears*)  Yes. He says
to the executioner: "Kill him slowly, so that he feels
what dying's like!"

CHEREA  No, there's a better one. After an execution

he yawns, and says quite seriously: "What I admire most is my imperturbability."

FIRST PATRICIAN  Do you hear . . . ?

(*A clanking of weapons is heard off stage*)

CHEREA  That remark betrays a weakness in his make-up.

THE OLD PATRICIAN  Would you be kind enough to stop philosophizing? It's something I particularly dislike.

(*A slave enters and deposits a sheaf of knives on a seat*)

CHEREA (*Who has not noticed him*)  Still, there's no denying it's remarkable, the effect this man has on all with whom he comes in contact. He forces one to think. There's nothing like insecurity for stimulating the brain. That, of course, is why he's so much hated.

THE OLD PATRICIAN (*Pointing a trembling finger*)  Look!

CHEREA (*Noticing the knives, in a slightly altered tone*)  Perhaps you were right.

FIRST PATRICIAN  Yes, waiting was a mistake. We should have acted at once.

CHEREA  I agree. Wisdom's come too late.

THE OLD PATRICIAN  But it's . . . it's crazy. I don't want to die.

(*He rises and begins to edge away. Two soldiers appear, and, after slapping his face, force him back onto his seat. The* FIRST PATRICIAN *squirms in his chair.* CHEREA *utters some inaudible words. Suddenly a queer music begins behind the curtain at the back of the stage; a thrumming and tinkling of zithers and cymbals. The patricians gaze at each other in silence. Outlined on the illuminated curtain, in shadow play,* CALIGULA *appears, makes some grotesque dance movements, and retreats from view. He is wearing ballet dancer's skirts and his head is garlanded with flowers. A moment later a* SOLDIER *announces gravely: "Gentlemen, the performance is over."* Meanwhile*

CÆSONIA *has entered soundlessly behind the watching patricians. She speaks in an ordinary voice, but none the less they give a start on hearing it.*)

CÆSONIA   Caligula has instructed me to tell you that, whereas in the past he always summoned you for affairs of state, today he invited you to share with him an artistic emotion. (*A short pause. Then she continues in the same tone*) He added, I may say, that anyone who has not shared in it will be beheaded. (*They keep silent*) I apologize for insisting, but I must ask you if you found that dance beautiful.

FIRST PATRICIAN (*After a brief hesitation*)   Yes, Cæsonia. It was beautiful.

THE OLD PATRICIAN (*Effusively*)   Lovely! Lovely!

CÆSONIA   And you, Cherea?

CHEREA (*Icily*)   It was . . . very high art.

CÆSONIA   Good. Now I can describe your artistic emotions to Caligula.

   (CÆSONIA *goes out*)

CHEREA   And now we must act quickly. You two stay here. Before the night is out there'll be a hundred of us.

   (*He goes out*)

THE OLD PATRICIAN   No, no. *You* stay. Let me go, instead. (*Sniffs the air*) It smells of death here.

FIRST PATRICIAN   And of lies. (*Sadly*) I said that dance was beautiful!

THE OLD PATRICIAN (*Conciliatingly*)   And so it was, in a way. Most original.

   (*Some patricians and knights enter hurriedly*)

SECOND PATRICIAN   What's afoot? Do you know anything? The Emperor's summoned us here.

THE OLD PATRICIAN (*Absent-mindedly*)   For the dance, maybe.

SECOND PATRICIAN   What dance?

THE OLD PATRICIAN   Well, I mean . . . er . . . the artistic emotion.

THIRD PATRICIAN   I've been told Caligula's very ill.

FIRST PATRICIAN   He's a sick man, yes . . .

THIRD PATRICIAN   What's he suffering from? (*In a joyful tone*) By God, is he going to die?

FIRST PATRICIAN   I doubt it. His disease is fatal—to others only.

THE OLD PATRICIAN   That's one way of putting it.

SECOND PATRICIAN   Quite so. But hasn't he some other disease less serious, and more to our advantage?

FIRST PATRICIAN   No. That malady of his excludes all others.

(*He goes out.* CÆSONIA *enters. A short silence*)

CÆSONIA (*In a casual tone*)   If you want to know, Caligula has stomach trouble. Just now he vomited blood.

(*The patricians crowd round her*)

SECOND PATRICIAN   O mighty gods, I vow, if he recovers, to pay the Treasury two hundred thousand sesterces as a token of my joy.

THIRD PATRICIAN (*With exaggerated eagerness*)   O Jupiter, take my life in place of his!

(CALIGULA *has entered, and is listening*)

CALIGULA (*Going up to the* SECOND PATRICIAN)   I accept your offer, Lucius. And I thank you. My Treasurer will call on you tomorrow. (*Goes to the* THIRD PATRICIAN *and embraces him*) You can't imagine how touched I am. (*A short silence. Then, tenderly*) So you love me, Cassius, as much as that?

THIRD PATRICIAN (*Emotionally*)   Oh, Cæsar, there's nothing, nothing I wouldn't sacrifice for your sake.

CALIGULA (*Embracing him again*)   Ah, Cassius, this is really too much; I don't deserve all this love. (CASSIUS *makes a protesting gesture*) No, no, really I don't! I'm not worthy of it. (*He beckons to two soldiers*) Take him away. (*Gently, to* CASSIUS) Go, dear friend, and remember that Caligula has lost his heart to you.

THIRD PATRICIAN (*Vaguely uneasy*)   But—where are they taking me?

CALIGULA   Why, to your death, of course. Your generous offer was accepted, and I feel better already. Even that nasty taste of blood in my mouth has gone. You've cured me, Cassius. It's been miraculous, and how proud you must feel of having worked the miracle by laying your life down for your friend—especially when that friend's none other than Caligula! So now you see me quite myself again, and ready for a festive night.

THIRD PATRICIAN (*Shrieking, as he is dragged away*) No! No! I don't want to die. You can't be serious!

CALIGULA (*In a thoughtful voice, between the shrieks*) Soon the sea roads will be golden with mimosas. The women will wear their lightest dresses. And the sky! Ah, Cassius, what a blaze of clean, swift sunshine! The smiles of life. (CASSIUS *is near the door.* CALIGULA *gives him a gentle push. Suddenly his tone grows serious*) Life, my friend, is something to be cherished. Had you cherished it enough, you wouldn't have gambled it away so rashly. (CASSIUS *is led off.* CALIGULA *returns to the table*) The loser must pay. There's no alternative. (*A short silence*) Come, Cæsonia. (*He turns to the others*) By the way, an idea has just waylaid me, and it's such an apt one that I want to share it with you. Until now my reign has been too happy. There's been no world-wide plague, no religious persecution, not even a rebellion—nothing in fact to make us memorable. And that, I'd have you know, is why I try to remedy the stinginess of fate. I mean—I don't know if you've followed me—that, well (*He gives a little laugh*), it's I who replace the epidemics that we've missed. (*In a different tone*) That's enough. I see Cherea's coming. Your turn, Cæsonia. (CALIGULA *goes out.* CHEREA *and the* FIRST PATRICIAN *enter.* CÆSONIA *hurries toward* CHEREA)

CÆSONIA   Caligula is dead.

(*She turns her head, as if to hide her tears; her*

*eyes are fixed on the others, who keep silence.
Everyone looks horrified, but for different reasons*)

FIRST PATRICIAN  You . . . you're *sure* this dreadful thing has happened? It seems incredible. Only a short while ago he was dancing.

CÆSONIA  Quite so—and the effort was too much for him. (CHEREA *moves hastily from one man to the other. No one speaks*) You've nothing to say, Cherea?

CHEREA  (*In a low voice*)  It's a great misfortune for us all, Cæsonia.

(CALIGULA *bursts in violently and goes up to* CHEREA)

CALIGULA  Well played, Cherea. (*He spins round and stares at the others. Petulantly*) Too bad! It didn't come off. (*To* CÆSONIA) Don't forget what I told you.

(CALIGULA *goes out.* CÆSONIA *stares after him without speaking*)

THE OLD PATRICIAN  (*Hoping against hope*)  Is he ill, Cæsonia?

CÆSONIA  (*With a hostile look*)  No, my pet. But what you don't know is that the man never has more than two hours' sleep and spends the best part of the night roaming about the corridors in his palace. Another thing you don't know—and you've never given a thought to—is what may pass in this man's mind in those deadly hours between midnight and sunrise. Is he ill? No, not ill—unless you invent a name and medicine for the black ulcers that fester in his soul.

CHEREA  (*Seemingly affected by her words*)  You're right, Cæsonia. We all know that Caius . . .

CÆSONIA  (*Breaking in emotionally*)  Yes, you know it—in your fashion. But, like all those who have none, you can't abide anyone who has too much soul. Healthy people loathe invalids. Happy people hate the sad. Too much soul! That's what bites you, isn't it? You prefer to label it a disease; that way all the dolts are justified and pleased. (*In a changed tone*)

Tell me, Cherea. Has love ever meant anything to you?

CHEREA (*Himself again*)　I'm afraid we're too old now, Cæsonia, to learn the art of love-making. And anyhow it's highly doubtful if Caligula will give us time to do so.

CÆSONIA (*Who has recovered her composure*)　True enough. (*She sits down*) Oh, I was forgetting. . . . Caligula asked me to impart some news to you. You know, perhaps, that it's a red-letter day today, consecrated to art.

THE OLD PATRICIAN　According to the calendar?

CÆSONIA　No, according to Caligula. He's convoked some poets. He will ask them to improvise a poem on a set theme. And he particularly wants those of you who are poets to take part in the competition. He specially mentioned young Scipio and Metellus.

METELLUS　But we're not ready.

CÆSONIA (*In a level tone, as if she has not heard him*)　Needless to say there are prizes. There will be penalties, too. (*Looks of consternation*) Between ourselves, the penalties won't be so very terrible.

(CALIGULA *enters, looking gloomier than ever*)

CALIGULA　All ready?

CÆSONIA　Yes. (*To a soldier*) Bring in the poets.

(*Enter, two by two, a dozen poets, keeping step; they line up on the right of the stage*)

CALIGULA　And the others?

CÆSONIA　Metellus! Scipio!

(*They cross the stage and take their stand beside the poets.* CALIGULA *seats himself, backstage on the left, with* CÆSONIA *and the patricians. A short silence*)

CALIGULA　Subject: death. Time limit: one minute.

(*The poets scribble feverishly on their tablets*)

THE OLD PATRICIAN　Who will compose the jury?

CALIGULA　I. Isn't that enough?

THE OLD PATRICIAN   Oh, yes, indeed. Quite enough.

CHEREA   Won't you take part in the competition, Caius?

CALIGULA   Unnecessary. I made my poem on that theme long ago.

THE OLD PATRICIAN (*Eagerly*)   Where can one get a copy of it?

CALIGULA   No need to get a copy. I recite it every day, after my fashion. (CÆSONIA *eyes him nervously.* CALIGULA *rounds on her almost savagely*) Is there anything in my appearance that displeases you?

CÆSONIA (*Gently*)   I'm sorry. . . .

CALIGULA   No meekness, please. For heaven's sake, no meekness. You're exasperating enough as it is, but if you start being humble . . . (CÆSONIA *slowly moves away.* CALIGULA *turns to* CHEREA) I continue. It's the only poem I have made. And it's proof that I'm the only true artist Rome has known—the only one, believe me—to match his inspiration with his deeds.

CHEREA   That's only a matter of having the power.

CALIGULA   Quite true. Other artists create to compensate for their lack of power. I don't need to make a work of art; I *live* it. (*Roughly*) Well, poets, are you ready?

METELLUS   I think so.

THE OTHERS   Yes.

CALIGULA   Good. Now listen carefully. You are to fall out of line and come forward one by one. I'll whistle. Number One will start reading his poem. When I whistle, he must stop, and the next begin. And so on. The winner, naturally, will be the one whose poem hasn't been cut short by the whistle. Get ready. (*Turning to* CHEREA, *he whispers*) You see, organization's needed for everything, even for art.

   (*Blows his whistle*)

FIRST POET   Death, when beyond thy darkling shore . . .
   (*A blast of the whistle. The poet steps briskly to the left. The others will follow the same pro-*

*cedure. These movements should be made with mechanical precision*)

SECOND POET   In their dim cave, the Fatal Sisters Three . . .
        (*Whistle*)

THIRD POET   Come to me death, beloved . . .
        (*A shrill blast of the whistle. The* FOURTH POET *steps forward and strikes a dramatic posture. The whistle goes before he has opened his mouth*)

FIFTH POET   When I was in my happy infancy . . .

CALIGULA (*Yelling*)   Stop that! What earthly connection has a blockhead's happy infancy with the theme I set? The connection! Tell me the connection!

FIFTH POET   But, Caius, I've only just begun, and . . .
        (*Shrill blast*)

SIXTH POET (*In a high-pitched voice*)   Ruthless, he goes his hidden ways . . .
        (*Whistle*)

SEVENTH POET (*Mysteriously*)   Oh, long, abstruse orison . . .
        (*Whistle, broken off as* SCIPIO *comes forward without a tablet*)

CALIGULA   You haven't a tablet?

SCIPIO   I do not need one.

CALIGULA   Well, let's hear you. (*He chews at his whistle*)

SCIPIO (*Standing very near* CALIGULA, *he recites listlessly, without looking at him*)

Pursuit of happiness that purifies the heart,
Skies rippling with light,
O wild, sweet, festal joys, frenzy without hope!

CALIGULA (*Gently*)   Stop, please. The others needn't compete. (*To* SCIPIO) You're very young to understand so well the lessons we can learn from death.

SCIPIO (*Gazing straight at* CALIGULA)   I was very young to lose my father.

CALIGULA (*Turning hastily*) Fall in, the rest of you. No, really a sham poet is too dreadful an infliction. Until now I'd thought of enrolling you as my allies; I sometimes pictured a gallant band of poets defending me in the last ditch. Another illusion gone! I shall have to relegate you to my enemies. So now the poets are against me—and that looks much like the end of all. March out in good order. As you go past you are to lick your tablets so as to efface the atrocities you scrawled on them. Attention! Forward! (*He blows his whistle in short rhythmic jerks. Keeping step, the poets file out by the right, tonguing their immortal tablets.* CALIGULA *adds in a lower tone*) Now leave me, everyone.

> (*In the doorway, as they are going out,* CHEREA *touches the* FIRST PATRICIAN'S *shoulder, and speaks in his ear*)

CHEREA Now's our opportunity.

> (SCIPIO, *who has overheard, halts on the threshold and walks back to* CALIGULA)

CALIGULA (*Acidly*) Can't you leave me in peace—as your father's doing?

SCIPIO No, Caius, all that serves no purpose now. For now I know, I *know* that you have made your choice.

CALIGULA Won't you leave me in peace!

SCIPIO Yes, you shall have your wish; I am going to leave you, for I think I've come to understand you. There's no way out left to us, neither to you nor to me—who am like you in so many ways. I shall go away, far away, and try to discover the meaning of it all. (*He gazes at* CALIGULA *for some moments. Then, with a rush of emotion*) Good-by, dear Caius. When all is ended, remember that I loved you. (*He goes out.* CALIGULA *makes a vague gesture. Then, almost savagely, he pulls himself together and takes some steps toward* CÆSONIA)

CÆSONIA What did he say?

CALIGULA   Nothing you'd understand.

CÆSONIA   What are you thinking about?

CALIGULA   About him. And about you, too. But it amounts to the same thing.

CÆSONIA   What is the matter?

CALIGULA (*Staring at her*)   Scipio has gone. I am through with his friendship. But you, I wonder why you are still here. . . .

CÆSONIA   Why, because you're fond of me.

CALIGULA   No. But I think I'd understand—if I had you killed.

CÆSONIA   Yes, that would be a solution. Do so, then. . . . But why, oh, why can't you relax, if only for a moment, and live freely, without constraint?

CALIGULA   I have been doing that for several years; in fact I've made a practice of it.

CÆSONIA   I don't mean that sort of freedom. I mean —Oh, don't you realize what it can be to live and love quite simply, naturally, in . . . in purity of heart?

CALIGULA   This purity of heart you talk of—every man acquires it, in his own way. Mine has been to follow the essential to the end. . . . Still all that needn't prevent me from putting you to death. (*Laughs*) It would round off my career so well, the perfect climax. (*He rises and swings the mirror round toward himself. Then he walks in a circle, letting his arms hang limp, almost without gestures; there is something feral in his gait as he continues speaking*) How strange! When I don't kill, I feel alone. The living don't suffice to people my world and dispel my boredom. I have an impression of an enormous void when you and the others are here, and my eyes see nothing but empty air. No, I'm at ease only in the company of my dead. (*He takes his stand facing the audience, leaning a little forward. He has forgotten* CÆSONIA's *presence*) Only the dead are real. They are of my kind. I see them waiting for me, straining toward me. And I have long talks with this man or that, who screamed to me for mercy and whose tongue I had cut out.

CÆSONIA  Come. Lie down beside me. Put your head on my knees. (CALIGULA *does so*) That's better, isn't it? Now rest. How quiet it is here!

CALIGULA  Quiet? You exaggerate, my dear. Listen! (*Distant metallic tinklings, as of swords or armor*) Do you hear those thousands of small sounds all around us, hatred stalking its prey? (*Murmuring voices, footsteps*)

CÆSONIA  Nobody would dare. . . .

CALIGULA  Yes, stupidity.

CÆSONIA  Stupidity doesn't kill. It makes men slow to act.

CALIGULA  It can be murderous, Cæsonia. A fool stops at nothing when he thinks his dignity offended. No, it's not the men whose sons or fathers I have killed who'll murder me. *They,* anyhow, have understood. They're with me, they have the same taste in their mouths. But the others—those I made a laughing-stock of—I've no defense against their wounded vanity.

CÆSONIA  (*Passionately*) *We* will defend you. There are many of us left who love you.

CALIGULA  Fewer every day. It's not surprising. I've done all that was needed to that end. And then— let's be fair—it's not only stupidity that's against me. There's the courage and the simple faith of men who ask to be happy.

CÆSONIA  (*In the same tone*)  No, *they* will not kill you. Or, if they tried, fire would come down from heaven and blast them, before they laid a hand on you.

CALIGULA  From heaven! There is no heaven, my poor dear woman! (*He sits down*) But why this sudden access of devotion? It wasn't provided for in our agreement, if I remember rightly.

CÆSONIA  (*Who has risen from the couch and is pacing*

*the room*) Don't you understand? Hasn't it been enough to see you killing others, without my also knowing you'll be killed as well? Isn't it enough to feel you hard and cruel, seething with bitterness, when I hold you in my arms; to breathe a reek of murder when you lie on me? Day after day I see all that's human in you dying out, little by little. (*She turns toward him*) Oh, I know. I know I'm getting old, my beauty's on the wane. But it's you only I'm concerned for now; so much so that I've ceased troubling whether you love me. I only want you to get well, quite well again. You're still a boy, really; you've a whole life ahead of you. And, tell me, what greater thing can you want than a whole life?

CALIGULA (*Rising, looks at her fixedly*) You've been with me a long time now, a very long time.

CÆSONIA Yes. . . . But you'll keep me, won't you?

CALIGULA I don't know. I only know that, if you're with me still, it's because of all those nights we've had together, nights of fierce, joyless pleasure; it's because you alone know me as I am. (*He takes her in his arms, bending her head back a little with his right hand*) I'm twenty-nine. Not a great age really. But today when none the less my life seems so long, so crowded with scraps and shreds of my past selves, so complete in fact, you remain the last witness. And I can't avoid a sort of shameful tenderness for the old woman that you soon will be.

CÆSONIA Tell me that you mean to keep me with you.

CALIGULA I don't know. All I know—and it's the most terrible thing of all—is that this shameful tenderness is the one sincere emotion that my life has given up to now. (CÆSONIA *frees herself from his arms.* CALIGULA *follows her. She presses her back to his chest and he puts his arms round her*) Wouldn't it be better that the last witness should disappear?

CÆSONIA That has no importance. All I know is: I'm

happy. What you've just said has made me very happy. But why can't I share my happiness with you?

CALIGULA   Who says I'm unhappy?

CÆSONIA   Happiness is kind. It doesn't thrive on bloodshed.

CALIGULA   Then there must be two kinds of happiness, and I've chosen the murderous kind. For I *am* happy. There was a time when I thought I'd reached the extremity of pain. But, no, one can go farther yet. Beyond the frontier of pain lies a splendid, sterile happiness. Look at me. (*She turns toward him*) It makes me laugh, Cæsonia, when I think how for years and years all Rome carefully avoided uttering Drusilla's name. Well, all Rome was mistaken. Love isn't enough for me; I realized it then. And I realize it again today, when I look at you. To love someone means that one's willing to grow old beside that person. That sort of love is right outside my range. Drusilla old would have been far worse than Drusilla dead. Most people imagine that a man suffers because out of the blue death snatches away the woman he loves. But his real suffering is less futile; it comes from the discovery that grief, too, cannot last. Even grief is vanity.

You see, I had no excuses, not the shadow of a real love, neither bitterness nor profound regret. Nothing to plead in my defense! But today—you see me still freer than I have been for years; freed as I am from memories and illusion. (*He laughs bitterly*) I know now that nothing, *nothing* lasts. Think what that knowledge means! There have been just two or three of us in history who really achieved this freedom, this crazy happiness. Well, Cæsonia, you have seen out a most unusual drama. It's time the curtain fell, for you.

(*He stands behind her again, linking his forearm round* CÆSONIA'S *neck*)

CÆSONIA (*Terrified*)   No, it's impossible! Now can you call it happiness, this terrifying freedom?

CALIGULA (*Gradually tightening his grip on* CÆSONIA'S *throat*)   Happiness it is, Cæsonia; I know what I'm saying. But for this freedom I'd have been a contented man. Thanks to it, I have won the godlike enlightenment of the solitary. (*His exaltation grows as little by little he strangles* CÆSONIA, *who puts up no resistance, but holds her hands half opened, like a suppliant's, before her. Bending his head, he goes on speaking, into her ear*) I live, I kill, I exercise the rapturous power of a destroyer, compared with which the power of a creator is merest child's play. And this, *this* is happiness; this and nothing else—this intolerable release, devastating scorn, blood, hatred all around me; the glorious isolation of a man who all his life long nurses and gloats over the ineffable joy of the unpunished murderer; the ruthless logic that crushes out human lives (*He laughs*), that's crushing yours out, Cæsonia, so as to perfect at last the utter loneliness that is my heart's desire.

CÆSONIA (*Struggling feebly*)   Oh, Caius . . .

CALIGULA (*More and more excitedly*)   No. No sentiment. I must have done with it, for the time is short. My time is very short, dear Cæsonia. (CÆSONIA *is gasping, dying.* CALIGULA *drags her to the bed and lets her fall on it. He stares wildly at her; his voice grows harsh and grating*) You, too, were guilty. But killing is not the solution. (*He spins round and gazes crazily at the mirror*) Caligula! You, too; you, too, are guilty. Then what of it—a little more, a little less? Yet who can condemn me in this world where there is no judge, where nobody is innocent? (*He brings his eyes close to his reflected face. He sounds genuinely distressed*) You see, my poor friend. Helicon has failed you. I won't have the moon. Never, never, never! But how bitter it is to know all, and

to have to go through to the consummation! Listen!
That was a sound of weapons. Innocence arming
for the fray—and innocence will triumph. Why am
I not in their place, among them? And I'm afraid.
That's cruelest of all, after despising others, to find
oneself as cowardly as they. Still, no matter. Fear,
too, has an end. Soon I shall attain that emptiness
beyond all understanding, in which the heart has rest.
(*He steps back a few paces, then returns to the mirror. He seems calmer. When he speaks again his voice
is steadier, less shrill*)

Yet, really, it's quite simple. If I'd had the moon, if
love were enough, all might have been different. But
where could I quench this thirst? What human heart,
what god, would have for me the depth of a great
lake? (*Kneeling, weeping*) There's nothing in this
world, or in the other, made to my stature. And yet
I know, and you, too, know (*Still weeping, he stretches
out his arms toward the mirror*) that all I need is
for the impossible to be. The impossible! I've searched
for it at the confines of the world, in the secret places
of my heart. I've stretched out my hands (*His voice
rises to a scream*); see, I stretch out my hands, but it's
always you I find, you only, confronting me, and I've
come to hate you. I have chosen a wrong path, a path
that leads to nothing. My freedom isn't the right one.
. . . Nothing, nothing yet. Oh, how oppressive is this
darkness! Helicon has not come; we shall be forever
guilty. The air tonight is heavy as the sum of human
sorrows. (*A clash of arms and whisperings are heard
in the wings.* CALIGULA *rises, picks up a stool, and
returns to the mirror, breathing heavily. He contemplates himself, makes a slight leap forward, and,
watching the symmetrical movement of his reflected
self, hurls the stool at it, screaming*) To history, Caligula! Go down to history! (*The mirror breaks and at
the same moment armed conspirators rush in.* CA-

LIGULA *swings round to face them with a mad laugh.*
SCIPIO *and* CHEREA, *who are in front, fling themselves
at him and stab his face with their daggers.* CALIGULA'S
*laughter turns to gasps. All strike him, hurriedly, con-
fusedly. In a last gasp, laughing and choking,* CA-
LIGULA *shrieks*) I'm still alive!

### *Curtain*

# *The*
# *Madwoman*
# *of Chaillot*

by
# JEAN GIRAUDOUX

A Play in Two Acts

*Adapted by*
*MAURICE VALENCY*

# CHARACTERS

THE WAITER
THE LITTLE MAN
THE PROSPECTOR
THE PRESIDENT
THE BARON
THERESE
THE STREET SINGER
THE PROFESSOR
THE FLOWER GIRL
THE RAGPICKER
PAULETTE
THE DEAF-MUTE
IRMA
THE SHOE-LACE PEDDLER
THE BROKER
THE STREET JUGGLER
DR. JADIN
COUNTESS AURELIA, *The Madwoman of Chaillot*
THE DOORMAN
THE POLICEMAN
PIERRE
THE SERGEANT
THE SEWER-MAN
CONSTANCE, *The Madwoman of Passy*
GABRIELLE, *The Madwoman of St. Sulpice*
JOSEPHINE, *The Madwoman of La Concorde*
THE PRESIDENTS
THE PROSPECTORS
THE PRESS AGENTS
THE LADIES
THE ADOLPHE BERTAUTS

The Madwoman of Chaillot *was first presented at the Théâtre de l'Athénée, Paris, in December, 1945.*

# Act One

SCENE  *The café terrace at* **Chez Francis,** *on the Place de l'Alma in Paris. The Alma is in the stately quarter of Paris known as Chaillot, between the Champs Élysées and the Seine, across the river from the Eiffel Tower.*

**Chez Francis** *has several rows of tables set out under its awning, and, as it is lunch time, a good many of them are occupied. At a table, downstage, a somewhat obvious* BLONDE *with ravishing legs is sipping a vermouth-cassis and trying hard to engage the attention of the* PROSPECTOR, *who sits at an adjacent table taking little sips of water and rolling them over his tongue with the air of a connoisseur. Downstage right, in front of the tables on the sidewalk, is the usual Paris bench, a stout and uncomfortable affair provided by the municipality for the benefit of those who prefer to sit without drinking. A* POLICEMAN *lounges about, keeping the peace without unnecessary exertion.*

TIME  *It is a little before noon in the Spring of next year.*

AT RISE  *The* PRESIDENT *and the* BARON *enter with importance, and are ushered to a front table by the* WAITER.

THE PRESIDENT  Baron, sit down. This is a historic occasion. It must be properly celebrated. The waiter is going to bring out my special port.

THE BARON  Splendid.

THE PRESIDENT (*Offers his cigar case*)   Cigar? My private brand.

THE BARON   Thank you. You know, this all gives me the feeling of one of those enchanted mornings in the *Arabian Nights* when thieves foregather in the market place. Thieves—pashas . . .
> (*He sniffs the cigar judiciously, and begins lighting it*)

THE PRESIDENT (*Chuckles*)   Tell me about yourself.

THE BARON   Well, where shall I begin?
> (*The* STREET SINGER *enters. He takes off a battered black felt with a flourish and begins singing an ancient mazurka*)

STREET SINGER (*Sings*)

> Do you hear, Mademoiselle,
> Those musicians of hell?

THE PRESIDENT   Waiter! Get rid of that man.

WAITER   He is singing *La Belle Polonaise*.

THE PRESIDENT   I didn't ask for the program. I asked you to get rid of him. (*The* WAITER *doesn't budge. The* SINGER *goes by himself*) As you were saying, Baron . . . ?

THE BARON   Well, until I was fifty . . . (*The* FLOWER GIRL *enters through the café door, center*) my life was relatively uncomplicated. It consisted of selling off one by one the various estates left me by my father. Three years ago, I parted with my last farm. Two years ago, I lost my last mistress. And now—all that is left me is . . .

THE FLOWER GIRL (*To the* BARON)   Violets, sir?

THE PRESIDENT   Run along. (*The* FLOWER GIRL *moves on*)

THE BARON (*Staring after her*)   So that, in short, all I have left now is my name.

THE PRESIDENT   Your name is precisely the name we need on our board of directors.

THE BARON (*With an inclination of his head*) Very flattering.

THE PRESIDENT You will understand when I tell you that mine has been a very different experience. I came up from the bottom. My mother spent most of her life bent over a washtub in order to send me to school. I'm eternally grateful to her, of course, but I must confess that I no longer remember her face. It was no doubt beautiful—but when I try to recall it, I see only the part she invariably showed me—her rear.

THE BARON Very touching.

THE PRESIDENT When I was thrown out of school for the fifth and last time, I decided to find out for myself what makes the world go round. I ran errands for an editor, a movie star, a financier. . . . I began to understand a little what life is. Then, one day, in the subway, I saw a face. . . . My rise in life dates from that day.

THE BARON Really?

THE PRESIDENT One look at that face, and I knew. One look at mine, and he knew. And so I made my first thousand—passing a boxful of counterfeit notes. A year later, I saw another such face. It got me a nice berth in the narcotics business. Since then, all I do is to look out for such faces. And now here I am—president of eleven corporations, director of fifty-two companies, and, beginning today, chairman of the board of the international combine in which you have been so good as to accept a post.

(*The* RAGPICKER *passes, sees something under the* PRESIDENT'S *table, and stoops to pick it up*)

Looking for something?

THE RAGPICKER Did you drop this?

THE PRESIDENT I never drop anything.

THE RAGPICKER Then this hundred-franc note isn't yours?

THE PRESIDENT Give it here.

(*The* RAGPICKER *gives him the note, and goes out*)

THE BARON   Are you sure it's yours?

THE PRESIDENT   All hundred-franc notes, Baron, are mine.

THE BARON   Mr. President, there's something I've been wanting to ask you. What exactly is the purpose of our new company? Or is that an indiscreet question . . . ?

THE PRESIDENT   Indiscreet? Not a bit. Merely unusual. As far as I know, you're the first member of a board of directors ever to ask such a question.

THE BARON   Do we plan to exploit a commodity? A utility?

THE PRESIDENT   My dear sir, I haven't the faintest idea.

THE BARON   But if you don't know—who does?

THE PRESIDENT   Nobody. And at the moment, it's becoming just a trifle embarrassing. Yes, my dear Baron, since we are now close business associates, I must confess that for the time being we're in a little trouble.

THE BARON   I was afraid of that. The stock issue isn't going well?

THE PRESIDENT   No, no—on the contrary. The stock issue is going beautifully. Yesterday morning at ten o'clock we offered 500,000 shares to the general public. By 10:05 they were all snapped up at par. By 10:20, when the police finally arrived, our offices were a shambles. . . . Windows smashed—doors torn off their hinges—you never saw anything so beautiful in your life! And this morning our stock is being quoted over the counter at 124 with no sellers, and the orders are still pouring in.

THE BARON   But in that case—what is the trouble?

THE PRESIDENT   The trouble is we have a tremendous capital, and not the slightest idea of what to do with it.

THE BARON   You mean all those people are fighting to buy stock in a company that has no object?

THE PRESIDENT   My dear Baron, do you imagine that

when a subscriber buys a share of stock, he has any idea of getting behind a counter or digging a ditch? A stock certificate is not a tool, like a shovel or a commodity, like a pound of cheese. What we sell a customer is not a share in a business, but a view of the Elysian Fields. A financier is a creative artist. Our function is to stimulate the imagination. We are poets!

THE BARON    But in order to stimulate the imagination, don't you need some field of activity?

THE PRESIDENT    Not at all. What you need for that is a name. A name that will stir the pulse like a trumpet call, set the brain awhirl like a movie star, inspire reverence like a cathedral. *United General International Consolidated!* Of course that's been used. That's what a corporation needs.

THE BARON    And do we have such a name?

THE PRESIDENT    So far we have only a blank space. In that blank space a name must be printed. This name must be a masterpiece. And if I seem a little nervous today, it's because—somehow—I've racked my brains, but it hasn't come to me. Oho! Look at that! Just like the answer to a prayer . . . ! (*The* BARON *turns and stares in the direction of the* PROSPECTOR) You see? There's one. And what a beauty!

THE BARON    You mean that girl?

THE PRESIDENT    No, no, not the girl. That face. You see . . . ? The one that's drinking water.

THE BARON    You call that a face? That's a tombstone.

THE PRESIDENT    It's a milestone. It's a signpost. But is it pointing the way to steel, or wheat, or phosphates? That's what we have to find out. Ah! He sees me. He understands. He will be over.

THE BARON    And when he comes . . . ?

THE PRESIDENT    He will tell me what to do.

THE BARON    You mean business is done this way? You mean, you would trust a stranger with a matter of this importance?

THE PRESIDENT    Baron, I trust neither my wife, nor my

daughter, nor my closest friend. My confidential
secretary has no idea where I live. But a face like
that I would trust with my inmost secrets. Though
we have never laid eyes on each other before, that
man and I know each other to the depths of our souls.
He's no stranger—he's my brother, he's myself. You'll
see. He'll be over in a minute. (*The* DEAF-MUTE *enters
and passes slowly among the tables, placing a small
envelope before each customer. He comes to the*
PRESIDENT's *table*) What is this anyway? A conspiracy?
We don't want your envelopes. Take them away. (*The*
DEAF-MUTE *makes a short but pointed speech in sign
language*) Waiter, what the devil's he saying?

WAITER   Only Irma understands him.

THE PRESIDENT   Irma? Who's Irma?

WAITER (*Calls*)   Irma! It's the waitress inside, sir. Irma!
(IRMA *comes out. She is twenty. She has the face
and figure of an angel*)

IRMA   Yes?

WAITER   These gentlemen would . . .

THE PRESIDENT   Tell this fellow to get out of here, for
God's sake! (*The* DEAF-MUTE *makes another manual
oration*) What's he trying to say, anyway?

IRMA   He says it's an exceptionally beautiful morning,
sir. . . .

THE PRESIDENT   Who asked him?

IRMA   But, he says, it was nicer before the gentleman
stuck his face in it.

THE PRESIDENT   Call the manager!
(IRMA *shrugs. She goes back into the restaurant.
The* DEAF-MUTE *walks off, Left. Meanwhile a*
SHOELACE PEDDLER *has arrived*)

PEDDLER   Shoelaces? Postcards?

THE BARON   I think I could use a shoelace.

THE PRESIDENT   No , no . . .

PEDDLER   Black? Tan?

THE BARON (*Showing his shoes*)   What would you recom-
mend?

PEDDLER   Anybody's guess.

THE BARON   Well, give me one of each.

THE PRESIDENT (*Putting a hand on the* BARON'S *arm*) Baron, although I am your chairman, I have no authority over your personal life—none, that is, except to fix the amount of your director's fees, and eventually to assign a motor car for your use. Therefore, I am asking you, as a personal favor to me, not to purchase anything from this fellow.

THE BARON   How can I resist so gracious a request? (*The* PEDDLER *shrugs, and passes on*) But I really don't understand . . . What difference would it make?

THE PRESIDENT   Look here, Baron. Now that you're with us, you must understand that between this irresponsible riff-raff and us there is an impenetrable barrier. *We* have no dealings whatever with *them.*

THE BARON   But without us, the poor devil will starve.

THE PRESIDENT   No, he won't. He expects nothing from us. He has a clientele of his own. He sells shoelaces exclusively to those who have no shoes. Just as the necktie peddler sells only to those who wear no shirts. And that's why these street hawkers can afford to be insolent, disrespectful, and independent. They don't need us. They have a world of their own. Ah! My broker. Splendid. He's beaming.

(*The* BROKER *walks up and grasps the* PRESIDENT'S *hand with enthusiasm*)

BROKER   Mr. President! My heartiest congratulations! What a day! What a day!

(*The* STREET JUGGLER *appears, Right. He removes his coat, folds it carefully, and puts it on the bench. Then he opens a suitcase, from which he extracts a number of colored clubs*)

THE PRESIDENT (*Presenting the* BROKER) Baron Tommard, of our Board of Directors. My broker. (*The* BROKER *bows. So does the* JUGGLER. *The* BROKER *sits down and signals for a drink. The* JUGGLER *prepares to juggle*) What's happened?

BROKER    Listen to this. Ten o'clock this morning. The market opens. (*As he speaks, the* JUGGLER *provides a visual counterpart to the* BROKER'S *lines, his clubs rising and falling in rhythm to the* BROKER'S *words*) Half million shares issued at par, par value a hundred, quoted on the curb at 124 and we start buying at 126, 127, 129—and it's going up—up—up—(*The* JUGGLER'S *clubs rise higher and higher*)—132—133 —138—141—141—141—141 . . .

THE BARON    May I ask . . . ?

THE PRESIDENT    No, no—any explanation would only confuse you.

BROKER    Ten forty-five we start selling short on rumors of a Communist plot, market bearish. . . . 141—138 —133—132—and it's down—down—down—102—and we start buying back at 93. Eleven o'clock, rumors denied—95—98—101—106—124—141—and by 11:30 we've got it all back—net profit three and a half million francs.

THE PRESIDENT    Classical. Pure. (*The* JUGGLER *bows again. A* LITTLE MAN *leans over from a near-by table, listening intently, and trembling with excitement*) And how many shares do we reserve to each member of the board?

BROKER    Fifty, as agreed.

THE PRESIDENT    Bit stingy, don't you think?

BROKER    All right—three thousand.

THE PRESIDENT    That's a little better. (*To the* BARON) You get the idea?

THE BARON    I'm beginning to get it.

BROKER    And now we come to the exciting part . . . (*The* JUGGLER *prepares to juggle with balls of fire*) Listen carefully: With 35 percent of our funded capital under Section 32 I buy 50,000 United at 36 which I immediately reconvert into 32,000 National Amalgamated two's preferred which I set up as collateral on 150,000 General Consols which I deposit against a credit of fifteen billion to buy Eastern Hennequin which I immediately turn into Argentine wheat realizing 136 percent of the original investment which naturally accrues as capital gain and not as corporate income thus saving twelve millions in taxes, and at once convert the 25 percent cotton reserve into lignite, and as our people swing into action in London and New York, I beat up the price on greige goods from 26 to 92—114—203—306—(*The* JUGGLER *by now is juggling his fire-balls in the sky. The balls no longer return to his hands*) 404 . . . (*The* LITTLE MAN *can stand no more. He rushes over and dumps a sackful of money on the table*)

LITTLE MAN　Here—take it—please, take it!

BROKER　(*Frigidly*)　Who is this man? What is this money?

LITTLE MAN　It's my life's savings. Every cent. I put it all in your hands.

BROKER　Can't you see we're busy?

LITTLE MAN　But I beg you . . . It's my only chance . . . Please don't turn me away.

BROKER　Oh, all right. (*He sweeps the money into his pocket*) Well?

LITTLE MAN　I thought— perhaps you'd give me a little receipt. . . .

THE PRESIDENT　My dear man, people like us don't give receipts for money. We take them.

LITTLE MAN　Oh, pardon. Of course. I was confused. Here it is. (*Scribbles a receipt*) Thank you—thank you—thank you. (*He rushes off joyfully. The* STREET SINGER *reappears*)

STREET SINGER　(*Sings*)

> Do you hear, Mademoiselle,
> Those musicians of hell?

THE PRESIDENT　What, again? Why does he keep repeating those two lines like a parrot?

WAITER   What else can he do? He doesn't know any more and the song's been out of print for years.

THE BARON   Couldn't he sing a song he knows?

WAITER   He likes this one. He hopes if he keeps singing the beginning someone will turn up to teach him the end.

THE PRESIDENT   Tell him to move on. We don't know the song.

(*The* PROFESSOR *strolls by, swinging his cane. He overhears*)

PROFESSOR (*Stops and addresses the* PRESIDENT *politely*) Nor do I, my dear sir. Nor do I. And yet, I'm in exactly the same predicament. I remember just two lines of my favorite song, as a child. A mazurka also, in case you're interested. . . .

THE PRESIDENT   I'm not.

PROFESSOR   Why is it, I wonder, that one always forgets the words of a mazurka? I suppose they just get lost in that damnable rhythm. All I remember is: (*He sings*)

From England to Spain
I have drunk, it was bliss . . . .

STREET SINGER (*Walks over, and picks up the tune*)
Red wine and champagne
And many a kiss.

PROFESSOR   Oh, God! It all comes back to me . . . ! (*He sings*)

Red lips and white hands I have known
Where the nightingales dwell. . . .

THE PRESIDENT (*Holding his hands to his ears*)   Please —please . . .

STREET SINGER

And to each one I've whispered, "My own,"
And to each one, I've murmured: "Farewell."

THE PRESIDENT    Farewell. Farewell.

STREET SINGER, PROFESSOR (*Duo*)
>    But there's one I shall never forget. . . .

THE PRESIDENT    This isn't a café. It's a circus!

>    (*The two go off, still singing: "There is one that's
>    engraved in my heart." The* PROSPECTOR *gets up
>    slowly and walks toward the* PRESIDENT's *table. He
>    looks down without a word. There is a tense
>    silence*)

PROSPECTOR    Well?

THE PRESIDENT    I need a name.

PROSPECTOR    (*Nods, with complete comprehension*)    I
need fifty thousand.

THE PRESIDENT    For a corporation.

PROSPECTOR    For a woman.

THE PRESIDENT    Immediately.

PROSPECTOR    Before evening.

THE PRESIDENT    Something . . .

PROSPECTOR    Unusual?

THE PRESIDENT    Something . . .

PROSPECTOR    Provocative?

THE PRESIDENT    Something . . .

PROSPECTOR    Practical.

THE PRESIDENT    Yes.

PROSPECTOR    Fifty thousand. Cash.

THE PRESIDENT    I'm listening.

PROSPECTOR    *International Substrate of Paris, Inc.*

THE PRESIDENT    (*Snaps his fingers*)    That's it! (*To the*
BROKER) Pay him off. (*The* BROKER *pays with the*
LITTLE MAN's *money*) Now—what does it mean?

PROSPECTOR    It means what it says. I'm a prospector.

THE PRESIDENT    (*Rises*)    A prospector! Allow me to shake
your hand. Baron. You are in the presence of one of
nature's noblemen. Shake his hand. This is Baron
Tommard. (*They shake hands*) It is this man, my dear
Baron, who smells out in the bowels of the earth those
deposits of metal or liquid on which can be founded

the only social unit of which our age is capable—the corporation. Sit down, please. (*They all sit*) And now that we have a name . . .

PROSPECTOR  You need a property.

THE PRESIDENT  Precisely.

PROSPECTOR  I have one.

THE PRESIDENT  A claim?

PROSPECTOR  Terrific.

THE PRESIDENT  Foreign?

PROSPECTOR  French.

THE BARON  In Indo-China?

BROKER  Morocco?

THE PRESIDENT  In France?

PROSPECTOR (*Matter of fact*)  In Paris.

THE PRESIDENT  In Paris? You've been prospecting in Paris?

THE BARON  For women, no doubt.

THE PRESIDENT  For art?

BROKER  For gold?

PROSPECTOR  Oil.

BROKER  He's crazy.

THE PRESIDENT  Sh! He's inspired.

PROSPECTOR  You think I'm crazy. Well, they thought Columbus was crazy.

THE BARON  Oil in Paris?

BROKER  But how is it possible?

PROSPECTOR  It's not only possible. It's certain.

THE PRESIDENT  Tell us.

PROSPECTOR  You don't know, my dear sir, what treasures Paris conceals. Paris is the least prospected place in the world. We've gone over the rest of the planet with a fine-tooth comb. But has anyone ever thought of looking for oil in Paris? Nobody. Before me, that is.

THE PRESIDENT  Genius!

PROSPECTOR  No. Just a practical man. I use my head.

THE BARON  But why has nobody ever thought of this before?

PROSPECTOR  The treasures of the earth, my dear sir, are not easy to find nor to get at. They are invariably guarded by dragons. Doubtless there is some reason for this. For once we've dug out and consumed the internal ballast of the planet, the chances are it will shoot off on some irresponsible tangent and smash itself up in the sky. Well, that's the risk we take. Anyway, that's not my business. A prospector has enough to worry about.

THE BARON  I know—snakes—tarantulas—fleas . . .

PROSPECTOR  Worse than that, sir. Civilization.

THE PRESIDENT  Does that annoy you?

PROSPECTOR  Civilization gets in our way all the time. In the first place, it covers the earth with cities and towns which are damned awkward to dig up when you want to see what's underneath. It's not only the real-estate people—you can always do business with them—it's human sentimentality. How do you do business with that?

THE PRESIDENT  I see what you mean.

PROSPECTOR  They say that where we pass, nothing ever grows again. What of it? Is a park any better than a coal mine? What's a mountain got that a slag pile hasn't? What would you rather have in your garden—an almond tree or an oil well?

THE PRESIDENT  Well . . .

PROSPECTOR  Exactly. But what's the use of arguing with these fools? Imagine the choicest place you ever saw for an excavation, and what do they put there? A playground for children! Civilization!

THE PRESIDENT  Just show us the point where you want to start digging. We'll do the rest. Even if it's in the middle of the Louvre. Where's the oil?

PROSPECTOR  Perhaps you think it's easy to make an accurate fix in an area like Paris where everything conspires to put you off the scent? Women—perfume —flowers—history. You can talk all you like about geology, but an oil deposit, gentlemen, has to be smelled out. I have a good nose. I go further. I have a phenomenal nose. But the minute I get the right whiff—the minute I'm on the scent—a fragrance rises from what I take to be the spiritual deposits of the past—and I'm completely at sea. Now take this very point, for example, this very spot.

THE BARON    You mean—right here in Chaillot?

PROSPECTOR    Right under here.

THE PRESIDENT    Good heavens! (*He looks under his chair*)

PROSPECTOR    It's taken me months to locate this spot.

THE BARON    But what in the world makes you think . . . ?

PROSPECTOR    Do you know this place, Baron?

THE BARON    Well, I've been sitting here for thirty years.

PROSPECTOR    Did you ever taste the water?

THE BARON    The water? Good God, no!

PROSPECTOR    It's plain to see that you are no prospector! A prospector, Baron, is addicted to water as a drunkard to wine. Water, gentlemen, is the one substance from which the earth can conceal nothing. It sucks out its innermost secrets and brings them to our very lips. Well—beginning at Notre Dame, where I first caught the scent of oil three months ago, I worked my way across Paris, glassful by glassful, sampling the water, until at least I came to this café. And here— just two days ago—I took a sip. My heart began to thump. Was it possible that I was deceived? I took another, a third, a fourth, a fifth. I was trembling like a leaf. But there was no mistake. Each time that I drank, my taste-buds thrilled to the most exquisite flavor known to a prospector—the flavor of— (*With utmost lyricism*) Petroleum!

THE PRESIDENT    Waiter! Some water and four glasses. Hurry. This round, gentlemen, is on me. And as a toast—I shall propose International Substrate of Paris, Incorporated. (*The* WAITER *brings a decanter and the*

*glasses. The* PRESIDENT *pours out the water amid
profound silence. They taste it with the air of con-
noisseurs savoring something that has never before
passed human lips. Then they look at each other
doubtfully. The* PROSPECTOR *pours himself a second
glass and drinks it off)* Well . . .

BROKER   Ye-es . . .

THE BARON   Mm . . .

PROSPECTOR   Get it?

THE BARON   Tastes queer.

PROSPECTOR   That's it. To the unpracticed palate it
tastes queer. But to the taste-buds of the expert—ah!

THE BARON   Still, there's one thing I don't quite understand . . .

PROSPECTOR   Yes?

THE BARON   This café doesn't have its own well, does
it?

PROSPECTOR   Of course not. This is Paris water.

BROKER   Then why should it taste different here than
anywhere else?

PROSPECTOR   Because, my dear sir, the pipes that carry
this water pass deep through the earth, and the earth
just here is soaked with oil, and this oil permeates
the pores of the iron and flavors the water it carries.
Ever so little, yes—but quite enough to betray its
presence to the sensitive tongue of the specialist.

THE BARON   I see.

PROSPECTOR   I don't say everyone is capable of tasting
it. No. But I—I can detect the presence of oil in water
that has passed within fifteen miles of a deposit. Under special circumstances, twenty.

THE PRESIDENT   Phenomenal!

PROSPECTOR   And so here I am with the greatest discovery of the age on my hands—but the blasted authorities won't let me drill a single well unless I show
them the oil! Now how can I show them the oil unless
they let me dig? Completely stymied! Eh?

THE PRESIDENT   What? A man like you?

PROSPECTOR   That's what they think. That's what they
want. Have you noticed the strange glamour of the
women this morning? And the quality of the sunshine? And this extraordinary convocation of vagabonds buzzing about protectively like bees around a
hive? Do you know why it is? Because they know.
It's a plot to distract us, to turn us from our purpose.
Well, let them try. I know there's oil here. And I'm
going to dig it up, even if I . . . (*He smiles*) Shall
I tell you my little plan?

THE PRESIDENT   By all means.

PROSPECTOR   Well . . . For heaven's sake, what's that?
   (*At this point, the* MADWOMAN *enters. She is
   dressed in the grand fashion of 1885, a taffeta
   skirt with an immense train—which she has gathered up by means of a clothespin—ancient button
   shoes, and a hat in the style of Marie Antoinette.
   She wears a lorgnette on a chain, and an enormous cameo pin at her throat. In her hand she
   carries a small basket. She walks in with great
   dignity, extracts a dinner bell from the bosom
   of her dress, and rings it sharply.* IRMA *appears*)

COUNTESS   Are my bones ready, Irma?

IRMA   There won't be much today, Countess. We had
broilers. Can you wait? While the gentleman inside
finishes eating?

COUNTESS   And my gizzard?

IRMA   I'll try to get it away from him.

COUNTESS   If he eats my gizzard, save me the giblets.
They will do for the tomcat that lives under the
bridge. He likes a few giblets now and again.

IRMA   Yes, Countess.
   (IRMA *goes back into the café. The* COUNTESS *takes
   a few steps and stops in front of the* PRESIDENT'S
   *table. She examines him with undisguised disap-
   proval*)

THE PRESIDENT   Waiter. Ask that woman to move on.

WAITER   Sorry, sir. This is her café.

THE PRESIDENT   Is she the manager of the café?

WAITER   She's the Madwoman of Chaillot.

THE PRESIDENT   A Madwoman? She's mad?

WAITER   Who says she's mad?

THE PRESIDENT   You just said so yourself.

WAITER   Look, sir. You asked me who she was. And I told you. What's mad about her? She's the Madwoman of Chaillot.

THE PRESIDENT   Call a policeman.

(*The* COUNTESS *whistles through her fingers. At once, the* DOORMAN *runs out of the café. He has three scarves in his hands*)

COUNTESS   Have you found it? My feather boa?

DOORMAN   Not yet, Countess. Three scarves. But no boa.

COUNTESS   It's five years since I lost it. Surely you've had time to find it.

DOORMAN   Take one of these, Countess. Nobody's claimed them.

COUNTESS   A boa like that doesn't vanish, you know. A feather boa nine feet long!

DOORMAN   How about this blue one?

COUNTESS   With my pink ruffle and my green veil? You're joking! Let me see the yellow. (*She tries it on*) How does it look?

DOORMAN   Terrific.

(*With a magnificent gesture, she flings the scarf about her, upsetting the* PRESIDENT'S *glass and drenching his trousers with water. She stalks off without a glance at him*)

THE PRESIDENT   Waiter! I'm making a complaint.

WAITER   Against whom?

THE PRESIDENT   Against her! Against you! The whole gang of you! That singer! That shoelace peddler! That female lunatic? Or whatever you call her!

THE BARON   Calm yourself, Mr. President. . . .

THE PRESIDENT   I'll do nothing of the sort! Baron, the

first thing we have to do is get rid of these people! Good heavens, look at them! Every size, shape, color and period of history imaginable. It's utter anarchy! I tell you, sir, the only safeguard of order and discipline in the modern world is a standardized worker with interchangeable parts. That would solve the entire problem of management. Here, the manager . . . And there—one composite drudge grunting and sweating all over the world. Just we two. Ah, how beautiful! How easy on the eyes! How restful for the conscience!

THE BARON    Yes, yes—of course.

THE PRESIDENT    Order. Symmetry. Balance. But instead of that, what? Here in Chaillot, the very citadel of management, these insolent phantoms of the past come to beard us with their raffish individualism— with the right of the voiceless to sing, of the dumb to make speeches, of trousers to have no seats and bosoms to have dinner bells!

THE BARON    But, after all, do these people matter?

THE PRESIDENT    My dear sir, wherever the poor are happy, and the servants are proud, and the mad are respected, our power is at an end. Look at that! That waiter! That madwoman! That flower girl! Do I get that sort of service? And suppose that I—president of twelve corporations and ten times a millionaire— were to stick a gladiolus in my buttonhole and start yelling— (*He tinkles his spoon in a glass violently, yelling*) Are my bones ready, Irma?

THE BARON    (*Reprovingly*)  Mr. President . . .
         (*People at the adjoining tables turn and stare with raised eyebrows. The* WAITER *starts to come over*)

THE PRESIDENT    You see? Now.

PROSPECTOR    We were discussing my plan.

THE PRESIDENT    Ah, yes, your plan. (*He glances in the direction of the* MADWOMAN'S *table*) Careful—she's looking at us.

PROSPECTOR   Do you know what a bomb is?

THE PRESIDENT   I'm told they explode.

PROSPECTOR   Exactly. You see that white building across the river. Do you happen to know what that is?

THE PRESIDENT   I do not.

PROSPECTOR   That's the office of the City Architect. That man has stubbornly refused to give me a permit to drill for oil anywhere within the limits of the city of Paris. I've tried everything with him—influence, bribes, threats. He says I'm crazy. And now . . .

THE PRESIDENT   Oh, my God! What is this one trying to sell us?

> (*A little* OLD MAN *enters left, and doffs his hat politely. He is somewhat ostentatiously respectable—gloved, pomaded, and carefully dressed, with a white handkerchief peeping out of his breast pocket*)

DR. JADIN   Nothing but health, sir. Or rather the health of the feet. But remember—as the foot goes, so goes the man. May I present myself . . . ? Dr. Gaspard Jadin, French Navy, retired. Former specialist in the extraction of ticks and chiggers. At present specializing in the extraction of bunions and corns. In case of sudden emergency, Martial the waiter will furnish my home address. My office is here, second row, third table, week days, twelve to five. Thank you very much.

> (*He sits at his table*)

WAITER   Your vermouth, Doctor?

DR. JADIN   My vermouth. My vermouths. How are your gallstones today, Martial?

WAITER   Fine. Fine. They rattle like anything.

DR. JADIN   Splendid. (*He spies the* COUNTESS) Good morning, Countess. How's the floating kidney? Still afloat? (*She nods graciously*) Splendid. Splendid. So long as it floats, it can't sink.

THE PRESIDENT   This is impossible! Let's go somewhere else.

PROSPECTOR    No. It's nearly noon.

THE PRESIDENT    Yes. It is. Five to twelve.

PROSPECTOR    In five minutes' time you're going to see that City Architect blown up, building and all— boom!

BROKER    Are you serious?

PROSPECTOR    That imbecile has no one to blame but himself. Yesterday noon, he got my ultimatum—he's had twenty-four hours to think it over. No permit? All right. Within two minutes my agent is going to drop a little package in his coal bin. And three minutes after that, precisely at noon . . .

THE BARON    You prospectors certainly use modern methods.

PROSPECTOR    The method may be modern. But the idea is old. To get at the treasure, it has always been necessary to slay the dragon. I guarantee that after this, the City Architect will be more reasonable. The new one, I mean.

THE PRESIDENT    Don't you think we're sitting a little close for comfort?

PROSPECTOR    Oh no, no. Don't worry. And, above all, don't stare. We may be watched. (*A clock strikes*) Why, that's noon. Something's wrong! Good God! What's this? (*A* POLICEMAN *staggers in bearing a lifeless body on his shoulders in the manner prescribed as "The Fireman's Lift"*) It's Pierre! My agent! (*He walks over with affected nonchalance*) I say, Officer, what's that you've got?

POLICEMAN    Drowned man. (*He puts him down on the bench*)

WAITER    He's not drowned. His clothes are dry. He's been slugged.

POLICEMAN    Slugged is also correct. He was just jumping off the bridge when I came along and pulled him back. I slugged him, naturally, so he wouldn't drag me under. Life Saving Manual, Rule 5: "In cases

where there is danger of being dragged under, it is
necessary to render the subject unconscious by means
of a sharp blow." He's had that. (*He loosens the
clothes and begins applying artificial respiration*)

PROSPECTOR   The stupid idiot! What the devil did he
do with the bomb? That's what comes of employing
amateurs!

THE PRESIDENT   You don't think he'll give you away?

PROSPECTOR   Don't worry. (*He walks over to the policeman*) Say, what do you think you're doing?

POLICEMAN   Lifesaving. Artificial respiration. First aid
to the drowning.

PROSPECTOR   But he's not drowning.

POLICEMAN   But he thinks he is.

PROSPECTOR   You'll never bring him round that way,
my friend. That's meant for people who drown in
water. It's no good at all for those who drown without
water.

POLICEMAN   What am I supposed to do? I've just been
sworn in. It's my first day on the beat. I can't afford
to get in trouble. I've got to go by the book.

PROSPECTOR   Perfectly simple. Take him back to the
bridge where you found him and throw him in. Then
you can save his life and you'll get a medal. This way,
you'll only get fined for slugging an innocent man.

POLICEMAN   What do you mean, innocent? He was just
going to jump when I grabbed him.

PROSPECTOR   Have you any proof of that?

POLICEMAN   Well, I saw him.

PROSPECTOR   Written proof? Witnesses?

POLICEMAN   No, but . . .

PROSPECTOR   Then don't waste time arguing. You're in
trouble. Quick—before anybody notices—throw him
in and dive after him. It's the only way out.

POLICEMAN   But I don't swim.

THE PRESIDENT   You'll learn how on the way down.
Before you were born, did you know how to breathe?

POLICEMAN (*Convinced*)  All right. Here we go. (*He starts lifting the body*)

DR. JADIN  One moment, please. I don't like to interfere, but it's my professional duty to point out that medical science has definitely established the fact of intra-uterine respiration. Consequently, this policeman, even before he was born, knew not only how to breathe but also how to cough, hiccup, and belch.

THE PRESIDENT  Suppose he did—how does it concern you?

DR. JADIN  On the other hand, medical science has never established the fact of intra-uterine swimming or diving. Under the circumstances, we are forced to the opinion, Officer, that if you dive in you will probably drown.

POLICEMAN  You think so?

PROSPECTOR  Who asked you for an opinion?

THE PRESIDENT  Pay no attention to that quack, Officer.

DR. JADIN  Quack, sir?

PROSPECTOR  This is not a medical matter. It's a legal problem. The officer has made a grave error. He's new. We're trying to help him.

BROKER  He's probably afraid of the water.

POLICEMAN  Nothing of the sort. Officially, I'm afraid of nothing. But I always follow doctor's orders.

DR. JADIN  You see, Officer, when a child is born . . .

PROSPECTOR  Now, what does he care about when a child is born? He's got a dying man on his hands. . . . Officer, if you want my advice . . .

POLICEMAN  It so happens, I care a lot about when a child is born. It's part of my duty to aid and assist any woman in childbirth or labor.

THE PRESIDENT  Can you imagine!

POLICEMAN  Is it true, Doctor, what they say, that when you have twins, the first born is considered to be the youngest?

DR. JADIN  Quite correct. And what's more, if the twins

happen to be born at midnight on December 31st, the
older is a whole year younger. He does his military
service a year later. That's why you have to keep
your eyes open. And that's the reason why a queen
always gives birth before witnesses. . . .

POLICEMAN   God! The things a policeman is supposed
to know! Doctor, what does it mean if, when I get up
in the morning sometimes . . .

PROSPECTOR (*Nudging the* PRESIDENT *meaningfully*) The
old woman . . .

BROKER   Come on, Baron.

THE PRESIDENT   I think we'd better all run along.

PROSPECTOR   Leave him to me.

THE PRESIDENT   I'll see you later. (*The* PRESIDENT *steals
off with the* BROKER *and the* BARON)

POLICEMAN (*Still in conference with* DR. JADIN)   But
what's really worrying me, Doctor, is this—don't you
think it's a bit risky for a man to marry after forty-
five?

　　　(*The* BROKER *runs in breathlessly*)

BROKER   Officer! Officer!

POLICEMAN   What's the trouble?

BROKER   Quick! Two women are calling for help—on
the sidewalk—Avenue Wilson!

POLICEMAN   Two women at once? Standing up or lying
down?

BROKER   You'd better go and see. Quick!

PROSPECTOR   You'd better take the Doctor with you.

POLICEMAN   Come along, Doctor, come along. . . .
(*Pointing to* PIERRE) Tell him to wait till I get back.
Come along, Doctor.

　　　(*He runs out, the* DOCTOR *following. The* PROS-
　　　PECTOR *moves over toward* PIERRE, *but* IRMA *crosses
　　　in front of him and takes the boy's hand*)

IRMA   How beautiful he is! Is he dead, Martial?

WAITER (*Handing her a pocket mirror*)   Hold this
mirror to his mouth. If it clouds over . . .

IRMA   It clouds over.

WAITER   He's alive. (*He holds out his hand for the mirror*)

IRMA   Just a sec— (*She rubs it clean and looks at herself intently. Before handing it back, she fixes her hair and applies her lipstick. Meanwhile the* PROSPECTOR *tries to get around the other side, but the* COUNTESS' *eagle eye drives him off. He shrugs his shoulders and exits with the* BARON) Oh, look—he's opened his eyes!

(PIERRE *opens his eyes, stares intently at* IRMA *and closes them again with the expression of a man who is among the angels*)

PIERRE (*Murmurs*)   Oh! How beautiful!

VOICE (*From within the café*)   Irma!

IRMA   Coming. Coming.

(*She goes in, not without a certain reluctance. The* COUNTESS *at once takes her place on the bench, and also the young man's hand.* PIERRE *sits up suddenly, and finds himself staring, not at* IRMA, *but into the very peculiar face of the* COUNTESS. *His expression changes*)

COUNTESS   You're looking at my iris? Isn't it beautiful?

PIERRE   Very. (*He drops back, exhausted*)

COUNTESS   The Sergeant was good enough to say it becomes me. But I no longer trust his taste. Yesterday, the flower girl gave me a lily, and he said it didn't suit me.

PIERRE   (*Weakly*)   It's beautiful.

COUNTESS   He'll be very happy to know that you agree with him. He's really quite sensitive. (*She calls*) Sergeant!

PIERRE   No, please—don't call the police.

COUNTESS   But I must. I think I hurt his feelings.

PIERRE   Let me go, Madame.

COUNTESS   No, no. Stay where you are. Sergeant! (PIERRE *struggles weakly to get up*)

PIERRE   Please let me go.

COUNTESS   I'll do nothing of the sort. When you let

someone go, you never see him again. I let Charlotte
Mazumet go. I never saw her again.

PIERRE  Oh, my head.

COUNTESS  I let Adolphe Bertaut go. And I was holding
him. And I never saw him again.

PIERRE  Oh, God!

COUNTESS  Except once. Thirty years later. In the market. He had changed a great deal—he didn't know
me. He sneaked a melon from right under my nose,
the only good one of the year. Ah, here we are. Sergeant! (*The* POLICE SERGEANT *comes in with importance*)

SERGEANT  I'm in a hurry, Countess.

COUNTESS  With regard to the iris. This young man
agrees with you. He says it suits me.

SERGEANT (*Going*)  There's a man drowning in the
Seine.

COUNTESS  He's not drowning in the Seine. He's drowning here. Because I'm holding him tight—as I should
have held Adolphe Bertaut. But if I let him go, I'm
sure he will go and drown in the Seine. He's a lot
better looking than Adolphe Bertaut, wouldn't you
say?

     (PIERRE *sighs deeply*)

SERGEANT  How would I know?

COUNTESS  I've shown you his photograph. The one
with the bicycle.

SERGEANT  Oh, yes. The one with the harelip.

COUNTESS  I've told you a hundred times! Adolphe
Bertaut had no harelip. That was a scratch in the
negative. (*The* SERGEANT *takes out his notebook and
pencil*) What are you doing?

SERGEANT  I am taking down the drowned man's name,
given name, and date of birth.

COUNTESS  You think that's going to stop him from
jumping in the river? Don't be silly, Sergeant. Put
that book away and try to console him.

SERGEANT  I should try and console him?

COUNTESS　When people want to die, it is your job as a guardian of the state to speak out in praise of life. Not mine.

SERGEANT　I should speak out in praise of life?

COUNTESS　I assume you have some motive for interfering with people's attempts to kill each other, and rob each other, and run each other over? If you believe that life has some value, tell him what it is. Go on.

SERGEANT　Well, all right. Now look, young man . . .

COUNTESS　His name is Roderick.

PIERRE　My name is not Roderick.

COUNTESS　Yes, it is. It's noon. At noon all men become Roderick.

SERGEANT　Except Adolphe Bertaut.

COUNTESS　In the days of Adolphe Bertaut, we were forced to change the men when we got tired of their names. Nowadays, we're more practical—each hour on the hour all names are automatically changed. The men remain the same. But you're not here to discuss Adolphe Bertaut, Sergeant. You're here to convince the young man that life is worth living.

PIERRE　It isn't.

SERGEANT　Quiet. Now then—what was the idea of jumping off the bridge, anyway?

COUNTESS　The idea was to land in the river. Roderick doesn't seem to be at all confused about that.

SERGEANT　Now how can I convince anybody that life is worth living if you keep interrupting all the time?

COUNTESS　I'll be quiet.

SERGEANT　First of all, Mr. Roderick, you have to realize that suicide is a crime against the state. And why is it a crime against the state? Because every time anybody commits suicide, that means one soldier less for the army, one taxpayer less for the . . .

COUNTESS　Sergeant, isn't there something about life that you really enjoy?

SERGEANT　That I enjoy?

COUNTESS  Well, surely, in all these years, you must
have found something worth living for. Some secret
pleasure, or passion. Don't blush. Tell him about it.

SERGEANT  Who's blushing? Well, naturally, yes—I have
my passions—like everybody else. The fact is, since
you ask me—I love—to play—casino. And if the gentleman would like to join me, by and by when I go
off duty, we can sit down to a nice little game in the
back room with a nice cold glass of beer. If he wants
to kill an hour, that is.

COUNTESS  He doesn't want to kill an hour. He wants
to kill himself. Well? Is that all the police force has
to offer by way of earthly bliss?

SERGEANT  Huh? You mean— (*He jerks a thumb in the
direction of the pretty* BLONDE, *who has just been
joined by a* BRUNETTE *of the same stamp*) Paulette?
(*The young man groans*)

COUNTESS  You're not earning your salary, Sergeant.
I defy anybody to stop dying on your account.

SERGEANT  Go ahead, if you can do any better. But you
won't find it easy.

COUNTESS  Oh, this is not a desperate case at all. A
young man who has just fallen in love with someone
who has fallen in love with him!

PIERRE  She hasn't. How could she?

COUNTESS  Oh, yes, she has. She was holding your hand,
just as I'm holding it, when all of a sudden . . . Did
you ever know Marshal Canrobert's niece?

SERGEANT  How could he know Marshal Canrobert's
niece?

COUNTESS  Lots of people knew her—when she was
alive. (PIERRE *begins to struggle energetically*) No, no,
Roderick—stop—stop!

SERGEANT  You see? You won't do any better than I did.

COUNTESS  No? Let's bet. I'll bet my iris against one of
your gold buttons. Right?—Roderick, I know very
well why you tried to drown yourself in the river.

PIERRE  You don't at all.

COUNTESS  It's because that Prospector wanted you to commit a horrible crime.

PIERRE  How did you know that?

COUNTESS  He stole my boa, and now he wants you to kill me.

PIERRE  Not exactly.

COUNTESS  It wouldn't be the first time they've tried it. But I'm not so easy to get rid of, my boy, oh, no . . . Because . . .

> (*The* DOORMAN *rides in on his bicycle. He winks at the* SERGEANT, *who has now seated himself while the* WAITER *serves him a beer*)

DOORMAN  Take it easy, Sergeant.

SERGEANT  I'm busy saving a drowning man.

COUNTESS  They can't kill me because—I have no desire to die.

PIERRE  You're fortunate.

COUNTESS  To be alive is to be fortunate, Roderick. Of course, in the morning, when you first awake, it does not always seem so very gay. When you take your hair out of the drawer, and your teeth out of the glass, you are apt to feel a little out of place in this world. Especially if you've just been dreaming that you're a little girl on a pony looking for strawberries in the woods. But all you need to feel the call of life once more is a letter in your mail giving you your schedule for the day—your mending, your shopping, that letter to your grandmother that you never seem to get around to. And so, when you've washed your face in rosewater, and powdered it—not with this awful rice-powder they sell nowadays, which does nothing for the skin, but with a cake of pure white starch—and put on your pins, your rings, your brooches, bracelets, earrings, and pearls—in short, when you are dressed for your morning coffee—and have had a good look at yourself—not in the glass, naturally—it lies—but in the side of the brass gong that once belonged to

Admiral Courbet—then, Roderick, then you're armed,
you're strong, you're ready—you can begin again.

(PIERRE *is listening now intently. There are tears
in his eyes*)

PIERRE   Oh, Madame . . . ! Oh, Madame . . . !

COUNTESS   After that, everything is pure delight. First
the morning paper. Not, of course, these current
sheets full of lies and vulgarity. I always read the
*Gaulois,* the issue of March 22, 1903. It's by far the
best. It has some delightful scandal, some excellent
fashion notes, and, of course, the last-minute bulletin
on the death of Leonide Leblanc. She used to live
next door, poor woman, and when I learn of her
death every morning, it gives me quite a shock. I'd
gladly lend you my copy, but it's in tatters.

SERGEANT   Couldn't we find him a copy in some library?

COUNTESS   I doubt it. And so, when you've taken your
fruit salts—not in water, naturally—no matter what
they say, it's water that gives you gas—but with a bit
of spiced cake—then in sunlight or rain, Chaillot
calls. It is time to dress for your morning walk. This
takes much longer, of course—without a maid, impossible to do it under an hour, what with your corset,
corset-cover, and drawers all of which lace or button
in the back. I asked Madame Lanvin, a while ago, to
fit the drawers with zippers. She was quite charming,
but she declined. She thought it would spoil the style.

(*The* DEAF-MUTE *comes in*)

WAITER   I know a place where they put zippers on anything.

(*The* RAGPICKER *enters*)

COUNTESS   I think Lanvin knows best. But I really
manage very well, Martial. What I do now is, I lace
them up in front, then twist them around to the back.
It's quite simple, really. Then you choose a lorgnette,
and then the usual fruitless search for the feather boa
that the prospector stole—I know it was he: he didn't

dare look me in the eye—and then all you need is a rubber band to slip around your parasol—I lost the catch the day I struck the cat that was stalking the pigeon—it was worth it—ah, that day I earned my wages!

THE RAGPICKER　Countess, if you can use it, I found a nice umbrella catch the other day with a cat's eye in it.

COUNTESS　Thank you, Ragpicker. They say these eyes sometimes come to life and fill with tears. I'd be afraid . . .

PIERRE　Go on, Madame, go on . . .

COUNTESS　Ah! So life is beginning to interest you, is it? You see how beautiful it is?

PIERRE　What a fool I've been!

COUNTESS　Then, Roderick, I begin my rounds. I have my cats to feed, my dogs to pet, my plants to water. I have to see what the evil ones are up to in the district—those who hate people, those who hate plants, those who hate animals. I watch them sneaking off in the morning to put on their disguises—to the baths, to the beauty parlors, to the barbers. But they can't deceive me. And when they come out again with blonde hair and false whiskers, to pull up my flowers and poison my dogs, I'm there, and I'm ready. All you have to do to break their power is to cut across their path from the left. That isn't always easy. Vice moves swiftly. But I have a good long stride and I generally manage. . . . Right, my friends? (*The* WAITER *and the* RAGPICKER *nod their heads with evident approval*) Yes, the flowers have been marvelous this year. And the butcher's dog on the Rue Bizet, in spite of that wretch that tried to poison him, is friskier than ever. . . .

SERGEANT　That dog had better look out. He has no license.

COUNTESS　He doesn't seem to feel the need for one.

THE RAGPICKER  The Duchess de la Rochefoucauld's whippet is getting awfully thin. . . .

COUNTESS  What can I do? She bought that dog full grown from a kennel where they didn't know his right name. A dog without his right name is bound to get thin.

THE RAGPICKER  I've got a friend who knows a lot about dogs—an Arab . . .

COUNTESS  Ask him to call on the Duchess. She receives Thursdays, five to seven. You see, then, Roderick. That's life. Does it appeal to you now?

PIERRE  It seems marvelous.

COUNTESS  Ah! Sergeant. My button. (*The* SERGEANT *gives her his button and goes off. At this point the* PROSPECTOR *enters*) That's only the morning. Wait till I tell you about the afternoon!

PROSPECTOR  All right, Pierre. Come along now.

PIERRE  I'm perfectly all right here.

PROSPECTOR  I said, come along now.

PIERRE (*To the* COUNTESS)  I'd better go, Madame.

COUNTESS  No.

PIERRE  It's no use. Please let go my hand.

PROSPECTOR  Madame, will you oblige me by letting my friend go?

COUNTESS  I will not oblige you in any way.

PROSPECTOR  All right. Then I'll oblige you . . . !

> (*He tries to push her away. She catches up a soda water siphon and squirts it in his face*)

PIERRE  Countess . . .

COUNTESS  Stay where you are. This man isn't going to take you away. In the first place, I shall need you in a few minutes to take me home. I'm all alone here and I'm very easily frightened.

> (*The* PROSPECTOR *makes a second attempt to drag* PIERRE *away. The* COUNTESS *cracks him over the skull with the siphon. They join battle. The* COUNTESS *whistles. The* DOORMAN *comes, then the*

*other* VAGABONDS, *and lastly the* POLICE SERGEANT)

PROSPECTOR    Officer! Arrest this woman!

SERGEANT    What's the trouble here?

PROSPECTOR    She refuses to let this man go.

SERGEANT    Why should she?

PROSPECTOR    It's against the law for a woman to detain a man on the street.

IRMA    Suppose it's her son whom she's found again after twenty years?

THE RAGPICKER (*Gallantly*)    Or her long-lost brother? The Countess is not so old.

PROSPECTOR    Officer, this is a clear case of disorderly conduct.

(*The* DEAF-MUTE *interrupts with frantic signals*)

COUNTESS    Irma, what is the Deaf-Mute saying?

IRMA (*Interpreting*)    The young man is in danger of his life. He mustn't go with him.

PROSPECTOR    What does he know?

IRMA    He knows everything.

PROSPECTOR    Officer, I'll have to take your number.

COUNTESS    Take his number. It's 2133. It adds up to nine. It will bring you luck.

SERGEANT    Countess, between ourselves, what are you holding him for, anyway?

COUNTESS    I'm holding him because it's very pleasant to hold him. I've never really held anybody before, and I'm making the most of it. And because so long as *I* hold him, he's free.

PROSPECTOR    Pierre, I'm giving you fair warning. . . .

COUNTESS    And I'm holding him because Irma wants me to hold him. Because if I let him go, it will break her heart.

IRMA    Oh, Countess!

SERGEANT (*To the* PROSPECTOR)    All right, you—move on. Nobody's holding you. You're blocking traffic. Move on.

PROSPECTOR (*Menacingly*)    I have your number. (*And murderously, to* PIERRE) You'll regret this, Pierre.

(*Exit* PROSPECTOR)

PIERRE   Thank you, Countess.

COUNTESS   They're blackmailing you, are they? (PIERRE *nods*) What have you done? Murdered somebody?

PIERRE   No.

COUNTESS   Stolen something?

PIERRE   No.

COUNTESS   What then?

PIERRE   I forged a signature.

COUNTESS   Whose signature?

PIERRE   My father's. To a note.

COUNTESS   And this man has the paper, I suppose?

PIERRE   He promised to tear it up, if I did what he wanted. But I couldn't do it.

COUNTESS   But the man is mad! Does he really want to destroy the whole neighborhood?

PIERRE   He wants to destroy the whole city.

COUNTESS (*Laughs*)   Fantastic.

PIERRE   It's not funny, Countess. He can do it. He's mad, but he's powerful, and he has friends. Their machines are already drawn up and waiting. In three months' time you may see the city covered by a forest of derricks and drills.

COUNTESS   But what are they looking for? Have they lost something?

PIERRE   They're looking for oil. They're convinced that Paris is sitting on a lake of oil.

COUNTESS   Suppose it is. What harm does it do?

PIERRE   They want to bring the oil to the surface, Countess.

COUNTESS (*Laughs*)   How silly! Is that a reason to destroy a city? What do they want with this oil?

PIERRE   They want to make war, Countess.

COUNTESS   Oh, dear, let's forget about these horrible men. The world is beautiful. It's happy. That's how God made it. No man can change it.

WAITER   Ah, Countess, if you only knew . . .

COUNTESS   If I only knew what?

WAITER    Shall we tell her now? Shall we tell her?

COUNTESS    What is it you are hiding from me?

THE RAGPICKER    Nothing, Countess. It's you who are hiding.

WAITER    You tell her. You've been a pitchman. You can talk.

ALL    Tell her. Tell her. Tell her.

COUNTESS    You're frightening me, my friends. Go on. I'm listening.

THE RAGPICKER    Countess, there was a time when old clothes were as good as new—in fact, they were better. Because when people wore clothes, they gave something to them. You may not believe it, but right this minute, the highest-priced shops in Paris are selling clothes that were thrown away thirty years ago. They're selling them for new. That's how good they were.

COUNTESS    Well?

THE RAGPICKER    Countess, there was a time when garbage was a pleasure. A garbage can was not what it is now. If it smelled a little strange, it was because it was a little confused—there was everything there —sardines, cologne, iodine, roses. An amateur might jump to a wrong conclusion. But to a professional— it was the smell of God's plenty.

COUNTESS    Well?

THE RAGPICKER    Countess, the world has changed.

COUNTESS    Nonsense. How could it change? People are the same, I hope.

THE RAGPICKER    No, Countess. The people are not the same. The people are different. There's been an invasion. An infiltration. From another planet. The world is not beautiful any more. It's not happy.

COUNTESS    Not happy? Is that true? Why didn't you tell me this before?

THE RAGPICKER    Because you live in a dream, Countess. And we don't like to disturb you.

COUNTESS  But how could it have happened?

THE RAGPICKER  Countess, there was a time when you could walk around Paris, and all the people you met were just like yourself. A little cleaner, maybe, or dirtier, perhaps, or angry, or smiling—but you knew them. They were you. Well, Countess, twenty years ago, one day, on the street, I saw a face in the crowd. A face, you might say, without a face. The eyes— empty. The expression—not human. Not a human face. It saw me staring, and when it looked back at me with its gelatine eyes, I shuddered. Because I knew that to make room for this one, one of us must have left the earth. A while after, I saw another. And another. And since then, I've seen hundreds come in —yes—thousands.

COUNTESS  Describe them to me.

THE RAGPICKER  You've seen them yourself, Countess. Their clothes don't wrinkle. Their hats don't come off. When they talk, they don't look at you. They don't perspire.

COUNTESS  Have they wives? Have they children?

THE RAGPICKER  They buy the models out of shop win- dows, furs and all. They animate them by a secret process. Then they marry them. Naturally, they don't have children.

COUNTESS  What work do they do?

THE RAGPICKER  They don't do any work. Whenever they meet, they whisper, and then they pass each other thousand-franc notes. You see them standing on the corner by the Stock Exchange. You see them at auc- tions—in the back. They never raise a finger—they just stand there. In theater lobbies, by the box office —they never go inside. They don't do anything, but wherever you see them, things are not the same. I remember well the time when a cabbage could sell itself just by being a cabbage. Nowadays it's no good being a cabbage—unless you have an agent and pay

him a commission. Nothing is free any more to sell
itself or give itself away. These days, Countess, every
cabbage has its pimp.

COUNTESS    I can't believe that.

THE RAGPICKER    Countess, little by little, the pimps have
taken over the world. They don't do anything, they
don't make anything—they just stand there and take
their cut. It makes a difference. Look at the shop-
keepers. Do you ever see one smiling at a customer
any more? Certainly not. Their smiles are strictly for
the pimps. The butcher has to smile at the meat-
pimp, the florist at the rose-pimp, the grocer at the
fresh-fruit-and-vegetable pimp. It's all organized down
to the slightest detail. A pimp for bird-seed. A pimp
for fishfood. That's why the cost of living keeps going
up all the time. You buy a glass of beer—it costs twice
as much as it used to. Why? 10 percent for the glass-
pimp, 10 percent for the beer-pimp, 20 percent for
the glass-of-beer-pimp—that's where our money goes.
Personally, I prefer the old-fashioned type. Some of
those men at least were loved by the women they sold.
But what feelings can a pimp arouse in a leg of lamb?
Pardon my language, Irma.

COUNTESS    It's all right. She doesn't understand it.

THE RAGPICKER    So now you know, Countess, why the
world is no longer happy. We are the last of the free
people of the earth. You saw them looking us over
today. Tomorrow, the street-singer will start paying
the song-pimp, and the garbage-pimp will be after
me. I tell you, Countess, we're finished. It's the end
of free enterprise in this world!

COUNTESS    Is this true, Roderick?

PIERRE    I'm afraid it's true.

COUNTESS    Did you know about this, Irma?

IRMA    All I know is the doorman says that faith is dead.

DOORMAN    I've stopped taking bets over the phone.

JUGGLER    The very air is different, Countess. You can't

trust it any more. If I throw my torches up too high, they go out.

THE RAGPICKER  The sky-pimp puts them out.

FLOWER GIRL  My flowers don't last over night now. They wilt.

JUGGLER  Have you noticed, the pigeons don't fly any more?

THE RAGPICKER  They can't afford to. They walk.

COUNTESS  They're a lot of fools and so are you! You should have told me at once! How can you bear to live in a world where there is unhappiness? Where a man is not his own master? Are you cowards? All we have to do is to get rid of these men.

PIERRE  How can we get rid of them? They're too strong.

(*The* SERGEANT *walks up again*)

COUNTESS (*Smiling*)  The Sergeant will help us.

SERGEANT  Who? Me?

IRMA  There are a great many of them, Countess. The Deaf-Mute knows them all. They employed him once, years ago, because he was deaf. (*The* DEAF-MUTE *wigwags a short speech*) They fired him because he wasn't blind. (*Another flash of sign language*) They're all connected like the parts of a machine.

COUNTESS  So much the better. We shall drive the whole machine into a ditch.

SERGEANT  It's not that easy, Countess. You never catch these birds napping. They change before your very eyes. I remember when I was in the detectives . . . You catch a president, pfft! He turns into a trustee. You catch him as trustee, and pfft! he's not a trustee —he's an honorary vice-chairman. You catch a Senator dead to rights: he becomes Minister of Justice. You get after the Minister of Justice—he is Chief of Police. And there you are—no longer in the detectives.

PIERRE  He's right, Countess. They have all the power.

And all the money. And they're greedy for more.

COUNTESS  They're greedy? Ah, then, my friends, they're lost. If they're greedy, they're stupid. If they're greedy —don't worry, I know exactly what to do. Roderick, by tonight you will be an honest man. And, Juggler, your torches will stay lit. And your beer will flow freely again, Martial. And the world will be saved. Let's get to work.

THE RAGPICKER  What are you going to do?

COUNTESS  Have you any kerosene in the house, Irma?

IRMA  Yes. Would you like some?

COUNTESS  I want just a little. In a dirty bottle. With a little mud. And some mange-cure, if you have it. (*To the* DEAF-MUTE) Deaf-Mute! Take a letter. (IRMA *interprets in sign language. To the* SINGER) Singer, go and find Madame Constance.

(IRMA *and the* WAITER *go into the café*)

SINGER  Yes, Countess.

COUNTESS  Ask her to be at my house by two o'clock. I'll be waiting for her in the cellar. You may tell her we have to discuss the future of humanity. That's sure to bring her.

SINGER  Yes, Countess.

COUNTESS  And ask her to bring Mademoiselle Gabrielle and Madame Josephine with her. Do you know how to get in to speak to Madame Constance? You ring twice, and then meow three times like a cat. Do you know how to meow?

SINGER  I'm better at barking.

COUNTESS  Better practice meowing on the way. Incidentally, I think Madame Constance knows all the verses of your mazurka. Remind me to ask her.

SINGER  Yes, Countess. (*Exit*)

(IRMA *comes in. She is shaking the oily concoction in a little perfume vial, which she now hands the* COUNTESS)

IRMA  Here you are, Countess.

COUNTESS   Thanks, Irma. (*She assumes a presidential manner*) Deaf-Mute! Ready?

> (IRMA *interprets in sign language. The* WAITER *has brought out a portfolio of letter paper and placed it on a table. The* DEAF-MUTE *sits down before it, and prepares to write*)

IRMA (*Speaking for the* DEAF-MUTE)   I'm ready.

COUNTESS   My dear Mr.— What's his name?

> (IRMA *wigwags the question to the* DEAF-MUTE, *who answers in the same manner. It is all done so deftly that it is as if the* DEAF-MUTE *were actually speaking*)

IRMA   They are all called Mr. President.

COUNTESS   My dear Mr. President: I have personally verified the existence of a spontaneous outcrop of oil in the cellar of Number 21 Rue de Chaillot, which is at present occupied by a dignified person of unstable mentality. (*The* COUNTESS *grins knowingly*) This explains why, fortunately for us, the discovery has so long been kept secret. If you should wish to verify the existence of this outcrop for yourself, you may call at the above address at three P.M. today. I am herewith enclosing a sample so that you may judge the quality and consistency of the crude. Yours very truly. Roderick, can you sign the prospector's name?

PIERRE   You wish me to?

COUNTESS   One forgery wipes out the other.

> (PIERRE *signs the letter. The* DEAF-MUTE *types the address on an envelope*)

IRMA   Who is to deliver this?

COUNTESS   The Doorman, of course. On his bicycle. And as soon as you have delivered it, run over to the prospector's office. Leave word that the President expects to see him at my house at three.

DOORMAN   Yes, Countess.

COUNTESS   I shall leave you now. I have many pressing

things to do. Among others, I must press my red gown.

RAGPICKER    But this only takes care of two of them, Countess.

COUNTESS    Didn't the Deaf-Mute say they are all connected like the works of a machine?

IRMA    Yes.

COUNTESS    Then, if one comes, the rest will follow. And we shall have them all. My boa, please.

DOORMAN    The one that's stolen, Countess?

COUNTESS    Naturally. The one the prospector stole.

DOORMAN    It hasn't turned up yet, Countess. But someone has left an ermine collar.

COUNTESS    Real ermine?

DOORMAN    Looks like it.

COUNTESS    Ermine and iris were made for each other. Let me see it.

DOORMAN    Yes, Countess. (*Exit* DOORMAN)

COUNTESS    Roderick, you shall escort me. You still look pale. I have some old Chartreuse at home. I always take a glass each year. Last year I forgot. You shall have it.

PIERRE    If there is anything I can do, Countess . . . ?

COUNTESS    There is a great deal you can do. There are all the things that need to be done in a room that no man has been in for twenty years. You can untwist the cord on the blind and let in a little sunshine for a change. You can take the mirror off the wardrobe door, and deliver me once and for all from the old harpy that lives in the mirror. You can let the mouse out of the trap. I'm tired of feeding it. (*To her friends*) Each man to his post. See you later, my friends. (*The* DOORMAN *puts the ermine collar around her shoulders*) Thank you, my boy. It's rabbit. (*One o'clock strikes*) Your arm, Valentine.

PIERRE    Valentine?

COUNTESS    It's just struck one. At one, all men become Valentine.

PIERRE (*He offers his arm*)  Permit me.

COUNTESS  Or Valentino. It's obviously far from the same, isn't it, Irma? But they have that much choice. (*She sweeps out majestically with* PIERRE. *The others disperse. All but* IRMA)

IRMA (*Clearing off the table*)  I hate ugliness. I love beauty. I hate meanness. I adore kindness. It may not seem so grand to some to be a waitress in Paris. I love it. A waitress meets all sorts of people. She observes life. I hate to be alone. I love people. But I have never said I love you to a man. Men try to make me say it. They put their arms around me—I pretend I don't see it. They pinch me—I pretend I don't feel it. They kiss me—I pretend I don't know it. They take me out in the evening and make me drink—but I'm careful, I never say it. If they don't like it, they can leave me alone. Because when I say I love you to Him, He will know just by looking in my eyes that many have held me and pinched me and kissed me, but I have never said I love you to anyone in the world before. Never. No. (*Looking off in the direction in which* PIERRE *has gone, she whispers softly:*) I love you.

VOICE (*From within the café*)  Irma!

IRMA  Coming. (*Exits*)

*Curtain*

# Act Two

SCENE    *The cellar of the* COUNTESS' *house. An ancient vault set deep in the ground, with walls of solid masonry, part brick and part great ashlars, mossy and sweating. A staircase of medieval pattern is built into the thickness of the wall, and leads up to the street level from a landing halfway down. In the corners of the cellar are piled casks, packing cases, birdcages, and other odds and ends—the accumulation of centuries—the whole effect utterly fantastic.*

*In the center of the vast underground room, some furniture has been arranged to give an impression of a sitting-room of the 1890's. There is a venerable chaise-longue piled with cushions that once were gay, three armchairs, a table with an oil lamp and a bowl of flowers, a shaggy rug. It is two* P.M., *the same day.*

AT RISE    *The* COUNTESS *is sitting over a bit of mending, in one of the armchairs.* IRMA *appears on the landing and calls down.*

IRMA    Countess! The Sewer Man is here.

COUNTESS    Thank goodness, Irma. Send him down. (*The* SEWER MAN *enters. He carries his hip-boots in his hand*) How do you do, Mr. Sewer Man? (*The* SEWER MAN *bows*) But why do you have your boots in your hand instead of on your feet?

SEWER MAN    Etiquette, Countess. Etiquette.

COUNTESS    How very American! I'm told that Americans nowadays apologize for their gloves if they happen to take one's hand. As if the skin of a human were nicer to touch than the skin of a sheep! And particularly if they have sweaty hands . . . !

SEWER MAN   My feet never sweat, Countess.

COUNTESS   How very nice! But please don't stand on ceremony here. Put your boots on. Put them on.

SEWER MAN (*Complying*)   Thanks very much, Countess.

COUNTESS (*While he draws on his boots*)   I'm sure you must have a very poor opinion of the upper world, from what you see of it. The way people throw their filth into your territory is absolutely scandalous! I burn all my refuse, and I scatter the ashes. All I ever throw in the drain is flowers. Did you happen to see a lily float by this morning? Mine. But perhaps you didn't notice?

SEWER MAN   We notice a lot more down there, Countess, than you might think. You'd be surprised the things we notice. There's lots of things come along that were obviously intended for us—little gifts, you might call them—sometimes a brand-new shaving brush—sometimes, *The Brothers Karamazov* . . . Thanks for the lily, Countess. A very sweet thought.

COUNTESS   Tomorrow you shall have this iris. But now, let's come to the point. I have two questions to ask you.

SEWER MAN   Yes, Countess?

COUNTESS   First—and this has nothing to do with our problem—it's just something that has been troubling me. . . . Tell me, is it true that the sewer men of Paris have a king?

SEWER MAN   Oh, now, Countess, that's another of those fairy tales out of the Sunday supplements. It just seems those writers can't keep their minds off the sewers! It fascinates them. They keep thinking of us moving around in our underground canals like gondoliers in Venice, and it sends them into a fever of romance! The things they say about us! They say we have a race of girls down there who never see the light of day! It's completely fantastic! The girls naturally come out—every Christmas and Easter. And orgies by torchlight with gondolas and guitars! With troops of rats that dance as they follow the piper! What nonsense! The rats are not allowed to dance. No, no, no. Of course we have no king. Down in the sewers, you'll find nothing but good Republicans.

COUNTESS   And no queen?

SEWER MAN   No. We may run a beauty contest down there once in a while. Or crown a mermaid Queen of the May. But no queen what you'd call a queen. And, as for these swimming races they talk so much about . . . possibly once in a while—in the summer—in the dog days . . .

COUNTESS   I believe you. I believe you. And now tell me. Do you remember that night I found you here in my cellar—looking very pale and strange—you were half-dead as a matter of fact—and I gave you some brandy . . .

SEWER MAN   Yes, Countess.

COUNTESS   That night you promised if ever I should need it—you would tell me the secret of this room.

SEWER MAN   The secret of the moving stone?

COUNTESS   I need it now.

SEWER MAN   Only the King of the Sewer Men knows this secret.

COUNTESS   I'm sure of it. I know most secrets, of course. As a matter of fact, I have three magic words that will open any door that words can open. I have tried them all—in various tones of voice. They don't seem to work. And this is a matter of life and death.

SEWER MAN   Look, Countess. (*He locates a brick in the masonry, and pushes it. A huge block of stone slowly pivots and uncovers a trap from which a circular staircase winds into the bowels of the earth*)

COUNTESS   Good heavens! Where do those stairs lead?

SEWER MAN　Nowhere.

COUNTESS　But they must go somewhere.

SEWER MAN　They just go down.

COUNTESS　Let's go and see.

SEWER MAN　No, Countess. Never again. That time you found me, I had a pretty close shave. I kept going down and around, and down and around for an hour, a year—I don't know. There's no end to it, Countess. Once you start you can't stop. . . . Your head begins to turn—you're lost. No—once you start down, there's no coming up.

COUNTESS　You came up.

SEWER MAN　I—I am a special case. Besides, I had my tools, my ropes. And I stopped in time.

COUNTESS　You could have screamed—shouted.

SEWER MAN　You could fire off a cannon.

COUNTESS　Who could have built a thing like this?

SEWER MAN　Paris is old, you know. Paris is very old.

COUNTESS　You don't suppose, by any chance, there is oil down there?

SEWER MAN　There's only death down there.

COUNTESS　I should have preferred a little oil too—or a vein of gold—or emeralds. You're quite sure there is nothing?

SEWER MAN　Not even rats.

COUNTESS　How does one lower this stone?

SEWER MAN　Simple. To open, you press here. And to close it, you push there. (*He presses the brick. The stone descends*) Now there's two of us in the world that knows it.

COUNTESS　I won't remember long. Is it all right if I repeat my magic words while I press it?

SEWER MAN　It's bound to help. (IRMA *enters*)

IRMA　Countess, Madame Constance and Mademoiselle Gabrielle are here.

COUNTESS　Show them down, Irma. Thank you very much, Mr. Sewer Man.

SEWER MAN　Like that story about the steam laundry

that's supposed to be running day and night in my sewer . . . I can assure you . . .

COUNTESS (*Edging him toward the door*)  Thank you very much.

SEWER MAN  Pure imagination! They never work nights. (*He goes off, bowing graciously*)

(CONSTANCE, *the Madwoman of Passy, and* GABRI-ELLE, *the Madwoman of St. Sulpice, come down daintily.* CONSTANCE *is all in white. She wears an enormous hat graced with ostrich plumes, and a lavender veil.* GABRIELLE *is costumed with the affected simplicity of the 1880's. She is atrociously made up in a remorseless parody of blushing innocence, and she minces down the stairs with macabre coyness*)

CONSTANCE  Aurelia! Don't tell us they've found your feather boa?

GABRIELLE  You don't mean Adolphe Bertaut has proposed at last! I knew he would.

COUNTESS  How are you, Constance? (*She shouts*) How are you, Gabrielle?

GABRIELLE  You needn't shout today, my dear. It's Wednesday. Wednesdays, I hear perfectly.

CONSTANCE  It's Thursday.

GABRIELLE  Oh, dear. Well, never mind. I'm going to make an exception just this once.

CONSTANCE (*To an imaginary dog who has stopped on the landing*)  Come along, Dickie. Come along. And stop barking. What a racket you're making! Come on, darling—we've come to see the longest boa and the handsomest man in Paris. Come on.

COUNTESS  Constance, it's not a question of my boa today. Nor of poor Adolphe. It's a question of the future of the human race.

CONSTANCE  You think it has a future?

COUNTESS  Please don't make silly jokes. Sit down and listen to me. Today we must make a decision which may alter the fate of the world.

CONSTANCE  Couldn't we do it tomorrow? I want to wash my slippers. Now, Dickie—please!

COUNTESS  We haven't a moment to waste. Where is Josephine? Well, we'd best have our tea, and the moment Josephine comes . . .

GABRIELLE  Josephine is sitting on her bench in front of the palace waiting for President Wilson to come out. She says she's sorry, but she positively must see him today.

CONSTANCE  Dickie!

COUNTESS  What a pity! (*She gets the tea things from the side table, pours tea and serves cake and honey*) I wish she were here to help us. She has a first-class brain.

CONSTANCE  Go ahead, dear. We're listening. (*To* DICKIE) What is it, Dickie? You want to sit in Aunt Aurelia's lap. All right, darling. Go on. Jump, Dickie.

COUNTESS  Constance, we love you, as you know. And we love Dickie. But this is a serious matter. So let's stop being childish for once.

CONSTANCE  And what does that mean, if you please?

COUNTESS  It means Dickie. You know perfectly well that we love him and fuss over him just as if he were still alive. He's a sacred memory and we wouldn't hurt his feelings for the world. But please don't plump him in my lap when I'm settling the future of mankind. His basket is in the corner—he knows where it is, and he can just go and sit in it.

CONSTANCE  So you're against Dickie too! You too!

COUNTESS  Constance! I'm not in the least against Dickie! I adore Dickie. But you know as well as I that Dickie is only a convention with us. It's a beautiful convention—but it doesn't have to bark all the time. Besides, it's you that spoil him. The time you went to visit your niece and left him with me, we got on marvelously together. He didn't bark, he didn't tear things, he didn't even eat. But when you're with him, one can pay attention to nothing else. I'm not going to take Dickie in my lap at a solemn moment like this, no, not for anything in the world. And that's that!

GABRIELLE (*Very sweetly*)    Constance, dear, I don't mind taking him in my lap. He loves to sit in my lap, don't you, darling?

CONSTANCE    Kindly stop putting on angelic airs, Gabrielle. I know you very well. You're much too sweet to be sincere. There's plenty of times that I make believe that Dickie is here, when really I've left him home, and you cuddle and pet him just the same.

GABRIELLE    I adore animals.

CONSTANCE    If you adore animals, you shouldn't pet them when they're not there. It's a form of hypocrisy.

COUNTESS    Now, Constance, Gabrielle has as much right as you . . .

CONSTANCE    Gabrielle has no right to do what she does. Do you know what she does? She invites *people* to come to tea with us. *People* whom we know nothing about. *People* who exist only in her imagination.

COUNTESS    You think that's not an existence?

GABRIELLE    I don't invite them at all. They come by themselves. What can I do?

CONSTANCE    You might introduce us.

COUNTESS    If you think they're only imaginary, there's no point in your meeting them, is there?

CONSTANCE    Of course they're imaginary. But who likes to have imaginary people staring at one? Especially strangers.

GABRIELLE    Oh, they're really very nice. . . .

CONSTANCE    Tell me just one thing, Gabrielle—are they here now?

COUNTESS    Am I to be allowed to speak? Or is this going to be the same as the argument about inoculating Josephine's cat, when we didn't get to the subject at all?

CONSTANCE    Never! Never! Never! I'll never give my

consent to that. (*To* DICKIE) I'd never do a thing like that to you, Dickie sweet. . . . Oh, no! Oh, no! (*She begins to weep softly*)

COUNTESS Good heavens! Now we have her in tears. What an impossible creature! With the fate of humanity hanging in the balance! All right, all right, stop crying. I'll take him in my lap. Come, Dickie, Dickie.

CONSTANCE No, He won't go now. Oh, how can you be so cruel? Don't you suppose I know about Dickie? Don't you think I'd rather have him here alive and woolly and frisking around the way he used to? You have your Adolphe. Gabrielle has her birds. But I have only Dickie. Do you think I'd be so silly about him if it wasn't that it's only by pretending that he's here all the time that I get him to come sometimes, really? Next time I won't bring him!

COUNTESS Now let's not get ourselves worked up over nothing. Come here, Dickie. . . . Irma is going to take you for a nice walk. (*She rings her bell*) Irma! (IRMA *appears on the landing*)

CONSTANCE No. He doesn't want to go. Besides, I didn't bring him today. So there!

COUNTESS Very well, then. Irma, make sure the door is locked.

IRMA Yes, Countess. (IRMA *exits*)

CONSTANCE What do you mean? Why locked? Who's coming?

COUNTESS If you'd let me get a word in, you'd know by now. A terrible thing has happened. This morning, this very morning, exactly at noon . . .

CONSTANCE (*Thrilled*) Oh, how exciting!

COUNTESS Be quiet. This morning, exactly at noon, thanks to a young man who drowned himself in the Seine . . . Oh, yes, while I think of it—do you know a mazurka called *La Belle Polonaise?*

CONSTANCE Yes, Aurelia.

COUNTESS    Could you sing it now? This very minute?

CONSTANCE    Yes, Aurelia.

COUNTESS    All of it?

CONSTANCE    Yes, Aurelia. But who's interrupting now, Aurelia?

COUNTESS    You're right. Well, this morning, exactly at noon, I discovered a horrible plot. There is a group of men who intend to tear down the whole city!

CONSTANCE    Is that all?

GABRIELLE    But I don't understand, Aurelia. Why should men want to tear down the city? It was they themselves who put it up.

COUNTESS    You are so innocent, my poor Gabrielle. There are people in the world who want to destroy everything. They have the fever of destruction. Even when they pretend that they're building, it is only in order to destroy. When they put up a new building, they quietly knock down two old ones. They build cities so that they can destroy the countryside. They destroy space with telephones and time with airplanes. Humanity is now dedicated to the task of universal destruction. I am speaking, of course, primarily of the male sex.

GABRIELLE (*Shocked*)    Oh . . . !

CONSTANCE    Aurelia! Must you talk sex in front of Gabrielle?

COUNTESS    There *are* two sexes.

CONSTANCE    Gabrielle is a virgin, Aurelia!

COUNTESS    Oh, she can't be as innocent as all that. She keeps canaries.

GABRIELLE    I think you're being very cruel about men, Aurelia. Men are big and beautiful, and as loyal as dogs. I preferred not to marry, it's true. But I hear excellent reports from friends who have had an opportunity to observe them closely.

COUNTESS    My poor darling! You are still living in a dream. But one day, you will wake up as I have, and then you will see what is happening in the world.

The tide has turned, my dear. Men are changing back
into beasts. They know it. They no longer try to hide
it. There was once such a thing as manners. I remember a time when the hungriest was the one who
took the longest to pick up his fork. The one with
the broadest grin was the one who needed most to
go to the . . . It was such fun to keep them grinning
like that for hours. But now they no longer pretend.
Just look at them—snuffling their soup like pigs, tearing their meat like tigers, crunching their lettuce like
crocodiles! A man doesn't take your hand nowadays.
He gives you his paw.

CONSTANCE   Would that trouble you so much if they
turned into animals? Personally, I think it's a good
idea.

GABRIELLE   Oh, I'd love to see them like that. They'd
be sweet.

CONSTANCE   It might be the salvation of the human
race.

COUNTESS (*To* CONSTANCE)   You'd make a fine rabbit,
wouldn't you?

CONSTANCE   I?

COUNTESS   Naturally. You don't think it's only the
men who are changing? You change along with them.
Husbands and wives together. We're all one race,
you know.

CONSTANCE   You think so? And why would my poor
husband have to be a rabbit if he were alive?

COUNTESS   Remember his front teeth? When he nib-
bled his celery?

CONSTANCE   I'm happy to say, I remember absolutely
nothing about him. All I remember on that subject
is the time that Father Lacordaire tried to kiss me
in the park.

COUNTESS   Yes, yes, of course.

CONSTANCE   And what does that mean, if you please,
"Yes, yes, of course"?

COUNTESS   Constance, just this once, look us in the

eye and tell us truly—did that really happen or did you read about it in a book?

CONSTANCE    Now I'm being insulted!

COUNTESS    We promise you faithfully that we'll believe it all over again afterwards, won't we, Gabrielle? But tell us the truth this once.

CONSTANCE    How dare you question my memories? Suppose I said your pearls were false!

COUNTESS    They were.

CONSTANCE    I'm not asking what they were. I'm asking what they are. Are they false or are they real?

COUNTESS    Everyone knows that little by little, as one wears pearls, they become real.

CONSTANCE    And isn't it exactly the same with memories?

COUNTESS    Now do not let us waste time. I must go on.

CONSTANCE    I think Gabrielle is perfectly right about men. There are still plenty who haven't changed a bit. There's an old Senator who bows to Gabrielle every day when he passes her in front of the palace. And he takes off his hat each time.

GABRIELLE    That's perfectly true, Aurelia. He's always pushing an empty baby carriage, and he always stops and bows.

COUNTESS    Don't be taken in, Gabrielle. It's all make-believe. And all we can expect from these make-believe men is itself make-believe. They give us facepowder made of stones, sausages made of sawdust, shirts made of glass, stockings made of milk. It's all a vulgar pretence. And if that is the case, imagine what passes, these days, for virtue, sincerity, generosity, and love! I warn you, Gabrielle, don't let this Senator with the empty baby carriage pull the wool over your eyes.

GABRIELLE    He's really the soul of courtesy. He seems very correct.

COUNTESS    Those are the worst. Gabrielle, beware! He'll make you put on black riding boots, while he dances

the can-can around you, singing God knows what
filth at the top of his voice. The very thought makes
one's blood run cold!

GABRIELLE You think that's what he has in mind?

COUNTESS Of course. Men have lost all sense of decency. They are all equally disgusting. Just look at
them in the evening, sitting at their tables in the
café, working away in unison with their toothpicks,
hour after hour, digging up roast beef, veal, onion . . .

CONSTANCE They don't harm anyone that way.

COUNTESS Then why do you barricade your door, and
make your friends meow before you let them come
up? Incidentally, we must make an interesting sight,
Gabrielle and I, yowling together on your doorstep
like a couple of tomcats!

CONSTANCE There's no need at all for you to yowl
together. One would be quite enough. And you know
perfectly well why I have to do it. It's because there
are murderers.

COUNTESS I don't quite see what prevents murderers
from meowing like anybody else. But why are there
murderers?

CONSTANCE Why? Because there are thieves.

COUNTESS And why are there thieves? Why is there
almost nothing but thieves?

CONSTANCE Because they worship money. Because
money is king.

COUNTESS Ah—now we've come to it. Because we live
in the reign of the Golden Calf. Did you realize that,
Gabrielle? Men now publicly worship the Golden
Calf!

GABRIELLE How awful! Have the authorities been
notified?

COUNTESS The authorities do it themselves, Gabrielle.

GABRIELLE Oh! Has anyone talked to the bishop?

COUNTESS Nowadays only money talks to the bishop.
And so you see why I asked you to come here today.
The world has gone out of its mind. Unless we do

something, humanity is doomed! Constance, have you any suggestions?

CONSTANCE   I know what I always do in a case like this. . . .

COUNTESS   You write to the Prime Minister.

CONSTANCE   He always does what I tell him.

COUNTESS   Does he ever answer your letters?

CONSTANCE   He knows I prefer him not to. It might excite gossip. Besides, I don't always write. Sometimes I wire. The time I told him about the Archbishop's frigidaire, it was by wire. And they sent a new one the very next day.

COUNTESS   There was probably a commission in it for someone. And what do you suggest, Gabrielle?

CONSTANCE   Now, how can she tell you until she's consulted her voices?

GABRIELLE   I could go right home and consult them, and we could meet again after dinner.

COUNTESS   There's no time for that. Besides, your voices are not real voices.

GABRIELLE   (*Furious*) How dare you say a thing like that?

COUNTESS   Where do your voices come from? Still from your sewing-machine?

GABRIELLE   Not at all. They've passed into my hot-water bottle. And it's much nicer that way. They don't chatter any more. They gurgle. But they haven't been a bit nice to me lately. Last night they kept telling me to let my canaries out. "Let them out. Let them out. Let them out."

CONSTANCE   Did you?

GABRIELLE   I opened the cage. They wouldn't go.

COUNTESS   I don't call that *voices*. Objects talk—everyone knows that. It's the principle of the phonograph. But to ask a hot-water bottle for advice is silly. What does a hot-water bottle know? No, all we have to consult here is our own judgment.

CONSTANCE   Very well then, tell us what you have

decided. Since you're asking our opinion, you've
doubtless made up your mind.

COUNTESS   Yes, I've thought the whole thing out. All
I really needed to discover was the source of the
infection. Today I found it.

CONSTANCE   Where?

COUNTESS   You'll see soon enough. I've baited a trap.
In just a few minutes, the rats will be here.

GABRIELLE (*In alarm*)   Rats!

COUNTESS   Don't be alarmed. They're still in human
form.

GABRIELLE   Heavens! What are you going to do with
them?

COUNTESS   That's just the question. Suppose I get these
wicked men all here at once—in my cellar—have I
the right to exterminate them?

GABRIELLE   To kill them? (COUNTESS *nods*)

CONSTANCE   That's not a question for us. You'll have
to ask Father Bridet.

COUNTESS   I have asked him. Yes. One day, in con-
fession, I told him frankly that I had a secret desire
to destroy all wicked people. He said: "By all means,
my child. And when you're ready to go into action,
I'll lend you the jawbone of an ass."

CONSTANCE   That's just talk. You get him to put that
in writing.

GABRIELLE   What's your scheme, Aurelia?

COUNTESS   That's a secret.

CONSTANCE   It's not so easy to kill them. Let's say you
had a tank full of vitriol all ready for them. You
could never get them to walk into it. There's nothing
so stubborn as a man when you want him to do something.

COUNTESS   Leave that to me.

CONSTANCE   But if they're killed, they're bound to be
missed, and then we'll be fined. They fine you for
every little thing these days.

COUNTESS   They won't be missed.

GABRIELLE   I wish Josephine were here. Her sister's husband was a lawyer. She knows all about these things.

COUNTESS   Do you miss a cold when it's gone? Or the germs that caused it? When the world feels well again, do you think it will regret its illness? No, it will stretch itself joyfully, and it will smile—that's all.

CONSTANCE   Just a moment! Gabrielle, are they here now? Yes or no?

COUNTESS   What's the matter with you now?

CONSTANCE   I'm simply asking Gabrielle if her friends are in the room or not. I have a right to know.

GABRIELLE   I'm not allowed to say.

CONSTANCE   I know very well they are. I'm sure of it. Otherwise you wouldn't be making faces.

COUNTESS   May I ask what difference it makes to you if her friends are in the room?

CONSTANCE   Just this: If they're here, I'm not going to say another word! I'm certainly not going to commit myself in a matter involving the death sentence in the presence of third parties, whether they exist or not.

GABRIELLE   That's not being very nice to my guests, is it?

COUNTESS   Constance, you must be mad! Or are you so stupid as to think that just because we're alone, there's nobody with us? Do you consider us so boring or repulsive that of all the millions of beings, imaginary or otherwise, who are prowling about in space, there's not one who might possibly enjoy spending a little time with us? On the contrary, my dear— my house is full of guests always. They know that here they have a place in the universe where they can come when they're lonely and be sure of a welcome. For my part, I'm delighted to have them.

GABRIELLE   Thank you, Aurelia.

CONSTANCE   You know perfectly well, Aurelia . . .

COUNTESS   I know perfectly well that at this moment

ber of the League for Decency. Experience shows it's the only way to get an acquittal.

COUNTESS   But we must not have an acquittal. That would mean the end of the world!

JOSEPHINE   Justice is justice, my dear.

(*The* RAGPICKER *comes down, with a stately air. Behind him, on the landing, appear the other* VAGABONDS)

THE RAGPICKER   Greetings, Countess. Greetings, ladies. My most sincere compliments.

COUNTESS   Has Irma told you . . . ?

THE RAGPICKER   She said something about a trial.

COUNTESS   You have been appointed attorney for the defense.

THE RAGPICKER   Terribly flattered, I'm sure.

COUNTESS   You realize, don't you, how much depends on the outcome of this trial?

JOSEPHINE   Do you know the defendants well enough to undertake the case?

THE RAGPICKER   I know them to the bottom of their souls. I go through their garbage every day.

CONSTANCE   And what do you find there?

THE RAGPICKER   Mostly flowers.

GABRIELLE   It's true, you know, the rich are always surrounded with flowers.

CONSTANCE   How beautiful!

COUNTESS   Are you trying to prejudice the court?

THE RAGPICKER   Oh no, Countess, no.

COUNTESS   We want a completely impartial defense.

THE RAGPICKER   Of course, Countess, of course. Permit me to make a suggestion.

COUNTESS   Will you preside, Josephine?

THE RAGPICKER   Instead of speaking as attorney, suppose you let me speak directly as defendant. It will be more convincing, and I can get into it more.

JOSEPHINE   Excellent idea. Motion granted.

the whole universe is listening to us—and that every word we say echoes to the remotest star. To pretend otherwise is the sheerest hypocrisy.

CONSTANCE   Then why do you insult me in front of everybody? I'm not mean. I'm shy. I feel timid about giving an opinion in front of such a crowd. Furthermore, if you think I'm so bad and so stupid, why did you invite me, in the first place?

COUNTESS   I'll tell you. And I'll tell you why, disagreeable as you are, I always give you the biggest piece of cake and my best honey. It's because when you come there's always someone with you—and I don't mean Dickie—I mean someone who resembles you like a sister, only she's young and lovely, and she sits modestly to one side and smiles at me tenderly all the time you're bickering and quarreling, and never says a word. That's the Constance to whom I give the cake that you gobble, and it's because of her that you're here today, and it's her vote that I'm asking you to cast in this crucial moment. And not yours, which is of no importance whatever.

CONSTANCE   I'm leaving.

COUNTESS   Be so good as to sit down. I can't let her go yet.

CONSTANCE   (*Crossing toward the stairs*)   No. This is too much. I'm taking her with me.

(IRMA *enters*)

IRMA   Madame Josephine.

COUNTESS   Thank heaven!

GABRIELLE   We're saved. (JOSEPHINE, *the Madwoman of La Concorde, sweeps in majestically in a get-up somewhere between the regal and the priestly*)

JOSEPHINE   My dear friends, today once again, I waited for President Wilson—but he didn't come out.

COUNTESS   You'll have to wait quite a while longer before he does. He's been dead since 1924.

JOSEPHINE   I have plenty of time.

COUNTESS  In anyone else, Josephine, these extravagances might seem a little childish. But a person of your judgment doubtless has her reasons for wanting to talk to a man to whom no one would listen when he was alive. We have a legal problem for you. Suppose you had all the world's criminals here in this room. And suppose you had a way of getting rid of them forever. Would you have the right to do it?

JOSEPHINE  Why not?

COUNTESS  Exactly my point.

GABRIELLE  But, Josephine, so many people!

JOSEPHINE  *De minimis non curat lex.* The more there are, the more legal it is. It's impersonal. It's even military. It's the cardinal principle of battle—you get all your enemies in one place, and you kill them all together at one time. Because if you had to track them down one by one in their houses and offices, you'd get tired, and sooner or later you'd stop. I believe your idea is very practical, Aurelia. I can't imagine why we never thought of it before.

GABRIELLE  Well, if you think it's all right to do it. . . .

JOSEPHINE  By all means. Your criminals have had a fair trial, I suppose?

COUNTESS  Trial?

JOSEPHINE  Certainly. You can't kill anybody without a trial. That's elementary. "No man shall be deprived of his life, liberty, and property without due process of law."

COUNTESS  They deprive us of ours.

JOSEPHINE  That's not the point. You're not accused of anything. Every accused—man, woman, or child— has the right to defend himself at the bar of justice. Even animals. Before the Deluge, you will recall, the Lord permitted Noah to speak in defense of his fellow mortals. He evidently stuttered. You know the result. On the other hand, Captain Dreyfus was not only innocent—he was defended by a marvelous orator.

The result was precisely the same. So you see, in having a trial, you run no risk whatever.

COUNTESS  But if I give them the slightest cause for suspicion—I'll lose them.

JOSEPHINE  There's a simple procedure prescribed in such cases. You can summon the defendants by calling them three times—mentally, if you like. If they don't appear, the court may designate an attorney who will represent them. This attorney can then argue their case to the court, *in absentia,* and a judgment can then be rendered, *in contumacio.*

COUNTESS  But I don't know any attorneys. And we have only ten minutes.

GABRIELLE  Hurry, Josephine, hurry!

JOSEPHINE  In case of emergency, it is permissible for the court to order the first passer-by to act as attorney for the defense. A defense is like a baptism. Absolutely indispensable, but you don't have to know anything to do it. Ask Irma to get you somebody. Anybody.

COUNTESS  The Deaf-Mute?

JOSEPHINE  Well—that's getting it down a bit fine. That might be questionable on appeal.

COUNTESS  (*Calls*) Irma! What about the Police Sergeant?

JOSEPHINE  He won't do. He's under oath to the state. (IRMA *appears*)

IRMA  Yes, Countess?

COUNTESS  Who's out there, Irma?

IRMA  All our friends, Countess. There's the Ragpicker and . . .

COUNTESS  Send down the Ragpicker.

CONSTANCE  Do you think it's wise to have all those millionaires represented by a ragpicker?

JOSEPHINE  It's a first-rate choice. Criminals are always represented by their opposites. Murderers, by someone who obviously wouldn't hurt a fly. Rapists, by a mem-

COUNTESS  We don't want you to be too convincing, remember.

THE RAGPICKER  Impartial, Countess, impartial.

JOSEPHINE  Well? Have you prepared your case?

THE RAGPICKER  How rich am I?

JOSEPHINE  Millions. Billions.

THE RAGPICKER  How did I get them? Theft? Murder? Embezzlement?

COUNTESS  Most likely.

THE RAGPICKER  Do I have a wife? A mistress?

COUNTESS  Everything.

THE RAGPICKER  All right. I'm ready.

GABRIELLE  Will you have some tea?

THE RAGPICKER  Is that good?

CONSTANCE  Very good for the voice. The Russians drink nothing but tea. And they talk like anything.

THE RAGPICKER  All right. Tea.

JOSEPHINE (*To the* VAGABONDS)  Come in. Come in. All of you. You may take places. The trial is public. (*The* VAGABONDS *dispose themselves on the steps and elsewhere*) Your bell, if you please, Aurelia.

COUNTESS  But what if I should need to ring for Irma?

JOSEPHINE  Irma will sit here, next to me. If you need her, she can ring for herself. (*To the* POLICE SERGEANT *and the* POLICEMAN)  Conduct the accused to the bar. (*The officers conduct the* RAGPICKER *to a bar improvised with a rocking chair and a packing case marked FRAGILE. The* RAGPICKER *mounts the box. She rings the bell*)  The court is now in session. (*All sit*)  Counsel for the defense, you may take the oath.

THE RAGPICKER  I swear to tell the truth, the whole truth, and nothing but the truth, so help me God.

JOSEPHINE  Nonsense! You're not a witness. You're an attorney. It's your duty to lie, conceal, and distort everything, and slander everybody.

THE RAGPICKER  All right. I swear to lie, conceal, and distort everything, and slander everybody.

(JOSEPHINE *rings stridently*)

JOSEPHINE    Quiet! Begin.

THE RAGPICKER    May it please the honorable, august and elegant Court . . .

JOSEPHINE    Flattery will get you nowhere. That will do. The defense has been heard. Cross-examination.

COUNTESS    Mr. President . . .

THE RAGPICKER (*Bowing with dignity*)    Madame.

COUNTESS    Do you know what you are charged with?

THE RAGPICKER    I can't for the life of me imagine. My life is an open book. My ways are known to all. I am a pillar of the church and the sole support of the Opera. My hands are spotless.

COUNTESS    What an atrocious lie! Just look at them!

CONSTANCE    You don't have to insult the man. He's only lying to please you.

COUNTESS    Be quiet, Constance! You don't get the idea at all. (*To the* RAGPICKER) You are charged with the crime of worshipping money.

THE RAGPICKER    Worshipping money? Me?

JOSEPHINE    Do you plead guilty or not guilty? Which is it?

THE RAGPICKER    Why, Your Honor . . .

JOSEPHINE    Yes or no?

THE RAGPICKER    Yes or no? No! I don't worship money, Countess. Heavens, no! Money worships me. It adores me. It won't let me alone. It's damned embarrassing, I can tell you.

JOSEPHINE    Kindly watch your language.

COUNTESS    Defendant, tell the Court how you came by your money.

THE RAGPICKER    The first time money came to me, I was a mere boy, a little golden-haired child in the bosom of my dear family. It came to me suddenly in the guise of a gold brick which, in my innocence, I picked out of a garbage can one day while playing. I was horrified, as you can imagine. I immediately tried to get rid of it by swapping it for a little run-down one-track railroad which, to my consternation, at once sold itself for a hundred times its value. In a desperate effort to get rid of this money, I began to buy things. I bought the Northern Refineries, the Galeries Lafayette, and the Schneider-Creusot Munition Works. And now I'm stuck with them. It's a horrible fate—but I'm resigned to it. I don't ask for your sympathy, I don't ask for your pity—all I ask for is a little common human understanding . . . . (*He begins to cry*)

COUNTESS   I object. This wretch is trying to play on the emotions of the Court.

JOSEPHINE   The Court has no emotions.

THE RAGPICKER   Everyone knows that the poor have no one but themselves to blame for their poverty. It's only just that they should suffer the consequences. But how is it the fault of the rich if they're rich?

COUNTESS   Dry your tears. You're deceiving nobody. If, as you say, you're ashamed of your money, why is it you hold onto it with such a death-grip?

THE RAGPICKER   Me?

STREET PEDDLER   You never part with a franc!

JUGGLER   You wouldn't even give the poor Deaf-Mute a sou!

THE RAGPICKER   Me, hold onto money? What slander! What injustice! What a thing to say to me in the presence of this honorable, august, and elegant Court! I spend all my time trying to spend my money. If I have tan shoes, I buy black ones. If I have a bicycle, I buy a motor car. If I have a wife, I buy . . .

JOSEPHINE (*Rings*)   Order!

THE RAGPICKER   I dispatch a plane to Java for a bouquet of flowers. I send a steamer to Egypt for a basket of figs. I send a special representative to New York to fetch me an ice-cream cone. And if it's not just exactly right, back it goes. But no matter what I do,

I can't get rid of my money! If I play a hundred to one shot, the horse comes in by twenty lengths. If I throw a diamond in the Seine, it turns up in the trout they serve me for lunch. Ten diamonds—ten trout. Well, now, do you suppose I can get rid of forty millions by giving a sou to a deaf-mute? Is it even worth the effort?

CONSTANCE   He's right.

THE RAGPICKER   Ah! You see, my dear? At last, there is somebody who understands me! Somebody who is not only beautiful, but extraordinarily sensitive and intelligent.

COUNTESS   I object!

JOSEPHINE   Overruled!

THE RAGPICKER   I should be delighted to send you some flowers, Miss—directly I'm acquitted. What flowers do you prefer?

CONSTANCE   Roses.

THE RAGPICKER   You shall have a bale every morning for the next five years. Money means nothing to me.

CONSTANCE   And amaryllis.

THE RAGPICKER   I'll make a note of the name. (*In his best lyrical style*) The lady understands, ladies and Gentlemen. The lady is no fool. She's been around and she knows what's what. If I gave the Deaf-Mute a franc, twenty francs, twenty million francs—I still wouldn't make a dent in the forty times a thousand million francs that I'm afflicted with! Right, little lady?

CONSTANCE   Right.

JOSEPHINE   Proceed.

THE RAGPICKER   Like on the Stock Exchange. If *you* buy a stock, it sinks at once like a plummet. But if *I* buy a stock, it turns around and soars like an eagle. If I buy it at 33 . . .

PEDDLER   It goes up to a thousand.

THE RAGPICKER   It goes to twenty thousand! That's

how I bought my twelve chateaux, my twenty villas, my 234 farms. That's how I endow the Opera and keep my twelve ballerinas.

FLOWER GIRL  I hope every one of them deceives you every moment of the day!

THE RAGPICKER  How can they deceive me? Suppose they try to deceive me with the male chorus, the general director, the assistant electrician, or the English horn—I own them all, body and soul. It would be like deceiving me with my big toe.

CONSTANCE  Don't listen, Gabrielle.

GABRIELLE  Listen to what?

THE RAGPICKER  No. I am incapable of jealousy. I have all the women—or I can have them, which is the same thing. I get the thin ones with caviar—the fat ones with pearls . . . .

COUNTESS  So you think there are no women with morals?

THE RAGPICKER  I mix morals with mink—delicious combination. I drip pearls into protests. I adorn resistance with rubies. My touch is jeweled; my smile, a motor car. What woman can withstand me? I lift my little finger—and do they fall?— Like leaves in autumn—like tin cans from a second-story window.

CONSTANCE  That's going a little too far!

COUNTESS  You see where money leads.

THE RAGPICKER  Of course. When you have no money, nobody trusts you, nobody believes you, nobody likes you. Because to have money is to be virtuous, honest, beautiful, and witty. And to be without is to be ugly and boring and stupid and useless.

COUNTESS  One last question. Suppose you find this oil you're looking for. What do you propose to do with it?

THE RAGPICKER  I propose to make war! I propose to conquer the world!

COUNTESS  You have heard the defense, such as it is. I demand a verdict of guilty.

THE RAGPICKER　What are you talking about? Guilty? I? I am never guilty!

JOSEPHINE　I order you to keep quiet.

THE RAGPICKER　I am never quiet!

JOSEPHINE　Quiet, in the name of the law!

THE RAGPICKER　I am the law. When I speak, that is the law. When I present my backside, it is etiquette to smile and to apply the lips respectfully. It is more than etiquette—it is a cherished national privilege, guaranteed by the Constitution.

JOSEPHINE　That's contempt of court. The trial is over.

COUNTESS　And the verdict?

ALL　Guilty!

JOSEPHINE　Guilty as charged.

COUNTESS　Then I have full authority to carry out the sentence?

ALL　Yes!

COUNTESS　I can do what I like with them?

ALL　Yes!

COUNTESS　I have the right to exterminate them?

ALL　Yes!

JOSEPHINE　Court adjourned!

COUNTESS (*To the* RAGPICKER)　Congratulations, Ragpicker. A marvelous defense. Absolutely impartial.

THE RAGPICKER　Had I known a little before, I could have done better. I could have prepared a little speech, like the time I used to sell the Miracle Spot Remover. . . .

JOSEPHINE　No need for that. You did very well, extempore. The likeness was striking and the style reminiscent of Clemenceau. I predict a brilliant future for you. Good-bye, Aurelia. I'll take our little Gabrielle home.

CONSTANCE　I'm going to walk along the river. (*To* DICKIE) Oh! So here you are. And your ear all bloody! Dickie! Have you been fighting again? Oh, dear . . . !

COUNTESS (*To the* RAGPICKER)　See that she gets home

all right, won't you? She loses everything on the way. And in the queerest places. Her prayer book in the butcher shop. And her corset in church.

THE RAGPICKER (*Bowing and offering his arm*) Permit me, Madame.

STREET SINGER Oh, Countess—my mazurka. Remember?

COUNTESS Oh, yes. Constance, wait a moment. (*To the* SINGER) Well? Begin.

SINGER (*Sings*)

> Do you hear, Mademoiselle,
> Those musicians of hell?

CONSTANCE Why, of course, it's *La Belle Polonaise.* . . . (*She sings*)

> From Poland to France
> Comes this marvelous dance,
>     So gracious,
>     Audacious,
> Will you foot it, perchance?

SINGER I'm saved!

JOSEPHINE (*Reappearing at the head of the stairs*)

> Now my arm I entwine
> Round these contours divine,
> So pure, so impassioned,
> Which Cupid has fashioned. . . .

GABRIELLE (*Reappearing also, she sings a quartet with the others*)

> Come, let's dance the mazurka, that devilish measure,
> 'Tis a joy that's reserved to the gods for their pleasure—
>     Let's gallop, let's hop,
>     With never a stop,
>     My blond Polish miss,

Let our heads spin and turn
As the dance-floor we spurn—
There was never such pleasure as this!

(*They all exit, dancing*)

IRMA   It's time for your afternoon nap.

COUNTESS   But suppose they come, Irma!

IRMA   I'll watch out for them.

COUNTESS   Thank you, Irma. I *am* tired. (*She smiles*)
Did you ever see a trial end more happily in your life?

IRMA   Lie down and close your eyes a moment.
(*The* COUNTESS *stretches out on the chaise-longue
and shuts her eyes.* IRMA *tiptoes out. In a moment,*
PIERRE *comes down softly, the feather boa in his
hands. He stands over the chaise-longue, looking
tenderly down at the sleeping woman, then kneels
beside her and takes her hand*)

COUNTESS   (*Without opening her eyes*) Is it you,
Adolphe Bertaut?

PIERRE   It's only Pierre.

COUNTESS   Don't lie to me, Adolphe Bertaut. These are
your hands. Why do you complicate things always?
Say that it's you.

PIERRE   Yes. It is I.

COUNTESS   Would it cost you so much to call me
Aurelia?

PIERRE   It's I, Aurelia.

COUNTESS   Why did you leave me, Adolphe Bertaut?
Was she so very lovely, this Georgette of yours?

PIERRE   No. You are a thousand times lovelier.

COUNTESS   But she was clever.

PIERRE   She was stupid.

COUNTESS   It was her soul, then, that drew you? When
you looked into her eyes, you saw a vision of heaven,
perhaps?

PIERRE   I saw nothing.

COUNTESS   That's how it is with men. They love you

because you are beautiful and clever and soulful—
and at the first opportunity they leave you for someone who is plain and dull and soulless. But why does
it have to be like that, Adolphe Bertaut? Why?

PIERRE  Why, Aurelia?

COUNTESS  I know very well she wasn't rich. Because
when I saw you that time at the grocer's, and you
snatched the only good melon from right under
my nose, your cuffs, my poor friend, were badly
frayed. . . .

PIERRE  Yes. She was poor.

COUNTESS  "Was" poor? Is she dead then? If it's because she's dead that you've come back to me—then
no. Go away. I will not take their leavings from the
dead. I refuse to inherit you. . . .

PIERRE  She's quite well.

COUNTESS  Your hands are still the same, Adolphe
Bertaut. Your touch is young and firm. Because it's
the only part of you that has stayed with me. The
rest of you is pretty far gone, I'm afraid. I can see
why you'd rather not come near me when my eyes
are open. It's thoughtful of you.

PIERRE  Yes. I've aged.

COUNTESS  Not I. I am young because I haven't had
to live down my youth, like you. I have it with me
still, as fresh and beautiful as ever. But when you
walk now in the park at Colombes with Georgette,
I'm sure . . .

PIERRE  There is no longer a park at Colombes.

COUNTESS  Is there a park still at St. Cloud? Is there
a park at Versailles? I've never gone back to see. But
I think, if they could move, those trees would have
walked away in disgust the day you went there with
Georgette. . . .

PIERRE  They did. Not many are left.

COUNTESS  You take her also, I suppose, to hear *Denise?*

PIERRE  No one hears *Denise* any more.

COUNTESS  It was on the way home from *Denise,* Adolphe Bertaut, that I first took your arm. Because it was windy and it was late. I have never set foot in that street again. I go the other way round. It's not easy, in the winter, when there's ice. One is quite apt to fall. I often do.

PIERRE  Oh, my darling—forgive me.

COUNTESS  No, never. I will never forgive you. It was very bad taste to take her to the very places where we'd been together.

PIERRE  All the same, I swear, Aurelia . . .

COUNTESS  Don't swear. I know what you did. You gave her the same flowers. You bought her the same chocolates. But has she any left? No. I have all your flowers still. I have twelve chocolates. No, I will never forgive you as long as I live.

PIERRE  I always loved you, Aurelia.

COUNTESS  You "loved" me? Then you too are dead, Adolphe Bertaut?

PIERRE  No. I love you. I shall always love you, Aurelia.

COUNTESS  Yes. I know. That much I've always known. I knew it the moment you went away, Adolphe, and I knew that nothing could ever change it. Georgette is in his arms now—yes. But he loves me. Tonight he's taken Georgette to hear *Denise*—yes. But he loves me. . . . I know it. You never loved her. Do you think I believed for one moment that absurd story about her running off with the osteopath? Of course not. Since you didn't love her, obviously she stayed with you. And, after that, when she came back, and I heard about her going off with the surveyor— I knew that couldn't be true, either. You'll never get rid of her, Adolphe Bertaut—never. Because you don't love her.

PIERRE  I need your pity, Aurelia. I need your love. Don't forget me. . . .

COUNTESS  Farewell, Adolphe Bertaut. Farewell. Let go my hand, and give it to little Pierre. (PIERRE *lets go*

*her hand, and after a moment takes it again. The*
COUNTESS *opens her eyes*) Pierre? Ah, it's you. Has he
gone?

PIERRE  Yes, Countess.

COUNTESS  I didn't hear him go. Oh, he knows how to
make a quick exit, that one. (*She sees the boa*) Good
heavens! Wherever did you find it?

PIERRE  In the wardrobe, Countess. When I took off
the mirror.

COUNTESS  Was there a purple felt shopping bag with it?

PIERRE  Yes, Countess.

COUNTESS  And a little child's sewing box?

PIERRE  No, Countess.

COUNTESS  Oh, they're frightened now. They're trembling for their lives. You see what they're up to?
They're putting back all the things they have stolen.
I never open that wardrobe, of course, on account of
the old woman in the mirror. But I have sharp eyes.
I don't need to open it to see what's in it. Up to this
morning, that wardrobe was empty. And now—you
see? But, dear me, how stupid they are! The one
thing I really miss is my little sewing box. It's something they stole from me when I was a child. They
haven't put it back? You're quite sure?

PIERRE  What was it like?

COUNTESS  Green cardboard with paper lace and gold
stamping. I got it for Christmas when I was seven.
They stole it the very next day. I cried my eyes out
every time I thought of it—until I was eight.

PIERRE  It's not there, Countess.

COUNTESS  The thimble was gilt. I swore I'd never use
any other. Look at my poor fingers. . . .

PIERRE  They've kept the thimble too.

COUNTESS  Splendid! Then I'm under no obligation to
be merciful. Put the boa around my neck, Pierre. I
want them to see me wearing it. They'll think it's a
real boa.

    (IRMA *runs in excitedly*)

IRMA   Here they come, Countess! You were right—it's a procession. The street is full of limousines and taxis!

COUNTESS   I will receive them. (*As* PIERRE *hesitates to leave her*) Don't worry. There's nothing to be frightened of. (PIERRE *goes out*) Irma, did you remember to stir the kerosene into the water?

IRMA   Yes, Countess. Here it is.

COUNTESS (*Looking critically at the bottle*)   You might as well pour in what's left of the tea. (IRMA *shakes up the liquid*) Don't forget, I'm supposed to be deaf. I want to hear what they're thinking.

IRMA   Yes, Countess.

COUNTESS (*Putting the finishing touches to her make-up*)   I don't have to be merciful—but, after all, I do want to be just. . . .

>   (IRMA *goes up to the landing and exits. As soon as she is alone, the* COUNTESS *presses the brick, and the trap door opens. There is a confused sound of auto horns in the street above, and the noise of an approaching crowd*)

IRMA (*Offstage*)   Yes, Mr. President. Come in, Mr. President. You're expected, Mr. President. This way, Mr. President. (*The* PRESIDENTS *come down, led by the* PRESIDENT. *They all look alike, are dressed alike, and all have long cigars*) The Countess is quite deaf, gentlemen. You'll have to shout. (*She announces*) The presidents of the boards of directors!

THE PRESIDENT   I had a premonition, Madame, when I saw you this morning, that we should meet again. (*The* COUNTESS *smiles vaguely. He continues, a tone louder*) I want to thank you for your trust. You may place yourself in our hands with complete confidence.

SECOND PRESIDENT   Louder. The old trot can't hear you.

THE PRESIDENT   I have a letter here, Madame, in which . . .

SECOND PRESIDENT   Louder. Louder.

THIRD PRESIDENT (*Shouting*) Is it true that you've located . . . ? (*The* COUNTESS *stares at him blankly. He shouts at the top of his voice*) Oil? (*The* COUNTESS *nods with a smile, and points down. The* PRESIDENT *produces a legal paper and a fountain pen*) Sign here.

COUNTESS What is it? I haven't my glasses.

THE PRESIDENT Your contract. (*He offers the pen*)

COUNTESS Thank you.

SECOND PRESIDENT (*Normal voice*) What is it?

THIRD PRESIDENT Waiver of all rights. (*He takes it back signed*) Thank you. (*He hands it to the* SECOND PRESIDENT) Witness. (*The* SECOND PRESIDENT *witnesses it. The* PRESIDENT *passes it on to the* THIRD PRESIDENT) Notarize. (*The paper is notarized. The* PRESIDENT *turns to the* COUNTESS *and shouts*) My congratulations. And now, Madame— (*He produces a gold brick wrapped in tissue paper*) If you'll show us the well, this package is yours.

COUNTESS What is it?

THE PRESIDENT Pure gold. Twenty-four karat. For you.

COUNTESS Thank you very much. (*She takes it*) It's heavy.

SECOND PRESIDENT Are you going to give her that?

THE PRESIDENT Don't worry. We'll pick it up again on the way out. (*He shouts at the* COUNTESS, *pointing at the trap door*) Is this the way?

COUNTESS That's the way.

(*The* SECOND PRESIDENT *tries to slip in first. The* PRESIDENT *pulls him back*)

THE PRESIDENT Just a minute, Mr. President. After me, if you don't mind. And watch those cigars. It's oil, you know.

(*But as he is about to descend, the* COUNTESS *steps forward*)

COUNTESS Just one moment . . .

THE PRESIDENT Yes?

COUNTESS  Did any of you happen to bring along a little sewing box?

THE PRESIDENT  Sewing box? (*He pulls back another impatient* PRESIDENT) Take it easy.

COUNTESS  Or a little gold thimble?

THE PRESIDENT  Not me.

THE PRESIDENTS  Not us.

COUNTESS  What a pity!

THE PRESIDENT  Can we go down now?

COUNTESS  Yes. You may go down now. Watch your step!

(*They hurry down eagerly. When they have quite disappeared,* IRMA *appears on the landing and announces the next echelon*)

IRMA  Countess, the Prospectors.

COUNTESS  Heavens! Are there more than one?

IRMA  There's a whole delegation.

COUNTESS  Send them down.

(*The* PROSPECTOR *comes in, following his nose*)

IRMA  Come in, please.

THE PROSPECTOR  (*Sniffing the air like a bloodhound*) I smell something. . . . Who's that?

IRMA  The Countess. She is very deaf.

THE PROSPECTOR  Good.

(*The* PROSPECTORS *also look alike. Sharp clothes, Western hats, and long noses. They crowd down the stairs after the* PROSPECTOR, *sniffing in unison. The* PROSPECTOR *is especially talented. He casts about on the scent until it leads him to the decanter on the table. He pours himself a glass, drinks it off, and belches with much satisfaction. The others join him at once, and follow his example. They all belch in unison*)

THE PROSPECTORS  Oil?

THE PROSPECTOR  Oil!

COUNTESS  Oil.

THE PROSPECTOR  Traces? Puddles?

COUNTESS   Pools. Gushers.

SECOND PROSPECTOR   Characteristic odor? (*He sniffs*)

THE PROSPECTOR   Chanel Number 5. Nectar! Undoubt-
edly—the finest—rarest! (*He drinks*) Sixty gravity
crude: straight gasoline! (*To the* COUNTESS) How
found? By blast? Drill?

COUNTESS   By finger.

THE PROSPECTOR (*Whipping out a document*)   Sign here,
please.

COUNTESS   What is it?

THE PROSPECTOR   Agreement for dividing the profits
. . . (*The* COUNTESS *signs*)

SECOND PROSPECTOR (*To* FIRST PROSPECTOR)   What is it?

THE PROSPECTOR (*Pocketing the paper*)   Application to
enter a lunatic asylum. Down there?

COUNTESS   Down there. (*The* PROSPECTORS *go down,
sniffing*)

　　(IRMA *enters*)

IRMA   The gentlemen of the press are here.

COUNTESS   The rest of the machine! Show them in.

IRMA   The Public Relations Counselors! (*They enter,
all shapes and sizes, all in blue pin-striped suits and
black homburg hats*) The Countess is very deaf, gentlemen. You'll have to shout!

FIRST PRESS AGENT   You don't say— Delighted to make
the acquaintance of so charming and beautiful a
lady . . . .

SECOND PRESS AGENT   Louder. She can't hear you.

FIRST PRESS AGENT   What a face! (*Shouts*) Madame, we
are the press. You know our power. We fix all values.
We set all standards. Your entire future depends
on us.

COUNTESS   How do you do?

FIRST PRESS AGENT   What will we charge the old trull?
The usual thirty?

SECOND PRESS AGENT   Forty.

THIRD PRESS AGENT   Sixty.

FIRST PRESS AGENT   All right—seventy-five. (*He fills in a form and offers it to the* COUNTESS) Sign here, Countess. This contract really gives you a break.

COUNTESS   That is the entrance.

FIRST PRESS AGENT   Entrance to what?

COUNTESS   The oil well.

FIRST PRESS AGENT   Oh, we don't need to see that, Madame.

COUNTESS   Don't need to see it?

FIRST PRESS AGENT   No, no—we don't have to see it to write about it. We can imagine it. An oil well is an oil well. "That's oil we know on earth, and oil we need to know." (*He bows*)

COUNTESS   But if you don't see it, how can you be sure the oil is there?

FIRST PRESS AGENT   If it's there, well and good. If it's not, by the time we get through, it will be. You underestimate the creative aspect of our profession, Madame. (*The* COUNTESS *shakes her head, handing back the papers*) I warn you, if you insist on rubbing our noses in this oil, it will cost you 10 percent extra.

COUNTESS   It's worth it. (*She signs. They cross toward the trapdoor*)

SECOND PRESS AGENT   (*Descending*) You see, Madame, we of the press can refuse a lady nothing.

THIRD PRESS AGENT   Especially, such a lady. (THIRD PRESS AGENT *starts going down*)

SECOND PRESS AGENT   (*Going down. Gallantly*) It's plain to see, Madame, that even fountains of oil have their nymphs. . . . I can use that somewhere. That's copy!

> (*The* PRESS AGENTS *go down. As he disappears, the* FIRST PRESS AGENT *steals the gold brick and blows a kiss gallantly to the* COUNTESS, *who blows one back*)
>
> (*There is a high-pitched chatter offstage, and* IRMA *comes in, trying hard to hold back* THREE WOMEN *who pay no attention to her whatever.*

*These* WOMEN *are tall, slender, and as soulless as if they were molded of wax. They march down the steps, erect and abstracted like animated window models, but chattering incessantly*)

IRMA  But, ladies, please—you have no business here —you are not expected. (*To the* COUNTESS) There are some strange ladies coming. . . .

COUNTESS  Show them in, Irma. (*The* WOMEN *come down, without taking the slightest interest in their surroundings*) Who are you?

FIRST WOMAN  Madame, we are the most powerful pressure group in the world.

SECOND WOMAN  We are the ultimate dynamic.

THIRD WOMAN  The mainspring of all combinations.

FIRST WOMAN  Nothing succeeds without our assistance. Is that the well, Madame?

COUNTESS  That is the well.

FIRST WOMAN  Put out your cigarettes, girls. We don't want any explosions. Not with my brand-new eyelashes.

(*They go down, still chattering. The* COUNTESS *crosses to the wall to close the trap. As she does so, there is a commotion on the landing*)

IRMA  Countess . . . (*A* MAN *rushes in breathlessly*)

MAN  Just a minute! Just a minute! (*He rushes for the trap door*)

COUNTESS  Wait! Who are you?

MAN  I'm in a hurry. Excuse me. It's my only chance! (*He rushes down*)

COUNTESS  But . . . (*But he is gone. She shrugs her shoulders, and presses the brick. The trap closes. She rings the bell for* IRMA) My gold brick! Why, they've stolen my gold brick! (*She moves toward the trap. It is now closed*) Well, let them take their god with them.

(IRMA *enters and sees with astonishment that the stage is empty of all but the* COUNTESS. *Little by little, the scene is suffused with light, faint at first, but increasing as if the very walls were glowing with the quiet radiance of universal joy. Only around the closed trap a shadow lingers)*

IRMA   But what's happened? They've gone! They've vanished!

COUNTESS   They've evaporated, Irma. They were wicked. Wickedness evaporates.

(PIERRE *enters. He is followed by the* VAGABONDS, *all of them. The new radiance of the world is now very perceptible. It glows from their faces)*

PIERRE   Oh, Countess . . . !

WAITER   Countess, everything's changed. Now you can breathe again. Now you can see.

PIERRE   The air is pure! The sky is clear!

IRMA   Life is beautiful again.

THE RAGPICKER   (*Rushes in*)   Countess—the pigeons! The pigeons are flying!

FLOWER GIRL   They don't have to walk any more.

THE RAGPICKER   They're flying. . . . The air is like crystal. And young grass is sprouting on the pavements.

COUNTESS   Is it possible?

IRMA   (*Interpreting for the* DEAF-MUTE)   Now, Juggler, you can throw your fireballs up as high as you please —they won't go out.

SERGEANT   On the street, utter strangers are shaking hands, they don't know why, and offering each other almond bars!

COUNTESS   Oh, my friends . . .

WAITER   Countess, we thank you. . . .

(*They go on talking with happy and animated gestures, but we no longer hear them, for their words blend into a strain of unearthly music which seems to thrill from the uttermost confines of the universe. And out of this music comes a voice)*

FIRST VOICE  Countess . . . (*Only the* COUNTESS *hears it. She turns from the group of* VAGABONDS *in wonder*)

SECOND VOICE  Countess . . .

THIRD VOICE  Countess . . . (*As she looks up in rapture, the* FIRST VOICE *speaks again*)

FIRST VOICE  Countess, we thank you. We are the friends of animals.

SECOND VOICE  We are the friends of people.

THIRD VOICE  We are the friends of friendship.

FIRST VOICE  You have freed us!

SECOND VOICE  From now on, there will be no hungry cats. . . .

THIRD VOICE  And we shall tell the Duchess her dog's right name!

(*The* VOICES *fade off. And now another group of voices is heard*)

FIRST VOICE  Countess, we thank you. We are the friends of flowers.

SECOND VOICE  From now on, every plant in Paris will be watered. . . .

THIRD VOICE  And the sewers will be fragrant with jasmine!

(*These voices, too, are silent. For an instant, the stage is vibrant with music. Then the* DEAF-MUTE *speaks, and his voice is the most beautiful of all*)

DEAF-MUTE  Sadness flies on the wings of the morning, and out of the heart of darkness comes the light.

(*Suddenly a group of figures detaches itself from the shadows. These are exactly similar in face and figure and in dress. They are shabby in the fashion of 1900 and their cuffs are badly frayed. Each bears in his hand a ripe melon*)

FIRST ADOLPHE BERTAUT  Countess, we thank you. We, too, are freed at last. We are the Adolphe Bertauts of the world.

SECOND ADOLPHE BERTAUT  We are no longer timid.

THIRD ADOLPHE BERTAUT　We are no longer weak.

FIRST ADOLPHE BERTAUT　From this day on, we shall hold fast to what we love. For your sake, henceforth, we shall be handsome, and our cuffs forever immaculate and new. Countess, we bring you this melon and with it our hearts . . . ! (*They all kneel*) Will you do us the honor to be our wife?

COUNTESS (*Sadly*)　Too late! Too late! (*She waves them aside. They take up their melons sadly and vanish. The voices of the* VAGABONDS *are heard again, and the music dies*) Too late! Too late!

PIERRE　Too late, Countess?

IRMA　Too late for what?

COUNTESS　I say that it's too late for them. On the twenty-fourth of May, 1881, the most beautiful Easter in the memory of man, it was not too late. And on the fifth of September, 1887, the day they caught the trout and broiled it on the open fire by the brook at Villeneuve, it was not too late. And it was even not too late for them on the twenty-first of August, 1897, the day the Czar visited Paris with his guard. But they did nothing and they said nothing, and now—kiss each other, you two, this very instant!

IRMA　You mean . . . ?

PIERRE　You mean . . . ?

IRMA　But, Countess . . .

COUNTESS　It's three hours since you've met and known and loved each other. Kiss each other quickly. (PIERRE *hesitates*) Look at him. He hesitates. He trembles. Happiness frightens him. . . . How like a man! Oh, Irma, kiss him, kiss him! If two people who love each other let a single instant wedge itself between them, it grows—it becomes a month, a year, a century; it becomes too late. Kiss him, Irma, kiss him while there is time, or in a moment his hair will be white and there will be another madwoman in Paris! Oh, make her kiss him, all of you! (*They kiss*) Bravo! Oh, if only you'd had the courage to do that thirty years ago, how different I would be today! Dear Deaf-Mute, be still—your words dazzle our eyes! And Irma is too busy to translate for you. (*They kiss once more*) Well, there we are. The world is saved. And you see how simple it all was? Nothing is ever so wrong in this world that a sensible woman can't set it right in the course of an afternoon. Only, the next time, don't wait until things begin to look black. The minute you notice anything, tell me at once.

THE RAGPICKER    We will, Countess. We will.

COUNTESS (*Puts on her hat. Her tone becomes business-like*)    Irma. My bones. My gizzard.

IRMA    I have them ready, Countess.

COUNTESS    Good. (*She puts the bones into her basket and starts for the stairs*) Well, let's get on to more important things. Four o'clock. My poor cats must be starved. What a bore for them if humanity had to be saved every afternoon. They don't think much of it, as it is.

*Curtain*

# About the Authors

JEAN ANOUILH was born in Bordeaux in 1910. His long and prolific career has been centered exclusively around the theater. Few playwrights have been able to match Anouilh in his ability to write both popular and artistic successes. His inventiveness as a dramatist can be seen in *Thieves' Carnival, Time Remembered, Waltz of the Toreadors, Poor Bitos, The Lark,* and *Becket.*

ALBERT CAMUS was born in Algeria in 1913 and died in an automobile accident in 1960. He gained fame as a novelist, philosopher and playwright, and in 1957 was awarded the Nobel Prize for Literature. Camus was the head of a theatrical company in the thirties and ran an underground newspaper during World War II. His plays include *The Misunderstanding, State of Siege,* and *The Just Assassins.*

JEAN GIRAUDOUX was born in Bellac, a town in southern France, in 1882, and died in 1944. A diplomat by career, he also became one of France's most famous playwrights. His poetic conception of drama mixed myth with fairy-tale in a succession of plays. Among his most famous are *Siegfried, Amphitryon 38, Judith, Tiger at the Gates, Electra, Intermezzo,* and *Ondine.*

JEAN-PAUL SARTRE was born in Paris in 1905. He received a doctorate in philosophy from L'École Normale Supérieure. Sartre declined the 1964 Nobel Prize for Literature. He is the author of philosophical works, novels, short stories, and plays, and a foremost exponent of the Existentialist school of philosophy. His plays include *The Flies, The Respectful Prostitute, Dirty Hands, The Devil and the Good Lord,* and *The Condemned of Altona.*

# The Best of the World's Best Books
## COMPLETE LIST OF TITLES IN
# THE MODERN LIBRARY

*A series of handsome, cloth-bound books, formerly available only in expensive editions.*

# MISCELLANEOUS